Entering the High Holy Days

by Reuven Hammer

The Jewish Publication Society
Philadelphia
5758 / 1998

Entering the High Holy Days

A Guide to the Origins, Themes, and Prayers

Reuven Hammer

2005 • 5765
THE JEWISH PUBLICATION SOCIETY
Philadelphia

The Jewish Publication Society
2100 Arch Street, 2nd floor
Philadelphia, PA 19103

Manufactured in the United States of America

05 06 07 08 09 10 11 12 13 14   10 9 8 7 6 5 4 3 2 1

Library of Congress Cataloging-in-Publication Data
Hammer, Rueven.
Entering the high holy Days: a guide to the origins,
themes, and prayers / by Rueven Hammer.
          p.   cm.
    Includes bibliographical references and index.
    ISBN 0-8276-0609-5
    1. Mahzor.   High Holidays.   2. High holidays—Liturgy.
3. Judaism—Liturgy.   I. Title
BM675.H5Z728   1998
296.4´31—dc21   97-41206
                                        CIP

To my first teacher and foremost mentor
Isaac Elhanan Simon z"l

"Appoint a teacher for yourself. . . ."
Avot 1:16

Contents

Preface

The *Yamim Nora'im,* the Days of Awe, or the High Holy Days, as we have become accustomed to call them, are days of remembrance. Not only does God remember, as the prayers and Torah readings tell us, but all of us remember. This season is a time of religious significance and of personal introspection; it is a time when images of family and of days gone by capture our imagination. The High Holy Days tie us to one another and convey the meaning of our lives, not only through ideas and concepts, but through feelings and memories. Those of us who have had these experiences are fortunate, and we hope that we are creating equally powerful ones for our children and grandchildren who come after us. The purpose of this book is to convey the spirit of these days and to enable those who have not experienced them fully before to begin to do so now.

From a personal point of view, the High Holy Days are forever mingled in my mind with the sight and the scent of autumn leaves, of chestnuts fallen from the trees, the brightness and chill of an upstate New York autumn, that particular sensation that comes from crisp fall air. I can almost feel myself again in the front yard of the building we always called the "little shule," which was not really a synagogue, and certainly not a "temple." I spent innumerable hours—probably fewer than it seemed to me then—playing outside with cousins and friends while our parents and grandparents *davened* (prayed) inside. We gathered chestnuts, broke open the pods, and polished the nuts to a burnished mahogany. We found the most colorful leaves we could, creating bouquets of deep red and gold. Inside, the New Year was being celebrated in prayer and melody, but outside we were performing the ritual of autumn.

When we went inside, it was not for junior congregation or for play groups, but for something much better—grandparents, or *bubbies* and *zadies,* as we called them. They waited within the small structure—an old house they had gutted, rebuilt, painted, and made into a shule. The marbled effect on the walls was the work of my grandfather, a house painter. The upper story had become a women's gallery where the women and girls could watch and hear what was going on below, where they could see their husbands, fathers, and brothers and be seen by them, and communicate by looks and hand signals.

The sight of all the men gathered together was a powerful one. My father's father was a short man who had seven tall sons. (Their height came from my grandmother.) They sat together on a bench at the front to the right of the ark, an impressive sight to behold. My other grandfather, a *cohen,* was a good *davener* with a beautiful voice. When he participated in the recitation of the priestly blessing—the *dukhening*—it was a haunting experience. I made certain to be inside when it took place. Without understanding what it meant, I was mesmerized by the sight of my grandfather standing with a group of men, wrapped in their *tallesim* so that their faces were hidden, chanting a combination of Hebrew words and wordless melodies. My grandfather's beautiful voice was stronger than the others. If the feel of autumn and its smells represent those Days of Awe in the sensuousness of sight and feeling, the blessing of the *cohanim* captures them for me in sound and emotion.

In the years that have passed, I have learned much about the prayers, concepts, and rituals that this book now consolidates to share with others. Still, there is probably nothing more important to me than the feelings I experienced on the High Holy Days as a child, when I came to recognize the importance of being part of a Jewish community, of our existence. That is what this season is all about: together we celebrate the fact that God has given us the opportunity to live and to experience this world. We celebrate a festival of life.

THE CELEBRATION OF LIFE

Few have prized the gift of life as fervently as the Jews. Perhaps the precarious nature of Jewish existence, the history of exiles and defeats, the memories of *autos-da-fé* and pogroms, of Cossacks and the Holocaust have taught us to value something that others may take for granted. But it is more than that: a life-affirming attitude underlies Judaism.

Jews have always had a dark sense of humor about the precariousness of their lives, an outlook hard-earned after centuries of living on the margins. A Jerusalem folk tale tells of a man who went from hospital to hospital, checking the lists of patients. When asked why, he said that he simply wanted to make certain that he was not on any of them but was still in good health. So it is with us: even in the best of times, we Jews are grateful, even awed, to be written once more in the Book of Life.

In Judaism we constantly celebrate the wonder of being alive. We take nothing for granted—not a day, not a moment. To awake to a new day is to feel that our soul has been revived, that life itself has been restored. Sleep, said the rabbis, is "one sixtieth of death"; to awaken is to be reborn. In our morning prayers we acknowledge that insight each day:

O my God,
the soul You have placed within me is pure.
You created it,
You formed it,
You breathed it within me . . .
Blessed are You, O Lord, who restores souls to the dead.

The prayer echoes the climactic moment of the biblical creation story, when God breathes the breath of life into the first human being: "And He blew into his nostrils the breath of life; and man became a living being" (Gen. 2:7). Thus each day's awakening is a recapitulation of the creation of Adam.

Judaism's love affair with life is expressed in the overriding rule of Jewish law: *pikuah nefesh doheh et ha-kol,* that is, saving a life comes before all else. Even when there is only a slight chance that our action will result in the saving of a life, we are nonetheless required to try to do so, in spite of the fact that it may mean violating the most stringent of ritual laws. In fact, the traditional description of a *hasid shoteh* (a foolish pious man) is of a man who stands by the shore when someone is drowning and says, "Just wait until I remove my *tefillin.* Then I will help you."

Certainly we should celebrate life each day, but it is difficult to overcome the routineness of daily activities that can all too easily dull our awe. Unfortunately, we come to take even the greatest gift for granted, and that is why Judaism has set aside these special days so that we can focus on celebrating life. The High Holy Days are a festival of life during which we can resensitize ourselves and renew our commitments. This is the time when we answer the call presented in Deuteronomy: "I call heaven and earth to witness against you this day: I have put before you life and death, blessing and curse. Choose life if you and your offspring would live" (Deut. 30:19). Time and time again the prayers of the High Holy Days return to the word *life.*

Remember us for life, *O King, who delights in* life.
Inscribe us in the Book of Life *for Your sake, King of* life.
In the Book of Life, *blessing and peace, may we be remembered and*
*   inscribed.*

Jewish tradition teaches that two books are open before the Heavenly Judge on Rosh Hashanah, the Book of Life and the Book of Death. Each of us is judged on the basis of our deeds and consigned to one book or the other, but the Merciful Judge grants each of us the time between Rosh Hashanah and Yom Kippur to change so that we may prove ourselves worthy of life.

We are also taught that the value of a human life is incalculable. The Sages declare: "If you save one life, it is equivalent to having saved an entire world. If you destroy one life, it is equivalent to having destroyed an entire world" (San. 4:5). Indeed, nothing is more precious than life, nothing as wondrous, and nothing as fragile. At this season especially, we are called upon to open our eyes and see the world, to feel that we are part of God's creative power. We are summoned to celebrate our lives and to ask, "What have we done to be worthy of this gift?"

Even Kohelet, cynic of cynics, proclaims, "God will hold you to account for everything you have not done and could have" (Eccles. 11:9). The Days of Awe are days for self-judgment. Celebrating life, we also judge the quality of our lives. Made aware as at no other time of how short life is, we ask ourselves the most difficult questions: During this past year, have we learned what we needed to? Have we helped others? Have we done enough? Have we created anything? Are we satisfied with what we have accomplished, with what we are? Where would we like to be when this season comes round again next year?

ENRICHING OUR LIVES

The High Holy Days have the power to enrich and even transform our lives. All too often, however, we let this unique opportunity slip through our fingers. Some of us treat the holidays as no more than an opportunity to see and be seen. Others regard these days as a burdensome obligation that must be fulfilled.

There are, however, many of us who would like to derive meaning and benefit from this season, but we find it difficult to do so. Language may be a problem, both because most of the prayers are in Hebrew and because even the English translations are not easily understood. For we are dealing here with ancient, classic texts. A simple reading will not suffice to bring them to life. And these prayers embody ancient concepts, too, often expressing a world-view that is radically different from our own. Because we come from a world of instant communication, thirty-second spots, and sound bites, we may often lack the patience that lengthy prayers require of us.

To make these holidays more meaningful, we need to acquire a deeper understanding of the many strands of text that have been woven together to create the tapestry of the High Holy Days and to fathom the concepts they embody. We need to read the individual prayers slowly and carefully, to learn what they are saying and how they are put together.

That is the purpose of this book: to provide a detailed map and a trustworthy compass to all those who seek to find greater meaning and personal fulfillment in their observance of the Days of Awe.

Acknowledgments

The idea of writing a book about the High Holy Days and the *Mahzor* was a natural outgrowth of writing *Entering Jewish Prayer*. When the decision was made not to include the liturgy of Rosh Hashanah and Yom Kippur in that work (mainly because of considerations of space, which would have made it impossible to do the subject justice), it seemed obvious that a volume on the High Holy Days was called for. In a sense, then, although other projects intervened between the two, *The High Holy Days* can be thought of as a companion volume to *Entering Jewish Prayer*. I was encouraged by the reactions to that book on the part of friends, colleagues, and even strangers whom I have met on my travels and who have indicated that it was helpful to them in their quest for meaningful prayer. I hope that this book will be similarly helpful to those who earnestly want the Days of Awe to have an influence upon them but have found participation in the lengthy and complex services difficult if not bewildering. This book may not address all their problems with the holidays, but perhaps it will help to clarify the themes of these days and explain the structure of the services and the import of the prayers. I hope that for many it will be a guide, enabling them to participate more fully in this important season.

The reading and research I had done in the past in order to prepare for teaching courses on the liturgy of the High Holy Days served as the kernel for this book. I recall with particular fondness teaching the material to students at the Seminario Rabinico Latinoamericano in Argentina. As usual, teaching is the best way to learn, and their insightful comments and questions were very helpful to me.

I have attempted to make use of the many books and articles on the subject of the High Holy Days (both in English and in Hebrew) written by past as well as contemporary scholars; I have acknowledged them in the notes and in references to various works. I would like to call special attention to three fine books that precede this one and that were useful to me in my own writing: S. Y. Agnon's comprehensive collection *Days of Awe,* Herman Kieval's learned and lucid volume *The High Holy Days,* and the informative and inspirational work of one of my beloved teachers, Max Arzt, *Justice and Mercy.* These texts are indispensable for anyone wishing to investigate the subject.

I am grateful that the Jewish Publication Society and its editor, Dr. Ellen Frankel, encouraged me to undertake this book. Dr. Frankel's wise editorial guidance was of great help to me in clarifying the goals of the book and improving it in substance and style. For her help, I give many thanks. Rena Potok's final editing contributed greatly to the literary style of the work. I am also very appreciative of the many hours my wife Raḥel put into reading the various versions of each chapter, correcting my mistakes and showing me where I was insufficiently lucid. She continues to be my first reader.

Any work on liturgy, or, for that matter, on any theological subject, must contend with the sensitive problem of gendered language. With regard to references to human beings, I have attempted to remain as neutral as possible and not to discriminate against either sex. With regard to God, I acknowledge that I have found using the language of reference a most difficult and clumsy endeavor. It is obvious to me that God is gender-neutral; God is no more a "He" than a "She." In fact, God is neither. Nevertheless, when referring to God and looking for a pronoun, I have chosen to use the traditional "He," since it is more appropriate than "It" and less provocative than "She." Similarly, many references in the liturgy are to masculine words (king, for example) and could not be easily avoided. I hope that all will understand and share my frustration at the limits of language. As we say in Hebrew, *itkhem ha-seliḥah*—forgiveness is yours.

I can think of no better phrase to articulate my relationship to this book than that of the prayer, *Modeh Ani*—I am thankful to the Almighty for the opportunity of undertaking this work and of completing it. It is my hope that it will prove useful and will enhance the most important season of the Jewish year, the season that can bring about profound changes for the better in our lives—the Days of Awe.

Jerusalem
5757, the forty-ninth year of Israel's independence

List of Abbreviations

Gen.	Genesis	Isa.	Isaiah
Exod.	Exodus	Jer.	Jeremiah
Lev.	Leviticus	Lam.	Lamentations
Num.	Numbers	Ezek.	Ezekiel
Deut.	Deuteronomy	Hos.	Hosea
Josh.	Joshua	Jon.	Jonah
Judg.	Judges	Mic.	Micah
1Sam.	1 Samuel	Zeph.	Zephaniah
2Sam.	2 Samuel	Zech.	Zechariah
1Chron.	1 Chronicles		
2Chron.	2 Chronicles	San.	Sanhedrin
Neh.	Nehemiah		
Ps.	Psalms	M.	Mishnah
Prov.	Proverbs	T.	Tosefta
Eccles.	Ecclesiastes	B.	Babylonian Talmud
Song	Song of Songs	J.	Jerusalem Talmud

1

The Days of Awe:
Origins and
Development

Rosh Hashanah and Yom Kippur—the Days of Awe, or *Yamim Nora'im*—are the most sacred days of the Jewish year, the time when more Jews attend synagogue services than at any other. (In fact, there is a close connection, at least in the Diaspora, between Jewish identification and High Holy Day observance; for years, school absenteeism on Yom Kippur has been one of the ways of measuring Jewish population figures.) These High Holy Days are a unique creation of the Jewish religious spirit. They embody the singular ideas and theology of Judaism and have the power to transform and renew human life.

"Awe" is a loose translation of the Hebrew word *nora*, which can also be translated as "reverence." The word characterizes this season of the year, which lasts from the first to the tenth of Tishre, the seventh month in the Jewish calendar. In post-biblical times this season was expanded to include Elul, the month prior to Tishre, and later was extended two weeks beyond Yom Kippur to Hoshana Rabba at the conclusion of the harvest festival of Sukkot. This High Holy Day period is a time of solemn rejoicing, of fear of judgment coupled with confidence of atonement, of both pleasant anticipation of the New Year and anxiety for the future. In the words of an old folk-saying, "Even the fish in the sea tremble at the approach of the Days of Awe."

Within the cycle of the Jewish year these days hold a peculiarly spiritual place, for they alone of Jewish holy days are devoid of agricultural or historical significance.[1] Paradoxically, these most "Jewish" of all days are, at the same time, the most universal. They touch on spiritual values that concern us as humans. Only the Sabbath, the weekly celebration of creation, approaches the universality of the Days of Awe, since it imposes a spiritual meaning upon an otherwise meaningless span of days. The Sabbath, however, is intended (in part) to be a commemoration of the exodus from Egypt,[2] whereas the *Yamim Nora'im* commemorate no historical events. Instead, they deal exclusively with the fundamental questions of human nature and human destiny and with the connections between God and humans, sin and repentance, and mercy and justice.

Of course, these overwhelmingly spiritual occasions did not spring full-blown from Sinai. The grew and developed over the centuries from modest beginnings until they attained their position of primacy in the Jewish sacred calendar.

In order to understand these holy days and participate in them more meaningfully, it is important to trace their development and to see the additions and transformations they have undergone over the centuries. This tracing will help us appreciate the various themes, sometimes contradictory, sometimes complementary, that come together at this time and to sense what it was that our spiritual leaders wanted us to contemplate and experience during these Days of Awe.

BIBLICAL ORIGINS

Little exists within the verses of the Torah to predict the central role these days would eventually play in Judaism; in fact, the biblical text focuses primarily on the dates and ritual practices of the holidays. The Torah notes the biblical calendar of the year in three different places: Leviticus 23:1–44, Numbers 28:9–39, and Deuteronomy 16:1–17.[3] Despite certain differences between them, these passages all depict a year characterized by an agricultural cycle of holidays, marking the seasons and the times of harvest. On three holidays, Israelite males were to "appear before God," that is, to make a pilgrimage to the sacred shrine that was eventually erected in Jerusalem: Passover, Shavuot (weeks), and Sukkot (tabernacles). The year was also divided into weeks. Each seventh day, the weekly Sabbath, was to be observed as a celebration of creation and a commemoration of the exodus. The first day of each month, which marked the appearance of a new moon, was also accorded a sacred status.

Two other dates appear on the lists in Leviticus and Numbers: a nameless holy day observed on the first day of the seventh month, and Yom Kippurim, the Day of Atonement, on the tenth day of the seventh month. Obviously, the three pilgrim festivals, agricultural in origin and augmented by significant historical associations, formed the sacred framework of the year. What, then, was the original meaning of these two other dates in the seventh month, which later were to become the most sacred days of our year?

Rosh Hashanah in the Torah

In Leviticus the first day of the seventh month is described as follows:

> In the seventh month on the first day of the month, you shall observe complete rest, a sacred occasion commemorated with loud blasts. You shall not work at your occupations; and you shall bring an offering by fire to the Lord (Lev. 23:24–25).

In Numbers we read:

> In the seventh month, on the first day of the month, you shall observe a sacred occasion: you shall not work at your occupations. . . .

You shall observe it as a day when the horn is sounded. You shall present a burnt offering of pleasing odor to the Lord (Num. 29:1–2).[4]

The sacred number seven seems critical here. Just as the seventh day of the week is holy, so the seventh month of the year has special significance. Since each new moon is a sacred time, it is logical that the seventh new moon—counting from Nisan, in the spring—should also acquire a special aura of holiness. That special sacredness is commemorated by the sounding of the shofar, the ram's horn. Aside from sacrifice, this is the only specific action mandated for this day in the Torah. Sounding the shofar is mentioned in both sets of verses, although no explanation or reason is offered. Taken together, the three elements of these verses—the lack of a name for the holiday, of a reason for the celebration, and of an explanation for sounding the shofar—pose a puzzle for us: why doesn't the Torah describe or emphasize this holy day any further?

Many scholars have suggested that the first day of the seventh month was popularly celebrated in ancient Israel as a divine coronation day, the time of God's assumption of the kingship and the beginning of a new cycle of the year.[5] There were two celebrations of a new annual cycle in ancient Israel, one in the spring month of Aviv (later called Nisan), "the first of the months of the year" (Exod. 12:2), and another in the fall at "the turn of the year" (Exod. 23:16; 34:22). The spring celebration was more cultic in nature, being connected to the cycle of sacred festivals and the reign of kings, while that of the fall emphasized the agricultural cycle.

The suggestion that a new year's festival was held in ancient Israel on the first day of the seventh month is based upon an analogy to Babylonian rites (two separate new year celebrations were held in Babylonia as well)[6] and upon allusions to such a commemoration found in the psalms. As Moshe Segal points out:

[T]hree principles, the creation of the world on the New Year, the manifestation of God's kingship over the world on the New Year, and the judgment of the world by God on the New Year . . . are already proclaimed together in a series of liturgical psalms which form a distinct group marked by a close affinity of tone, of language and of thought. These are the joyous and triumphant songs contained in Psalms 95–100, to which belong also Psalm 93 and the first part of Psalm 94. The constantly recurring thoughts in these beautiful songs are God as creator, God as King, God as judge.[7]

Several of these psalms allude to the one commandment specifically connected to this day, the sounding of the shofar. The *teru'ah*, one of the sounds of the shofar, is referred to in Psalms 95:1, 2; 98:4, 6; and 100:1 and should be differentiated from another sound mentioned in the Bible in connection to other holy days—the *teki'ah*, the sound of the trumpet.[8] In these particular psalms, the shofar sound is a joyous proclamation of God's ascendancy to the kingship and has none of the other connotations it received in later Jewish thought.[9] Another scholar, Baruch Levine, offers a different suggestion, that the day was commemorated by blasting the shofar in order to announce that the festival of Sukkot was to commence two weeks later.[10]

Although the Bible had not yet conferred a title on Rosh Hashanah (literally, the beginning or head of the year),[11] and although it had not yet connected that holiday to Yom Kippur, it is nonetheless conceivable that the first of Tishre was thought of, even in early times, as a time of "cosmic judgment . . . when the destiny of the world was fixed."[12]

Why, then, this reticence on the part of the Torah to ascribe all these meanings more explicitly to "the first day of the seventh month"? Perhaps the pagan connotations of this day were still too strong. After all, the Babylonian celebration centered upon struggles between gods and demons for dominance and was characterized by the use of magic and incantations.[13] Nothing of paganism remains, however, in the psalms. Mosaic monotheism had already transformed this day completely into the prototype of Rosh Hashanah as we now know it. If these psalms were indeed intended for recitation on the first of the seventh month, then even at this early date the Israelite new year festival celebrated the Lord as the sole creator of the world, who on this day ascended the throne and ruled over all of creation; the holiday was intended (at least in part) to acknowledge God by the people Israel as the righteous judge who dispenses justice for all humankind.

Yom Kippur in the Torah

Unlike the first day of the seventh month, the tenth day has a specific designation and purpose in the Torah, with elaborate rites connected to it:

> Mark, the tenth day of the seventh month is the Day of Atonement. It shall be a sacred occasion for you; you shall practice self-denial, and you shall bring an offering by fire to the Lord; and you shall do no work throughout that day. For it is a Day of Atonement, on which expiation is made on your behalf before the Lord your God. . . . Do no work whatever; it is a law for all time, throughout the generations in all your settlements. It shall be a Sabbath of complete rest for you, and you shall practice self-denial; on the ninth day of the month at evening, from evening to evening, you shall observe this your Sabbath (Lev. 23:27–32).

The designation of this day is reiterated in Numbers:

> On the tenth of the same seventh month you shall observe a sacred occasion when you shall practice self-denial. You shall do no work (Num. 29:7).

Self-denial—*inui nefesh* in Hebrew (literally, afflicting one's soul)—traditionally has been understood to refer to fasting.[14] For the Israelites, this Day of Atonement was therefore a day for fasting and complete cessation of work, observed by individuals in their homes and settlements.

While observed today as a time for individual atonement, the biblical Yom Kippur is primarily a priestly institution:

> The priest who has been anointed and ordained to serve as priest in place of his father shall make expiation. He shall put on the linen

vestments, the sacral vestments. He shall purge the inmost Shrine; he shall purge the Tent of Meeting and the altar; and he shall make expiation for the priests and for all the people of the congregation (Lev. 16:29–33).

Since Yom Kippur rites were performed in the sanctuary by the High Priest, the presence of the common people was not required. Individual observance was merely an accompaniment to the work of the High Priest, who was engaged in "rites of purgation,"[15] or "rites of riddance,"[16] in the sanctuary.

The Torah emphasizes these rituals of purging or cleansing the sanctuary and the altar, and the priests' atonement for themselves and for the people. *Kaparah* (atonement) means to cleanse that which has been defiled or contaminated. The sanctuary was a place of holiness and of ritual purity, which was tainted over the years by human beings who entered it in states of ritual impurity. If the sanctuary was to function as a holy place, as the dwelling place of the Holy One, it had to be purged of this impurity.

The rites of purgation described in Leviticus 16 resemble those found in other ancient religions.[17] In fact, the entire biblical ritual of *kaparah* can best be understood against the background of ancient Near Eastern religions. The fifth day of the ten-day Babylonian new year festival, for example, included a rite called *kuppuru*, in which a ram was beheaded and its body used to absorb the impurity of the sacred rooms of the temple. Other parts of the animal were thrown into the river, while the officiants were quarantined in the wilderness. The temple was doused and fumigated. Later, sins were confessed, and a criminal was paraded and beaten.[18]

The biblical ritual contains many similar features but, as Theodor Gaster points out, has transformed its pagan antecedent. Carried out "before the Lord," it is no longer "a mere mechanical act of purgation. . . . The people had to be cleansed not for themselves but for their God: 'before the Lord shall you be clean' (Lev. 16:30). Sin and corruption were now regarded as impediments not merely to their material welfare and prosperity but to the ful-

fillment of their duty to God."[19] The priest was to bring a sin offering that would "make expiation for himself and his household"
(Lev. 16:11), to enter the Holy of Holies and place sacrificial blood
on the cover of the ark, known as the "atonement seat" (Lev.
16:12–14), and thus to "make expiation in the Shrine" (Lev.
16:17). He then purged the altar by applying sacrificial blood to
it: "Thus he shall cleanse it of the uncleanness of the Israelites
and consecrate it" (Lev. 16:18–19). Thus, although similar concepts existed in all religions of the time, the Torah eliminated the
demonic and magical elements of impurity from the Yom Kippur
ritual. Instead, it emphasized that the closer the worshiper came
to the presence of God—that is, to holiness—the more restric-
tions there were in order to ensure ritual cleanliness.

The Scapegoat Ritual.   The purification ritual began by taking two goats and casting lots that determined their fate. One
goat, "marked for the Lord," was slaughtered as a sin offering,
and the other was "designated by lot for Azazel" (Lev. 16:8). That
goat was "left standing alive before the Lord, to make expiation
with it and to send it off to the wilderness for Azazel" (Lev. 16:10).
At the conclusion of all the rituals, the priest was to "lay his hands
upon the head of the live goat and confess over it all the iniquities and transgressions of the Israelites, whatever their sins,
putting them on the head of the goat; and it shall be sent off to
the wilderness through a designated man. Thus the goat shall
carry on him all their iniquities to an inaccessible region" (Lev.
16:21–22).

The final "rite of riddance" involving the scapegoat—called
se'ir la-azazel, or the goat for *azazel*—is one of the strangest and
yet most powerful of all rituals found in the Torah. "Scapegoat"
is short for "escape goat," an interpretation of the Hebrew word
azazel, which is understood as a contraction of the two words, *ez*
and *ozel,* that is, the goat that departs.[20]

But who or what is "Azazel"? Traditional commentators have
interpreted it either as the name of a place or as a goat-demon,[21]
while modern scholars generally agree that the latter is correct.
The word *ez,* the first part of the name, means "goat." The last

part of the name originally would have been *el* (the order of the Hebrew letters *aleph* and *zayin* have been transposed), meaning "god" or "divine being," often the suffix in the name of angelic beings such as Michael and Gabriel.[22] Thus, the name was originally *Az-el*, a goat of supernatural qualities or, simply, a goat-demon.

Yehezkel Kaufman identifies Azazel as a satyr living in the wilderness, one who inhabits the desert as a shade and whose sole apparent function is to receive the burden of sin and pollution annually sent off to him.[23] Moshe Segal notes that in an ancient Mideastern myth Azazel refers to a fallen angel who was banished and sent to an uninhabited land.[24] Based on these interpretations, sending the goat to Azazel may indeed have indicated sending it to "a locality named after the demon, the land and prison home of Azazel, a figurative name of a desert from which there can be no return."[25] In any case, there can be no question of a sacrifice to a demon in the Israelite tradition, not only because this goat was not sacrificed, but also because the very next chapter of Leviticus contains a specific prohibition against offering sacrifices to the goat-demons after whom the people strayed (Lev. 17:7). Clearly, the compilers of the Torah were familiar with the rites of their neighbors—such as goat-demon worship—and made sure to differentiate Israelite practice from them.

Before considering the meaning of the scapegoat ritual, several things should be noted. First, before this ritual was performed, the sins of the people had *already* been expiated. Slaughtering the other goat (the one designated for the Lord) and sprinkling its blood on the atonement seat were said to have purged the Shrine of both Israel's uncleanness and transgressions, "whatever their sins." Once the priest had performed those acts, he had "made expiation for himself and his household and for the whole congregation of Israel" (Lev. 16:16). Thus, the scapegoat rite was either an alternative act of riddance that had been added to the first ones or it was merely symbolic, emphasizing a cleansing from sins, which had already taken place. Secondly, this goat was not slaughtered but set free. There was no offering made to another "power" but a sending of sin into "an inaccessible region."[26] Finally, it is important to emphasize the element of confession. For, before sending the goat away, the sins of the people were not merely placed upon it, but were confessed. Sin was, therefore, both acknowledged verbally and atoned for ritually, through sacrifice. Only then could the sins be sent off into the wilderness.

We misunderstand this ritual if we think of the biblical goat as taking the place of the people and paying for their sins, as we popularly understand the term "scapegoat" today. Whatever may have been the case in other religions and cultures,[27] in the Torah the people could not rid themselves of sin by this simple procedure alone. Sending away the scapegoat was merely the *last* ritual act that completed a process of atonement.

Although ritual purity remains the main focus of the day in the biblical account, Leviticus 16:30 expands its thematic scope by including on the day's agenda the general topic of "sin"; the purpose of the day is thus "to cleanse you of all your sins; you shall be clean before the Lord." Over time, this idea of cleansing ourselves of the guilt of ethical as well as ritual misdeeds became the central focus of Yom Kippur. Furthermore, even at this early stage, the inclusion of the sin offering in the day's rites indicates that more was involved than mere expiation: there was also forgiveness and a return to holiness. All of this, of course, became more explicit in the later interpretations and observances added to the day.

It is also important to note the major differences between ancient pagan practices and those described in the Torah. In the Babylonian ritual the rites were performed by those who served in the temple, not by the High Priest. However, since the Holy of Holies—the inner room of the Israelite sanctuary in which the Ark of the Covenant was kept—was considered the dwelling place of the Presence of God, only the High Priest could enter it and perform these rites. In addition, in the Babylonian rite the sanctuary was purged while human sins were dealt with only secondarily; the emphasis is quite different in the biblical description.[28]

The Date of Yom Kippur.   What is the significance of the date of Yom Kippur?

The Israelite calendar is a lunar one in which sacred importance is given to the fifteenth day of the month, when the moon is full, and to the first, when it is new. The tenth of the month holds no specific significance. Why, then, was such a sacred day designated for the tenth of Tishre?

It is worth noting that the tenth of Nisan (another important month) is also singled out in the Torah; that is when the Passover lamb was to be chosen, although it was not slaughtered until the evening of the fourteenth (Exod. 12:2–7). Clearly, there is a connection, in the Passover doctrine, between the tenth day of the month and the festival observance that follows it: the one is a preparation for the other. Some scholars believe that the same connection applies to Yom Kippur, since that holiday was intended to prepare the sanctuary for the Sukkot rites. Furthermore, just as Passover focuses national religious energies in the spring, so too the festival of Sukkot, falling on the fifteenth of the seventh month, serves as the most elaborate and sanctuary-centered of the fall festivals. The later designation of Sukkot as *he-ḥag* (*the* festival) was an accurate description of its significance. Since it was important that the sanctuary, the priesthood, and the people be in a state of absolute purity for the proper observance of Sukkot, a day shortly before it was designated as a time for cleansing and purification.[29]

Another theory about the date of Yom Kippur is based on the fact that the ancient new year festivities of the Babylonians included a time for *kuppuru* (atonement), observed several days after the beginning of the festival. Thus the Israelite New Year (the first of the seventh month) also preceded an atonement day.[30] We will see that in post-biblical times a strong connection was established between the first and the tenth of Tishre, a connection that created the period now known as the High Holy Days, the Days of Awe.

THE PERIOD OF THE SECOND TEMPLE

Drastic changes occurred in the observance of these holy days during the period of the Second Temple and in the rabbinic period that followed. In rabbinic writings dating from the end of that period and edited at the beginning of the second century C.E., the High Holy Days as we know them are already fully described. These descriptions in the Mishnah (Rabbi Judah the Prince's codification of Jewish law) and in the Tosefta (a text containing other rabbinic material on the same topics) differ significantly from the biblical references. Unfortunately, there is little documentation in the literature of the Second Temple period about how these changes came about.

The first day of the seventh month is mentioned in the Book of Nehemiah as a holy day upon which an important event took place in the year 444 B.C.E.:

> When the seventh month arrived—the Israelites being [settled] in their towns—the entire people assembled as one man in the square before the Water Gate, and they asked Ezra the scribe to bring the scroll of the Teaching of Moses with which the Lord had charged Israel. On the first day of the seventh month, Ezra the priest brought the Teaching before the congregation, men and women and all who could listen with understanding. He read from it, facing the square before the Water Gate, from the first light until midday . . . (Neh. 8:1–3).

At this impressive gathering, the people of Israel renewed their covenant with God and accepted the Torah as their basic law. The people wept when they realized how far they had strayed from the teachings that were in the Torah. But they were admonished not to mourn because "this day is holy to the Lord your God" (Neh. 8:9). The holiness of the first day of the seventh month—made plain in this biblical narrative—may constitute the reason that it was chosen for this ceremony of reading and accepting the Law. At the same time, the Bible does not describe any specific New Year customs observed on that day.

Philo of Alexandria, the first-century B.C.E. Jewish philosopher, describes the first day of the seventh month as the great "Trumpet Feast" and connects it with the sounding of the horn at Mount Sinai when revelation took place.[31] He also interprets the trumpet as an instrument and symbol of war:

> Therefore the law instituted this feast figured by that instrument of war the trumpet, which gives it its name, to be as a thank-

offering to God the peace-maker and peace-keeper, who destroys faction both in cities and in the various parts of the universe and creates plenty and fertility and abundance of other good things. . . .[32]

If Philo accurately represents the general understanding prevalent in his day—rather than an interpretation particular to him or to the Alexandrian community where he lived—then clearly the first day of the seventh month was not celebrated at that time as the "New Year."[33] If we are to assume that the New Year was popularly celebrated during the First Temple period, we must conclude that this tradition was forgotten during the exile and not renewed until later.

The changes that took place in the observance of Yom Kippur during the Second Temple period were significant. Philo describes the day as one in which it was customary to spend the entire time, from morning to evening, in prayer.[34] Regarding the ritual of the Temple itself, the descriptions that we have in the Mishnah and Tosefta were not edited in their present form until a century or more after the destruction of the Temple in 70 C.E. There is little doubt, however, that they reflect an authentic tradition dedicated to preserving the rituals of the Temple—in the hope that they would one day be restored.

The most significant changes were:

1. the expansion of the confessions made by the High Priest;
2. the expansion of the role of the people in the Temple ritual;
3. the inclusion of prayer both by the priest and by the people;
4. changes in the ceremony of the scapegoat.

Most of these changes can be ascribed to the general trend of democratization within Judaism. The people came to participate more and more in the rituals so that the Temple became less the realm of the priests than the center of national worship. The role of verbal prayer also increased at that time. And people became more aware of their need to attain forgiveness and atonement for their own sins as opposed to focusing on purely ritual matters.

These changes mark an overall trend toward inwardness and ethical-moral concern within Jewish spiritual practice. What had

begun as a problem of ritual impurity developed into a concern
with human decency. The Prophets' focus upon moral concerns became incorporated into ritual observance. Isaiah's words challenging the value of fasts, incorporated later by the Rabbis into the Yom
Kippur services as the prophetic reading, took on new significance:

Is such the fast I desire,
A day for men to starve their bodies?
Is it bowing the head like a bulrush
And lying in sackcloth and ashes?
Do you call that a fast,
A day when the Lord is favorable?
No, this is the fast I desire:
To unlock the fetters of wickedness,
And untie the cords of the yoke
To let the oppressed go free;
To break off every yoke.
It is to share your bread with the hungry,
And to take the wretched poor into your home;
When you see the naked, to clothe him,
And not to ignore your own kin.
Then shall your light burst through like the dawn
And your healing spring up quickly (Isa. 58:5–8).

Despite this change in focus, the ancient rituals of the day were in
no way devalued or minimized. On the contrary, ceremonies in the
Second Temple were much more magnificent than those in the
wilderness Tabernacle or the First Temple, as was the building itself. Rituals in the Second Temple were carried out with great splen-
dor. If anything, the presence of so many pilgrims at these rites
made them more solemn and impressive than ever before.

RABBINIC ACCOUNTS OF THE YOM KIPPUR RITUAL

When we compare the Torah's account of the Yom Kippur
ritual with the Mishnah's, we notice that "expiation" is mentioned

in the Torah six times and that there are further references to "purging" and "cleansing," to slaughtering and sprinkling blood. But confession is mentioned only once: "Aaron shall lay both his hands upon the head of the live goat and confess over it all the iniquities and transgressions of the Israelites" (Lev. 16:21).

In the Mishnah's account of the ritual, on the other hand, the High Priest confessed his sins and those of his household (M. Yoma 3.8), those of the house of Aaron (M. Yoma 4.2), and those of the people of Israel (M. Yoma 6.2); there are, then, three separate confessions. While the Torah is silent about the content of the Priest's confession, the Mishnah gives a specific formula:

> Please Lord! I have transgressed, I have done wrong, I have sinned before You, I and my household. Please Lord! Atone for the transgressions, the wrongs and the sins that I have transgressed, done wrong and sinned before You, I and my household, as it is written in the Torah of Moses Your servant, "For on this day atonement shall be made for you to cleanse you of all your sins; you shall be clean before the Lord" (Lev. 16:30) (M. Yoma 3.8).[35]

After each of these confessions, the other priests and the people who were in the Temple courts would answer, "Blessed is the Name of His glorious Majesty forever" and would bow, prostrating themselves completely (M. Yoma 6.2).

According to the mishnaic account, the Torah's description of the ritual of the day (Lev. 16:1–34; 23:26–32) was read in the Temple either by the High Priest himself or by another high official. He also read Numbers 29:7–11, describing the offerings of the day, and then recited seven blessings: Torah, the Temple service, acknowledgment (*Modim*), the forgiveness of transgression, the Temple itself, the Priests, and the acceptance of prayer (M. Yoma 7.1).

As for the goat sent to Azazel, it was not set free, as the Torah mandates, but instead was taken in procession, accompanied by a distinguished delegation of leaders of Jerusalem, several miles into the wilderness along a pre-designated route. One end of a scarlet thread was attached to its horns and the other to a rocky precipice. When the goat was pushed off, "he tumbled down and was split limb from limb before reaching half way down the mountain" (M. Yoma 6.6). According to the Tosefta, if the goat was not killed in the fall, someone was to go down and kill it deliberately (T. Kippurim 3.14). Later rabbinic sources explain this ceremonial killing of the goat with the biblical verse, "it shall be left standing alive before the Lord, to make expiation with it and to send it off to the wilderness" (Lev. 16:10). The Rabbis understood this verse to imply that the goat was to be kept alive *at that time,* but was to die afterwards.[36] Perhaps they were also wary lest anyone think that the goat was being sent as a gift to gods, spirits, or demons. That speculation may also explain why some interpreted the word *azazel* as referring to the place where the goat was being sent, meaning "rough and difficult," rather than as the name of any demon or spiritual being.[37] It may also be that it was considered a bad sign if the goat were somehow to return carrying the sins back into the community.[38] As one midrash puts it, "If they saw the goat that had been sent away returning, they knew that the Holy One was angry with His world."[39]

POST-TEMPLE OBSERVANCES

Rosh Hashanah

The further development of the High Holy Days may be traced through sources compiled in the period following the destruction of the Second Temple (in the year 70 C.E.) and later recorded in the Mishnah (edited in 200 C.E. by Rabbi Judah the Prince). How much of the material was created only *after* the destruction and how much may have been produced earlier is a matter for conjecture. One should note, however, that discussions about the prayers of Rosh Hashanah are already recorded in the teachings of the schools of Hillel and Shammai, which would date these materials to the first century C.E.[40]

More significant is the specific designation in these sources of the first day of the seventh month, Tishre, as Rosh Hashanah, the beginning of the year, and a definition of what this title means:

"The first of Tishre is the beginning of the year [Rosh Hashanah] for years, sabbatical cycles and the jubilee . . ." (M. Rosh Hashanah 1.1). That is, the first of the seventh month was the time to begin the numbering of the year and the counting of the years for the seven-year cycle (the sabbatical) and the fifty-year cycle (the jubilee).

Of greatest import, however, is the information given in the Mishnah about the role of judgment on the first of Tishre, now designated simply "Rosh Hashanah":

> On Rosh Hashanah all human beings pass before Him as troops, as it is said, "the Lord looks down from heaven; He sees all mankind. From His dwelling place He gazes on all the inhabitants of the earth—He who fashions the hearts of them all, who discerns all their doings" (Ps. 33:13–15) (M. Rosh Hashanah 1.2).

The Mishnah also describes the basic prayers and shofar-blowing practices for Rosh Hashanah, which form the heart of the synagogue service today (M. Rosh Hashanah 4.5–6; 4.9).[41] The three major themes of the day—kingship, remembrance, and *shofrot*—are also established in the Mishnah, as are specific regulations concerning the sounding of the shofar during the prayers (M. Rosh Hashanah 4.5).

Yom Kippur

The explicit connection between Rosh Hashanah and Yom Kippur is made for the first time in the Tosefta (edited c. 300 C.E.): "All are judged on Rosh Hashanah and the verdict is issued on Yom Kippur" (T. Rosh Hashanah 1.13). Rabbi Yohanan, a second-century Sage, teaches that three books are open on Rosh Hashanah: one for the completely righteous, one for the completely wicked, and one for those in between, that is, average human beings. The first two books are sealed on Rosh Hashanah; the last is kept in suspension until Yom Kippur so that "if they do well, they are inscribed in the Book of Life and if they do not do well, they are inscribed in the Book of Death" (B. Rosh

Hashanah 16b). The period of time from the first day of the month to the tenth eventually came to be known as the "Ten Days of Penitence" and thus links them together.

With the destruction of the Second Temple, the Yom Kippur rituals associated with that institution could no longer be performed. Although rituals atoning for the impurities of the Temple were not necessary, the people still needed to atone for their own sins, both those against God and those between themselves and their fellows. In fact, the absence of the Temple rendered the problem of attaining atonement all the more acute. The story of Rabbi Yohanan ben Zakkai and Rabbi Joshua illustrates the void left by the destruction:

> [T]hey beheld the Temple ruins. "Woe is us!" cried Rabbi Joshua, "that the place where the iniquities of Israel were atoned for is now laid waste!" "My son," replied Rabbi Yohanan, "do not be grieved. We have another atonement as effective as this. And what is it? Acts of loving-kindness."[42]

Ritually, the power of atonement was now vested in the Day of Atonement itself. As always, *teshuvah* (repentance) was required before any sin could be atoned, but for the most severe sins atonement was "suspended until the Day of Atonement which then atones" (M. Yoma 8.8).[43] But it was now made clear that sins between human beings could only be atoned if "one pacified one's fellow" first (M. Yoma 8.9).

It was during this post-destruction period that the liturgy of Yom Kippur was developed, including the recitation of five daily services, something that was done on other fast days and that may reflect practices already in existence before the destruction (M. Ta'anit 4.1). Rabbinic teaching also spelled out the specific prohibitions of Yom Kippur for each individual. Although fasting remained the basic method of "afflicting one's soul," prohibitions were added against washing, anointing with oil, wearing shoes, and having sexual relations (M. Yoma 8.1)—prohibitions that are also associated with mourning practices. Thus, the Sages were attempting to eliminate all pleasures on that day, for Yom Kippur, like all fasts, is considered a time of mourning.

The Season of Awe

During the talmudic period in the centuries that followed, the specific liturgy of the High Holy Days was developed, drawing upon the regulations and concepts formulated in the Mishnah by the early Sages. Afterwards, the Geonim added the finishing touches to the work, giving us the liturgy we have today. Of course, liturgical creativity continued, as we shall see, but the basic components were in place by the Middle Ages. Rosh Hashanah, originally a one-day holiday, was expanded in later times—in the Diaspora—to two days. In fact, all major holidays were doubled this way because it was impossible for the court in the Land of Israel to notify the Diaspora communities when they proclaimed the beginning of the new month. In the case of Rosh Hashanah, the holiday was declared *Yoma Arikhta* (one long day).[44] Eventually, even in the Land of Israel it was, and still is, observed for two days.[45]

The vision of Rosh Hashanah as "one long day" rather than two separate ones led to certain liturgical consequences. For example, why recite the *She-heheyanu* blessing, said only when something new is done, on the second evening if the holiday constitutes only a *single* long day? To retain the traditional practice of reciting this blessing on both days, the custom arose of eating a new fruit on the second evening, thus justifying this blessing.

Sometime in the second millennium of the common era, the concluding day of Sukkot, known as Hoshana Rabba, came to be commonly regarded as the end of this period of judgment. The thirteenth-century kabbalist Bahya ben Asher of Saragossa called it the "day of the great sealing on high aside from the first sealing of Yom Kippur." He described it as something that "has come down from mouth to mouth and is the tradition of wisdom."[46] The eighteenth-century mystical work *Hemdat Yamim*, which describes all of the holy days, speaks about the night of Hoshana Rabba, using the exact vocabulary of Yom Kippur—sin, atonement, forgiveness, repentance—and dubs it "the night of great holiness on which judgment is pronounced."[47]

During these centuries, the season of awe was also extended
backwards by a month. The thirteenth-century halakhic authority, the Mordekai, mentions the custom of reciting special forgiveness prayers *(Selihot)* prior to Rosh Hashanah. In some communities it became the custom to begin reciting these prayers at
the beginning of Elul, the month before Tishre, and to sound the
shofar each day of that month.[48] Thus, the period of the Days of
Awe extended backwards and forwards until it encompassed
nearly two full months of the year!

Formulating and formalizing the Days of Awe took at least a
millennium and a half. In time, practices once connected only to
the priests and the Temple became part of the observances of the
entire people. Specific communal rituals and prayers centering
around the synagogue supplanted both individual observance and
Temple ceremonials. Discrete days originally important because
of their attachment to the agricultural festivals, to a conception
of God's enthronement, and to a ritual of purification eventually
became a constellation of days during which the Jewish people
prepared for judgment, prayed for forgiveness, reconciled themselves with their neighbors and with God, and purified themselves from sin and error. Thus the New Year became a time for
a new beginning.

2

The Meaning of the Yamim Nora'im

As we have seen, the High Holy Days we celebrate today are the product of thousands of years of religious creativity. They contain ideas that originated in biblical days, some concepts developed by the Sages in rabbinic times, and others that stem from more modern periods. We experience these days primarily through the prism of the synagogue service and secondarily through home rituals. Like the proverbial forest that cannot be seen for the trees, the sheer quantity of the prayers and the complexity of the services can seem overwhelming. We read a prayer, hear a melody, or listen to a biblical reading but are hard-pressed to understand how they relate to one another or what we are supposed to feel or experience when participating in the service. Although the individual services and prayers will be discussed in greater detail in later chapters of this book, some general observations may prove helpful at this point. Examining the writings of the early Sages and the later interpreters of Judaism will help us understand the basic ideas and concepts underlying the High Holy Days and will show how they are woven together to form a magnificent tapestry that encompasses the many facets of life.

DIVINE JUDGMENT AND HUMAN RESPONSIBILITY

The *Yamim Nora'im* have two main foci: judgment and forgiveness. Rosh Hashanah stresses judgment, which includes the concepts of kingship and remembrance. These ideas teach us that the world is meaningful because it has a ruler who makes demands upon human beings and who remembers and judges them. They also indicate that people are responsible, and therefore accountable, for their own actions.

The notion of judgment is nowhere mentioned in the Torah in connection with Rosh Hashanah. What, then, inspired it? When we examine the psalms connected with a possible ancient New Year celebration, we see that they already embody this concept. After describing the proclamation of God as king, Psalms 96 and 98 conclude with the idea that God is coming "to judge the earth; He will judge the world in righteousness and its peoples in faithfulness." In God's role as judge and ruler of the world, God is responsible for judgment. There is, then, a direct ideological connection between the New Year, marking the beginning of God's reign, and the idea of a godly judgment of the earth.

While the focus of Rosh Hashanah is on human responsibility and divine judgment, that of Yom Kippur is on human failure and divine forgiveness. We sin, but our failure can be mitigated; we can attain forgiveness. By striving for forgiveness (which we do during *Seliḥot*), we gain atonement (*kaparah*).

Judgment and forgiveness are connected by the possibility of repentance (*teshuvah*), which is emphasized in the interval between Rosh Hashanah and Yom Kippur, the ten days of repentance (*aseret yemei teshuvah*). Judgment does not lead to automatic punishment. The possibility of change, of repentance, allows us to achieve atonement.

THE DAY OF REMEMBRANCE

Judgment is an extension of the biblical term "remembrance" (*zikaron*), used in connection with the first of Tishre: "In the seventh month, on the first day of the month, you shall observe complete rest, remembrance through loud blasts, *teru'ah,* a sacred occasion" (Lev. 23:24).

The most ancient prayers of the High Holy Day liturgy call Rosh Hashanah *Yom Ha-zikaron*—"the Day of Remembrance." When God "remembers" or "visits" us, His favors and promises to us are granted and fulfilled.

Remembrance is one of the three major themes of the special prayers recited in the *Amidah* of Rosh Hashanah:[1] kingship (*malkhuyot*), remembrance (*zikhronot*), and *shofrot*. These themes are linked together in a rabbinic saying: "Proclaim Him *king* so that He may *remember* you with the shofar of redemption."[2] We are called to appear before God, who then judges us and apportions our degree of "remembrance" for the coming year, taking note of us and fulfilling His promises to us. If, however, we are judged not worthy, we cannot expect to benefit from God's favor. In this way, the idea of God's remembering us is expanded to mean that God judges our actions and either rewards them or decrees punishment. However, the tradition asserts that when God judges us, His justice is tempered by mercy and leniency; God's mercy far outweighs His justice.

It is easy to misunderstand the idea of the Day of Remembrance, confusing it with a deterministic view of life, a fatalistic attitude that our future is preordained, that like Oedipus we are doomed to live out some preordained force of destiny. But the concept of "remembrance" means exactly the opposite: we have complete freedom of choice. God judges us on the basis of what we have done. As for our fate, we alone determine it. In the words of one of the *piyyutim*—the special poems compiled for this season—"the hand of every person has written it."

Thus, God's judgment is enacted through the consequences of human actions. We are responsible for what we do; our actions have consequences. Rabbinic Judaism characterized an atheist as one who says, "There is no judge and no judgment." On Rosh Hashanah we affirm our belief that there is indeed a judge and there is judgment.

Taken on the most literal level, these assertions are difficult to accept. How simplistic to believe that whatever happens to us in our lives has been ordained by God, that we are rewarded or punished on Rosh Hashanah on the basis of our actions. Kohelet long ago remarked that "time and accident overtake them all" (Eccles. 9:11). When we look around us, we see that the wicked often go unpunished. We note with bitterness and anger that the consequences of sin frequently are prosperity, power, and prestige, while the consequences of virtue are often deprivation, despair, even death. But we are not the first generation to ask the question: Why do the wicked prosper? The psalmist challenges:

How long shall the wicked, O Lord,
how long shall the wicked exult,
shall they utter insolent speech,
shall all evildoers vaunt themselves? (Ps. 94:3–4)

But if we do not literally believe that everything that happens to us in the coming year is determined by God on the *Yamim Nora'im,* what can remembrance and judgment mean to us?

DETERMINING OUR LIVES

The High Holy Days teach us that what we do and what we are determine what we will make of our lives. True, much is out of our own hands. We have only limited control over our health and over experiences we have that are caused by others, by accident, or by nature. The often cynical but realistic Kohelet writes of the sage and the fool that "the same fate awaits them both" (Eccles. 2:14). Certainly, on Rosh Hashanah when we contemplate what the year has in store for us, we think of fate. Nothing is more frightening than the unknown. Perhaps that is what we leave in the "hands of God," without necessarily believing that God determines everything. The most we can ask is that God help us to meet whatever happens and that God give us the ability and strength to cope with life's difficulties, and the humility and grace to appreciate its blessings. But we must take responsibility for those things that we *can* determine: our own character, our own actions, and thus our own fate. Although we cannot determine what will happen to us, we can control our reactions. For these we can blame no one but ourselves. As Viktor Frankl wrote: "Man's freedom is no freedom from conditions but rather freedom to take a stand on whatever conditions might confront him."[3]

In this sense, judgment means taking responsibility and being accountable for our actions. There is ultimate meaning in what we do. God cares. We face not an unfathomable universe in which human striving meets with cosmic indifference, but a power concerned with human action and with moral meaning. The world is not an unformed, void place of chaos, not "a tale . . . full of sound and fury, signifying nothing," as Shakespeare put it, but a place of meaning and responsibility. Belief in God offers us a sense that our lives matter—that God "remembers."

THE DAY OF JUDGMENT

The ancient Rabbis base their description of Rosh Hashanah on an analogy drawn from Roman military life. Just as a Roman commander reviews the troops who pass before him, so "[o]n Rosh Hashanah all human being pass before [God] as troops,[4] as it is said [in Ps. 33:15], 'He who fashions the heart of them all, who discerns all their doings'" (M. Rosh Hashanah 1.2). Seeing how they conduct themselves, the commander, like God, decrees each person's fate. The liturgy of the day draws upon a second analogy: a great trial. On this day, the world is judged. The *payytanim,* the liturgical poets (such as the writer of the poem *U-netanah tokef),* expand upon this theme. The poets describe the great day of judgment when all—even the heavenly creatures—are judged by God.[5] There are many other references to this idea, such as the *piyyut Le-el orekh din* (God who sits in judgment) with its repeated emphasis on the word *din,* judgment,[6] as well as the expression "the King of judgment" inserted into the main prayers of Rosh Hashanah.

The idea that we, as human beings, are on trial before God is a frightening one. Franz Kafka took this concept to an extreme in his novel *The Trial*. His hero, K., the helpless victim, does not even know what his crime is. Just before he is killed, he puzzles: "Where was the Judge whom he had never seen? Where was the High Court, to which he had never penetrated? He raised his hands and spread out all his fingers."[7] For us, on the contrary, Rosh Hashanah is no trial before a cruel or unknown judge on arbitrary charges, but a summing up of our deeds, an acknowledgment of responsibility for our actions.

The Days of Awe are a magnificent opportunity for us to review the past year, our deeds, misdeeds, and missed opportunities. God can and does judge us daily, but we seldom take the time to think about our actions in more than a superficial fashion. Judaism has a term for true self-contemplation: *heshbon hanefesh*—taking an account of one's soul. Without this act, there is no possibility for change, and change is a central concept of the Days of Awe.

THE KINGSHIP OF GOD

Celebrating God's ascension as ruler of the universe is one of the most ancient themes of Rosh Hashanah. Although in the pagan world such an event was celebrated as a ceremony of coronation, only traces of this rite were preserved in Jewish observance. Such things were more appropriate for gods who attained power by overcoming forces of fate or other divine rivals, than for the God of Israel, sole and eternal ruler of the universe. Nevertheless, the concept of kingship, or sovereignty, remains one of the basic themes of Rosh Hashanah. Along with judgment, kingship is the major thematic focus of the *piyyutim*. One of the most popular refrains in these poems is "the Lord is King, the Lord was King, the Lord will be King for ever and ever."

Since Judaism could not really conceive of a time when God was *not* the sovereign of the universe, the notion of God's kingship entailed recognizing God as our sovereign and bringing His kingdom to the entire world. An individual does this daily when reciting the *Shema*.[8] On Rosh Hashanah, we not only celebrate the kingship of God, but also voice the hope that in the near future all humanity will join in this proclamation. That is what the prophet Zechariah meant when he declared: "And the Lord shall be king over all the earth; in that day the Lord will be one and His Name one" (Zech. 14:9). God will truly be king only when humans accept God's sovereignty.

The hasidim tell the tale of a rabbi who calls people together in the public square for an important announcement. With great anticipation they gather to hear what it is that he wants them to know. At last the rabbi appears and says simply, "There is a God." This deceptively simple tale contains a profound theological truth. This acknowledgment of the sovereignty of God is a major goal of the Days of Awe.

REPENTANCE, FORGIVENESS, AND ATONEMENT

Although rabbinic tradition has created a strong connection between Rosh Hashanah and Yom Kippur, there are major points of distinction between the two. On Rosh Hashanah we proclaim God King and acknowledge that we are responsible for our actions. Yet despite the day's solemnity, the over-all tone is positive and celebratory. The affirmative connotations of God's remembering and visiting outweigh the seriousness of judgment. The Rabbis deliberately decreed that the biblical verses to be recited in the three special prayers on kingship, remembrance, and *shofrot*[9] should contain only positive ideas, and nothing indicating punishment.[10] However, as we move toward Yom Kippur, even though we retain our basic optimism that the verdict will be positive (hence the wearing of white garb rather than black), the atmosphere darkens and turns somber. We begin to concentrate on the problem of sin, on the flawed nature of human beings, and on the removal of sin and guilt through repentance, for-giveness, and atonement.

As human beings, we try to define our place in the vast, mys-terious universe in which we live. We want to understand our nature and how we relate to other living things. We think about what came before us and what will come after. We envision the end of life and ponder what follows.

The *Yamim Nora'im* respond to this need to understand our-selves and our place in the universe. At one point during the con-fession of the Yom Kippur *Ne'ilah* service, we articulate these ques-tions in a way that seems to indicate a pessimistic, negative valuation of human beings and human life:

> What are we? What is our life? What is our piety? What is our virtue? What is our salvation? What is our strength? What is our accomplishment? What shall we say before You, O Lord our God and God of our ancestors? Are not all the mighty as nothing be-fore You, men of renown as if they did not exist? The wise as if they lacked knowledge, the discerning as if they had no wisdom, for most of their deeds are valueless and the days of their lives a mere nothing before You. Man's superiority to the beast is non-existent, for all is futile.

What an apt commentary on the pessimistic words of Kohelet:

Utter futility! said Kohelet.
Utter futility! All is futile!
What real value is there for a man
In all the gains he makes beneath the sun?
One generation goes, another comes,
But the earth remains the same forever (Eccles. 1:1–4).

U-netanah tokef also expresses these feelings of awe at the enormity of God's universe:

> In truth You are their creator and You understand what motivates them, for they are but flesh and blood. Man's origin is dust and his end is dust. He earns his bread with the exertion of his life. He

is like broken pottery, like dry grass, like a withered flower, like a passing shadow, like a vanishing cloud, like a breeze that passes by, like floating dust, like a dream that flies away.

Yet, while these parts of the liturgy clearly indicate the insignificance of humankind in the face of divine presence, other parts raise a different point. The *Ne'ilah* prayer quoted above goes on to state: "You have set man aside from the very beginning, permitting him to stand before You." On the one hand, then, human life seems to have very little value in the vast scheme of things, but on the other hand, we sense a special relationship between us and our Creator. Thus, for all our limitations, we are nonetheless creatures of worth.

On this matter the Sages gave us excellent advice. They said that each person should carry two notes in his or her pockets. On one would be the words: for my sake the world was created. On the other: I am but dust and ashes. When we despair of our value we look at the first. When we are too haughty, we look at the second.

This dichotomy is not between body and spirit, but between good and evil. Although we separate ourselves on Yom Kippur from bodily needs as much as possible, we do so only in order to emphasize the importance of the spiritual side of life, which we usually ignore, afflicting ourselves in order to gain a higher degree of holiness. The object is not to make this asceticism a part of everyday life, but to be able to return to normal life with greater self-knowledge and awareness. The central dichotomy established by the Yom Kippur fast and prayers is therefore not between body and spirit, but between worth and lack of worth, between impulses toward evil and impulses toward good.

The *Yamim Nora'im* are about choice. We are not toys of fate. We are not destined for sin and evil. We have the possibility of choosing the path to life. No matter what we have been, we can change and become better. If we seem to emphasize the dark side of life and of human beings, it is only in order to come to terms with our limitations, to recognize our faults, and to prepare to better ourselves.

THE MEANING OF SIN

Judaism teaches that human beings are not basically sinful. We come into the world neither carrying the burden of sin committed by our ancestors nor tainted by it. Rather, sin, *het,* is the result of our human inclinations, the *yetzer,* which must be properly channeled.

Het literally means something that goes astray. It is a term used in archery to indicate that the arrow has missed its target. This concept of sin suggests a straying from the correct ways, from what is good and straight. Can humans be absolved of their failure and rid themselves of their guilt? The ideology of Yom Kippur answers: Yes.

These concepts are already found in biblical stories, including those at the beginning of the Torah, those concerning Israel and its sins in the wilderness, and in the teachings of the prophets. These writings contemplate the nature of human beings, the meaning of sin, and the possibility of forgiveness. The early stories in Genesis teach that the "devisings *[yetzer]* of man's mind are evil from his youth" (Gen. 8:21). This is the source of the rabbinic concept of the *yetzer,* human instincts, similar to the Freudian id. Later, the rabbis spoke of the *yetzer ha-tov,* the good inclination, and the *yetzer ha-ra,* the evil inclination.

The word "forgiveness" or "pardon" (in Hebrew, *s-l-h*) appears for the first time in the story of the golden calf: "pardon our iniquity and our sin" (Exod. 34:9). The story of the spies contains a similar idea: "Pardon, I pray, the iniquity of this people according to Your great kindness, as You have tolerated [carried] this people ever since Egypt" (Num. 13:5). This text is followed by the verse that is central to the Yom Kippur liturgy: "And the Lord said, 'I pardon, as you have asked'" (Num. 14:37).

These narratives establish the concept of the God of Israel as a God of mercy and forgiveness. In revealing His nature to Moses, God indicates His forgiving nature much more fully than He did in the Ten Commandments. God emphasizes mercy, "carrying sin" and extending lovingkindness far beyond the extent of punishment. Thus, Moses learns that God's essence is not only

His absolute Being and His absolute freedom, but His fundamental mercy. It is not surprising that the passage in which these
attributes of God are detailed (Exod. 34:6–7) became the cor-
nerstone of the liturgy of forgiveness during the High Holy Day
season.[11]

In rabbinic Judaism, these ideas evolved into the concept of
the two attributes of God, the attribute of justice and the attribute
of mercy, the latter being the dominant mode of God's activity.
The medieval morality code *Mesillat Yesharim* suggested that the
attribute of mercy means that God gives respite to the sinner, not
meting out His full punishment at once, but granting the sinner
the opportunity to repent and thus be rid of the power of the evil
inclination.[12]

THE POSSIBILITY OF REPENTANCE

But even these biblical narratives lack the element of repentance, which wipes out sin, changes the individual, and elimi-
nates the consequences of sin. The complete realization of this
idea does not appear until the prophets and the Book of Deuteronomy (30:2–10), which emanates from the prophetic period. It is
perhaps best exemplified by the imaginary description in Jeremiah of the people realizing their sin and returning to God:

Hark! On the bare heights is heard
The suppliant weeping of the people of Israel.
For they have gone a crooked way,
Ignoring the Lord their God.
Turn back, O rebellious children,
I will heal your afflictions!
"Here we are, we come to You,
For You, O Lord, are our God! . . .
Let us lie down in our shame,
Let our disgrace cover us;
For we have sinned against the Lord our God,

We and our fathers from our youth to this day,
And we have not heeded the Lord our God."
If you return, O Israel, *declares the Lord,*
If you return to Me,
If you remove your abominations from My presence
And do not waver (Jer. 3:21–4:1).

To return to God *(la-shuv)* means to repent *(teshuvah)*, from the same Hebrew root. It means to acknowledge wrongdoing, to change one's conduct, and to experience regret for what one has done. As a result of these actions, God accepts the individual back, as illustrated in this passage from Hosea:

And I will espouse you forever:
I will espouse you with righteousness and justice,
And with goodness and mercy,
And I will espouse you with faithfulness
Then you shall be devoted to the Lord (Hos. 2:21–22).

The best illustration of this concept may be found in the Book of Jonah, a story very similar to that of Sodom and Gomorrah, except that here we find a call to repent followed by the people's change of heart and God's forgiveness. Small wonder that this book is read in its entirety on Yom Kippur afternoon.[13]

The concepts of repentance and forgiveness are also expressed by the authors of the psalms. Consider, for example, Psalm 51, which purports to be the words of David acknowledging his sin with Bathsheba:

Wash me thoroughly of my iniquity,
and purify me of my sin;
for I recognize my transgressions,
and am ever conscious of my sin . . .
Purge me with hyssop till I am pure;
wash me till I am whiter than snow . . .
Hide Your face from my sins;
blot out all my iniquities . . .

I will teach transgressors Your ways,
that sinners may return to You.

ACHIEVING ATONEMENT

From the beginning of the religion of Israel, atonement rituals existed which were connected with the sanctuary and the
observance of the commandments. Any slight of a commandment
had to be atoned for through sacrifice. Numbers 15:24–27, for
example, outlines the sacrifices to be brought by the community
or the individual for inadvertent trespass against God's commandments. Moral sins, however, could not simply be atoned for
by rituals. As the Mishnah later expressed it:

For sins between man and God, Yom Kippur atones.
For sins between humans and other humans, Yom Kippur atones
only when one has appeased his fellow (M. Yoma 8.9).

Thus, the forgiving nature of God came to be regarded as
more than the willingness to overlook sin. It was God's desire
that the sinner change and attain forgiveness through repentance.
Atonement for sin is the result of repentance and indicates that
the transgression no longer exists.

The liturgy speaks of three actions that help us to attain full
atonement: *tefilah* (prayer), *teshuvah* (repentance), and *tzedakah*
(charity). The medieval *Sefer Ha-ḥinukh* lists four things that can
"change the outcome of the trial," that is, the judgment on these
Days of Awe:

1. *tzedakah* (charity);
2. *tza'akah* (prayer);
3. *shinui ha-shem* (change of one's nature),
4. *shinui ma'aseh* (change of performance).[14]

The medieval morality code *Mesillat Yesharim* outlines these
steps:

1. acknowledgment and confession of sin;

2. realization of wickedness and feelings of remorse;
3. uprooting the desire to repeat the sin.[15]

The scholar Saadiah Gaon also gave his four steps to repentance:
1. renunciation of sin;
2. remorse;
3. quest for forgiveness;
4. obligation not to relapse into sin.

He based these on the verses from Hosea:

Return, O Israel, to the Lord your God,
For you have fallen because of your sin.
Take words with you
And return to the Lord.
Say to Him:
"Forgive all guilt
And accept what is good;
Instead of bulls we will pay
[The offering of] our lips.
Nor ever again will we call
Our handiwork our god . . ."
I will heal their affliction,
Generously will I take them back in love;
For My anger has turned away from them (14:2–5).[16]

In addition, Saadiah recommends increased prayer, charity, and the attempt to restore others to the proper path.[17]

The most detailed discussion of the process of repentance is that of Maimonides. According to him, *teshuvah* begins by confessing one's sins and is fully achieved if one finds oneself in the same situation and does not commit the sin again.[18] One must abandon the sin and determine never to do it again.[19] One must pray, perform acts of charity, and remake oneself into another person and also change one's actions.[20] Only then, when one's character has been thus transformed, has true repentance been achieved.

The full rabbinic concept of atonement is expressed well in the following midrash:

> They asked Wisdom, "What is the punishment of the sinner?" Wisdom replied, "Misfortune pursues the sinner". . . (Prov. 13:21).
> They asked Prophecy, "What is the punishment of the sinner?" Prophecy replied, "The person who sins shall die" (Ezek. 18:4).
> They asked Torah, "What is the punishment of the sinner?" Torah replied, "Let him bring his guilt offering, and it will be forgiven him, as it is said: 'that it may be acceptable in his behalf, in expiation for him'" (Lev. 1:4).
> They asked the Holy One Blessed Is He, "What is the punishment of the sinner?" The Holy One replied, "Let him repent and his sin will be atoned, as it is written: 'Good and upright is the Lord; therefore He shows sinners the way'" (Ps. 25:8).[21]

If the *Yamim Nora'im* taught us nothing more than that human beings have the power to change, to remake themselves and be renewed and reborn, that in itself would be a major accomplishment. As Viktor Frankl remarks,

> Man . . . may well change himself, otherwise he would not be man. It is a prerogative of being human, and a constituent of human existence, to be capable of shaping and reshaping oneself. In other words, it is a privilege of man to become guilty, and his responsibility to overcome guilt.[22]

Indeed, Yom Kippur helps us to accomplish one of the most important steps in achieving mental health: mitigating the feelings of guilt that often plague us when we acknowledge that we have done wrong. As much as we may want to make amends for what we have done, that is not always possible. And even if we do make amends, we can be haunted by the thought of what we have done. The ancient rituals of the scapegoat were intended to carry away our sins, to rid us of that burden. Although we no longer have the scapegoat, we still have the entire ritual of Yom Kippur, as well as the Rosh Hashanah custom of *Tashlikh*,[23] to help us rid ourselves of these feelings of guilt and to come to terms with our imperfect humanity.

THE FESTIVAL OF LIFE

And yet, despite all the concern with sin, atonement, forgiveness, mercy, and justice that pervades the High Holy Days, if pressed to condense their significance into one word I would choose "life," *hayim.* Indeed, life and death are the overriding concerns of these days. Rosh Hashanah emphasizes life and its renewal; Yom Kippur deals with death and renunciation, but only so that we may return to life purified and reinvigorated. Together, these two holy days help us realize that life is God's most precious gift and humankind's most precious possession, something we must not only prize but that we must also deserve. In doing so, they concretize one of Judaism's most basic value-concepts, life itself.

The Days of Awe, a unique creation in the annals of religion, were created in order to permit us to contemplate life, its meaning, its beauty, its fragility, its demands. This "festival of life" resensitizes us and renews our commitment to life. It helps us realize fully the meaning of the biblical text:

> I call heaven and earth to witness against you this day: I have put before you life and death, blessing and curse. Choose life . . . (Deut. 30:19).

These Days of Awe teach us to appreciate the gift of life and to affirm the freedom and responsibility of each human being to conduct his or her life with morality and decency as God has taught us. They confirm for us that what we do or do not do matters, and they make us aware how easily we can stray and how possible it is to change, to improve and remake our lives.

The journey from the beginning of the New Year to the end of the Day of Atonement takes us from hopeful celebration of God's promises to an awareness that we stand in judgment for our deeds. We move through feelings of sin and guilt until we emerge cleansed by God's mercy and forgiveness. As the Rabbis taught:

> The Holy One said to them, "Since you came before me for judgment on Rosh Hashanah and emerged successfully, I look upon you as if you had been created anew" (J. Rosh Hashanah 4:8, 59c).

Beginning the Journey: Preparing for the High Holy Days

THE MONTH OF ELUL

Although the month of Elul—the sixth month of the year, which immediately precedes Rosh Hashanah—has no special importance in the Bible or in early rabbinic writings, various customs arose sometime during the first millennium that designated Elul as the time to prepare for the High Holy Days.[1] Because these days are filled with so much meaning and potency, they require a special measure of readiness. We are called upon to enter them thoughtfully and to consider what they mean. As the Maharal of Prague said, "All the month of Elul, before eating and sleeping, a person should look into his soul and search his deeds, that he may make confession."[2]

Jewish tradition points to the name of the month as symbolically appropriate—the letters of Elul form an acronym for the words in the verse *Ani le-dodi ve-dodi li,* "I am my beloved's and my beloved is mine" (Song 6:3). Believing that the "beloved" refers to God, the Sages take this verse to describe the particularly loving and close relationship between God and Israel. Elul, then, is our time to establish this closeness so that we can approach the *Yamim Nora'im* in trusting acceptance of God's judgment. We approach the trial not out of fear but out of love.

SOUNDING THE SHOFAR

One of the earliest traditions to develop in connection with the High Holy Days was the daily sounding of the shofar during the entire month of Elul. The eighth-century work *Pirke derebbi eli'ezer* mentions the practice, connecting it with the ascension of Moses to receive the second set of tablets, an event that occurred, according to tradition, on the first day of Elul. According to the Midrash, this is the period described in the verse, "God ascends midst acclamation; the Lord, to the blasts of the horn" (Ps. 47:6).[3] Since these second tablets represented the reconciliation between God and Israel after the sin of the Golden Calf, sounding the shofar reminds us that Elul too is a time of favor.

During the entire month, the shofar is blown at the conclusion of the morning services (with the exception of the day before Rosh Hashanah). Hearing this sound calls us to search our souls and reminds us that judgment is upon us.

SELIHOT (PENITENTIAL PRAYERS)

A more complex practice that has emerged is the recitation of special penitential prayers, known as *Selihot,* late at night or early each morning during the month of Elul. They begin with *Ashrei* (Psalm 145), followed by *Kaddish,* "verses of mercy," special *Selihot* prayers, and the confession. The *Mahzor Vitry,* an eleventh-century work describing the yearly cycle of observances and prayers, tells us that "it is a custom to begin on the Saturday night before Rosh Hashanah to rise early to the synagogue, before the sun rises, and beg for mercy."[4] In the words of one of the poetic texts recited at this service:

At the conclusion of the day of rest, we come first to meet You.
Incline Your ear from above, You who dwells amongst praise,
To hear the song and the prayer.

Selihot, prayers for forgiveness, are ancient prayers already mentioned in the Mishnah.[5] They originated as prayers for fast days. The Mishnah describes public fast days and the order of prayer for such occasions as featuring a series of exhortations that end with the words "He will answer us," recalling the times in Jewish history when God answered those who called upon Him.[6]

The *Tanna deve eliyahu zuta,* a midrashic work that dates at the latest to the ninth century, mentions a special service for forgiveness instituted by King David when he realized that the Temple would be destroyed. "How will they attain atonement?" he asked the Lord and was told that the people would recite the order of *Selihot* and would then be forgiven. God even showed David that this act of contrition would include a recitation of the "Thirteen Attributes of God," a descriptive passage from Exodus that expresses God's merciful nature:

> The Lord! The Lord! A God compassionate and gracious, slow to anger, rich in steadfast kindness, extending kindness to the thousandth generation, forgiving iniquity, transgression, and sin; yet He does not remit all punishment . . . (Exod. 34:6–7).[7]

The name "Lord" was consistently understood by the Rabbis as referring to the appearance of God in His attribute of mercy. Therefore, its repetition in this passage indicated that God was merciful at all times. As the Talmud put it:

> "The Lord! the Lord!"—I am the same before one sins and after one sins and repents—"A God compassionate and gracious. . . ." Says Rabbi Judah, "A covenant has been made concerning these Thirteen Attributes. They will never be turned away empty handed. . . ."[8]

The *Seliḥot* service also emphasizes the recitation of "The Thirteen Attributes." Over the centuries, special poems embellishing this passage were added to the *Seliḥot*. The exact poems to be recited may differ from place to place, but the basic elements of the service have remained the same throughout the Jewish world.[9] Because of its emphasis on God's forgiving nature, this text describing "The Thirteen Attributes" plays an important role in the Yom Kippur liturgy as well.

The tradition of reciting *Seliḥot* throughout the month of Elul may stem from the fact that it was customary to fast six days before Rosh Hashanah. Since the *Seliḥot* originated as prayers for fast days, it followed naturally that they would be recited at this time.[10]

Sephardic communities begin reciting *Seliḥot* at the beginning of Elul so that a period of forty days, similar to the time Moses spent on Mount Sinai, is devoted to prayers of forgiveness. The practice among Ashkenazim is to begin saying them on the Saturday night prior to Rosh Hashanah. However, if there are fewer than four days between the beginning of *Seliḥot* and Rosh Hashanah, the prayers are begun the previous Saturday night. The conclusion of the Sabbath was considered particularly propitious for such prayers of forgiveness, since it marks the beginning of a new week and the completion of a sacred day of rest and study.[11]

Originally, *Seliḥot* prayers were recited early in the morning, prior to dawn. There was a custom in Eastern Europe that the person in charge of prayers would make the rounds of the village, knocking three times on each door and saying, "Israel, holy people, awake, arouse yourselves and rise for the service of the Creator!"[12] It later became common practice to hold the first *Seliḥot* service—considered the most important—at a time more convenient for the masses of people. Therefore, the Saturday night service was moved forward to midnight.

The effect of a *Seliḥot* service can be quite moving. The mere gathering together of people at a time when they are usually asleep is impressive. We sense the extraordinary nature of the prayer and turn introspectively within ourselves. The prayers themselves are pleas for mercy. The melodies are sad and full of longing.

Properly chanted, they form an oratorio expressing the despair that accompanies separation from God and the desire to change and repent. The self-deprecation contained in the words, which express the feeling of life's fleetingness, and the burden of vanity that motivates so much of what one does, all cause us to ponder how we can break the cycle of our lives and change ourselves for the better. The possibility of change and of a better life is inherent in these prayers:

> "O Lord, hear our voice in the morning; in the morning we set them before You with hopeful expectation. Hear our voice. . . ."

It is always darkest before the dawn. Yet the dawn is not far off, both literally and figuratively.

THE PENITENTIAL PSALM

During the month of Elul and even through Hoshana Rabba at the end of Sukkot, the daily services are augmented by the recitation of Psalm 27 every morning and evening. The psalm begins with these words:

The Lord is my light and my help;
whom should I fear?
The Lord is the stronghold of my life,
whom should I dread?

The theme of this psalm, confidence and trust in God, is most appropriate to the holy days. We enter this time of judgment not with fear, but with trust that God's verdict will be positive. The next part of the psalm indicates that nevertheless we feel trepidation and ask that God not hide Himself from us:

Hear, O Lord, when I cry aloud;
Have mercy on me, answer me.

In Your behalf my heart says:
"Seek My face!"

Regardless of our doubts, the psalm concludes with words
of hope, without which life would be unbearable:

Had I not the assurance
That I would enjoy the goodness of the Lord
In the land of the living . . .
Look to the Lord;
Be strong and of good courage!
O look to the Lord!

It is often pointed out that the Hebrew word for "had I not"
is *lulei,* which (in Hebrew) is Elul backwards. By the conclusion
of Elul we should be ready for the most important days of the
year. We have become alert to the need for self-scrutiny, we are
aware of the approach of the day of judgment, and yet we are assured by the promise of God's love and closeness. The sounds of
the warning shofar have already entered our consciousness, and
the feeling of forgiveness has been awakened. Tishre, the month
of judgment, whose zodiac sign is the scale of justice, is now upon
us.

ROSH HASHANAH IN THE HOME

The observance of the New Year begins at home with the
lighting of the holiday candles before sunset and continues there
after evening services with the festival meal. Unlike Passover and
Sukkot, when holiday activities center on the home, the focus of
Rosh Hashanah is on the synagogue. Nevertheless, the observances in the home on Rosh Hashanah do set a tone and create
an atmosphere that is important to the celebration and appreciation of the holiday as a time that raises hopes for a year full of
good news and happiness.

The pattern of home observances of Rosh Hashanah eve is basically that of any of the biblical festivals, with the addition of special foods (including apples and honey). These mitzvot and customs are brief and simple and are performed in the following order:

lighting candles;
Kiddush;
washing the hands;
Ha-motzi (the blessing over bread);
eating apples and honey;
festival meal;
Birkat Ha-mazon (the blessing after meals).

The blessing recited when lighting the candles is the one recited at all the festivals: "Blessed are You O Lord, our God, Sovereign of the universe, who has sanctified us by His commandments and commanded us to kindle the festival light" (*ner shel yom tov*). This blessing is followed by the *She-heheyanu,* the blessing recited upon reaching a new season or festival, or upon eating a new food, or wearing a new garment: "Blessed are You O Lord, our God, Sovereign of the universe, who has kept us alive, sustained us, and brought us to this moment."

The festival meal, usually eaten after returning from the evening service, begins, as do all festival meals, with the recitation of the *Kiddush,* the prayer recited over wine, which signifies the sanctification (*kiddush*) of the holy day. Wine is the ancient symbol of that which is most pleasing in life. In the words of the psalm, "Wine cheers the hearts of men" (Ps. 104:15). It is not the wine itself, however, that is sanctified in the *Kiddush,* but the festival day:

Blessed are You O Lord, our God, Sovereign of the universe, who chose and exalted us from all peoples and tongues, and sanctified us by His commandments. You granted us, O Lord our God, this Day of Remembrance, a day of sounding [the shofar], a holy season in remembrance of the Exodus from Egypt. For You have chosen us and sanctified us from all people and Your words are truth-

ful and everlasting. Blessed are You O Lord, Sovereign of the entire world, who sanctifies Israel and the Day of Remembrance.

The *Kiddush* for Rosh Hashanah follows the same pattern as
the *Kiddush* recited on other festivals. Two sections are unique to
Rosh Hashanah: the first names the occasion—"Day of Remembrance *[zikaron]*," and "a day of sounding [the shofar]," both of
which are based on the biblical verses concerning the day—and
the second is the concluding blessing, which repeats the formula
found throughout the prayers for Rosh Hashanah, proclaiming
God as "Sovereign *[melekh]* of the entire world." At the very beginning of our celebration, then, we emphasize the three most
important concepts of this day: the proclamation of God's sovereignty (*malkhuyot*), God's remembrance and judgment of the
world (*zikhronot*), and the sounding of the shofar, the symbol of
the messianic hope of humankind (*shofrot*).

The *Kiddush,* like the candle lighting, also concludes with the
She-heheyanu blessing. In order to justify saying this blessing—
which is made only over new things—on the second night (since
the second day is essentially a continuation of the previous one),
a new fruit that has not yet been eaten that year is put on the
table and eaten with the holiday meal.

As at any meal, we wash our hands and recite the blessing
netilat yadayim (washing the hands), which emphasizes that the
table is a sacred place, a kind of altar, and the food a sacred offering. We then say the blessing over bread, *Ha-motzi,* over hal-
lot shaped like crowns, a reminder of God's sovereignty, or like
ladders, a reminder that humans are exalted or brought low at
this season, as they are judged for the future.

Next, it is customary to dip an apple in honey and say: "May
it be Your will, O Lord our God, and God of our ancestors, to
grant us a new year of goodness and sweetness." The idea of eating special food to symbolize the meaning of the festival is an ancient one. The Talmud teaches us that Abaye, the third-century
Babylonian Amora, as the talmudic Sages are called, advised eating pumpkin, fenugreek, leek, beet, and dates on Rosh
Hashanah—all of which were symbols of prosperity.[13] On the ba-

sis of this suggestion, various customs developed in France of eating apples, grapes, figs, and even the head of a sheep. (In the case of this last example, it may be the word *rosh*, head, that determined the custom. Heads of animals or fish were eaten in other places as well.) Jews in other parts of the world have developed their own customs regarding foods (including eating sweet carrots in one form or another, or pomegranates), but all the different culinary traditions reflect the same hope for a sweet and fruitful year.

Birkat Ha-mazon, the blessing after meals, is said after concluding the meal. It is the same as that of any holiday and includes *Ya'aleh Ve-yavo*, the special festival blessing.

The afternoon meal following morning services follows the same formula as the evening meal the day before, except that there is no candle lighting preceding it, and the *Kiddush* is brief. This afternoon *Kiddush* begins with the verses:

Blow the shofar on the new moon,
On the full moon for our feast day.
For it is a law for Israel,
A ruling of the God of Jacob (Ps. 81:4–5).

Kiddush concludes with the blessing over the wine, *Borei peri ha-gafen* (creator of the fruit of the vine).

It is customary is greet one another on Rosh Hashanah with the words, *Le-shanah tovah tikateivu* (may you be inscribed for a good year).

4

The Rosh Hashanah Liturgy I: Arvit and Shaḥarit

THE *MAḤZOR*: THE HIGH HOLY DAY PRAYER BOOK

The magnificent poems, prayers, and readings created over the centuries by the great Jewish sages and poets are all contained in the *Maḥzor*, the High Holy Day prayer book. Understanding this work helps us participate in the holiday services in a more meaningful way. The word *Maḥzor* means "a cycle" and refers to the books containing the prayers for the various festivals; it is distinguished from the *Siddur*, which contains the Sabbath and weekday liturgy. *Maḥzor* is an appropriate name for the festival prayer book, since it refers to the "cycle of the year" rather than to daily or weekly events.

There are many different editions of the High Holy Day *Maḥzor* today, some more and some less traditional. This prayer book is not the work of a single person or group, but a collection of writings built around a core of prayers; it is, in a sense, a liturgical outline created by the tannaitic Sages (second century B.C.E. to 200 C.E.) and later refined and added to by teachers, *payytanim* (poets), Geonim (leaders of the academies), and *Poskim* (religious authorities). Even before the modern period there was no single *Mahzor*, since the liturgy of the *Yamim Nora'im* is different for various groups of Jews. Although the central prayers are similar for all, there are some major differences concerning the additional poetic selections, called *piyyutim*, which have been added over the centuries. The discussion in this book concentrates on the traditional *Mahzor* of European Jewry (Ashkenazim) used today in Europe, America, and Israel.

LITURGICAL THEMES: KINGSHIP, CREATION, JUDGMENT, REMEMBRANCE

The liturgy of Rosh Hashanah reflects the dominant thematic strands that are woven together in this holiday: the celebration of God's coronation and kingship; the creation of the world and the beginning of a new yearly cycle; and the recognition of the seventh new month as the time when individuals, nations, and indeed all humankind are judged. These themes convey a variety of feelings, and the prayers and observances of the day likewise impart a mixture of rejoicing and apprehension, of confidence and trepidation.

The idea of kingship is, as we have seen, an ancient one that may have been connected to Rosh Hashanah from its inception. The concept of creation is closely allied to that of kingship. God becomes king when the work of creation is completed and God rules over all He has made. This link between the themes of kingship and creation is reiterated in that between creation and judgment. Rabbi Eliezer offers the following commentary on this subject, in his reading of the verse, "In the seventh month, on the first day of the month" (Lev. 23:24):

> The world was created on the twenty-fifth of Elul. . . . Thus we find that Primal Adam was created on the first of Tishre . . . at the tenth hour he disobeyed God's command, at the eleventh he was judged . . . . The Holy One said to him: Adam, you are a precedent for your progeny. Just as you came before me for judgment and I ab-

solved you, so shall your progeny come before Me for judgment and I will absolve them. When? On Rosh Hashanah, "In the seventh month, on the first day of the month."[1]

This midrash explains why days of judgment such as Rosh Hashanah can be celebrated with joy: God's pardon is built into the scheme of judgment.

The centrality of judgment as a theme in the Rosh Hashanah liturgy stems from the teachings of the early Sages:

> There are four periods of judgment: Passover for produce; Shavuot for the fruit of trees; on Rosh Hashanah all creatures of the world pass before Him as a troop of soldiers, as it is said, "He who fashions the hearts of them all, who discerns all their doings" (Ps. 33:15); and on Sukkot for water (M. Rosh Hashanah 1:2).

> All are judged on Rosh Hashanah and their sentence is sealed on Yom Kippur. So taught Rabbi Meir. Rabbi Judah says: All [fruits, produce, humans, and water] are judged on Rosh Hashanah and their sentence is sealed at its appropriate time [as above] ... so that the sentence of human beings is sealed on Yom Kippur. Rabbi Yose says: Human beings are judged daily, as it is said [in Job 7:18], "You inspect him every morning, examine him every minute" (T. Rosh Hashanah 1.13).

Judgment, as we have seen,[2] stems from the idea that Rosh Hashanah is the time of God's remembrance, when God fulfills His word and remembers us for good. Throughout the *Maḥzor,* these themes repeat themselves, reminding us that we live in a created world, under the sovereignty of a God who cares for us and holds us responsible for our actions.

ROSH HASHANAH PRAYERS

The first references that we have to specific prayers for the *Yamim Nora'im* are in the Mishnah (c. 200 C.E.) and in the Tosefta (c. 300 C.E.). These references make it clear that a liturgical out-

line was already in use in those times although there were variations and disagreements concerning what should be recited in the
service. In many cases, the specific words and verses to be included remained flexible. The talmudic discussions settled many
of these issues, and the Babylonian Geonim (especially those in
the ninth century and after) contributed a great deal to the ultimate formulation of the liturgy.[3] The poetic additions—the *piyyutim,* which enhance the fixed prayers—are frequently the most
well-known sections of the service. These emanate from the Land
of Israel in the early centuries of this era and from Italy, Spain,
Germany, England, and France in the Middle Ages.

The most ancient section of the Rosh Hashanah liturgy consists of additions to the various *Amidah* prayers. These include:
paragraphs beginning with the word *u-vekhen* (therefore); three
sets of verses on the themes of kingship, remembrance, and the
shofar (including the introductions and conclusions to each of
them); the sounding of the shofar, at first in connection with these
verses and then by itself after the Torah reading; and a special
paragraph of the *Amidah* called *Kedushat ha-yom* (the sanctity of
the day). The emphasis in this section of the prayers is on God's
assumption of the kingly throne and on "remembrance," that is,
positive deeds for the good of Israel that God performs when act-
ing as our judge.

The second layer of liturgy is composed of several brief sections added by the Geonim of Babylonia. These phrases were inserted into various blessings of the *Amidah* and have one common theme: the books of life and death that are opened on Rosh
Hashanah. Although this theme is an ancient one that appears already in the Mishnah (edited in 200 C.E.), it was not stressed as
overtly in the ancient liturgy as it was to be later.

The third layer is the works of the *payytanim,* the liturgical
poets who flourished in the Land of Israel and in the European
Diaspora from the early days of the sixth or seventh century (or
even earlier) and throughout the Middle Ages. The *payytanim*
composed poetry not only for the Rosh Hashanah liturgy but for
that of the Sabbath and other holy days as well. They created additions to many parts of the service, particularly the prayers be-

fore the *Shema* and various blessings in the repetition of the *Amidah.* Their Rosh Hashanah poems stress and elaborate on the concept of God as king and judge. It is in the *piyyutim,* the liturgical poems, that we find the most dramatic depictions of judgment and the most moving accounts of God's relationship to Israel and to the world. Freed of the constraints of the fixed, official liturgy created by the Sages, the *payytanim* employed imaginative imagery, rhyme, rhythm, and sound repetition in dazzling displays of creative erudition.

The ancient core of the liturgy remains closest to the origins of Rosh Hashanah as the exultant proclamation of God as king and the time of God's remembrance of human beings. The most important prayers are the three sets of verses connected with the themes of kingship, remembrance, and shofar. Each of these is expressed in the liturgy as a source of celebration. The kingship section of the prayers rejoices over God as ruler of the newly created world; the remembrance section stresses that God fulfills all the covenants made with Israel and humankind at this time; and the shofar section serves as an opportunity to recall revelation and anticipate redemption.

AN OVERVIEW OF THE SERVICES

The Rosh Hashanah liturgy is a multi-layered one developed through the centuries. The services on Rosh Hashanah follow the basic structure of other festival services, with the addition of special prayers; in fact, the Rosh Hashanah services closely resemble those of the three pilgrim festivals—Passover, Shavuot, and Sukkot. The main difference between them is the omission on Rosh Hashanah of the Hallel, the special collection of psalms of praise that is recited on the pilgrim festivals, on the New Month, and on Hanukkah. Historically speaking, the reason it is not recited on Rosh Hashanah is that Hallel was originally confined to the special Temple-centered pilgrimage festivals when all males were required to come to the Temple. Rosh Hashanah was not one of these. The later Sages, however, offered a different explanation:

> The angels said to the Holy One: Master of the Universe, why does Israel not sing a song of praise to You on Rosh Hashanah and Yom Kippur? He replied: Is it possible that when a king sits on his throne of justice with books of life and death open before him, Israel should sing a song of praise?! (T. Rosh Hashanah 32b).

Here again we see the tension between the festive aspect of Rosh Hashanah and its solemn face. For all the celebration, it remains the day of destiny when judgment is held.

The main services for Rosh Hashanah are *Arvit*, the evening service; *Shaharit*, the morning service, which includes the Torah and shofar services; *Musaf*, the additional service; *Minhah*, the afternoon service; and *Tashlikh*, the ritual involving a symbolic casting of sins into a body of water. This chapter will deal with the *Arvit* and *Shaharit* services; *Musaf, Minhah,* and *Tashlikh* will be addressed in the following chapter.

Arvit: *The Evening Service*

The first service for Rosh Hashanah is *Arvit* (also called *Ma'ariv*), the evening service. All Jewish holidays begin in the evening, since the Hebrew calendar marks the start of a new day with the setting of the sun. *Arvit* is the briefest service and contains the least amount of material specific to Rosh Hashanah. Nevertheless, the service does impart a holiday atmosphere, as it includes the gaonic additions concerning the Book of Life as well as the special blessing in the *Amidah* called *Kedushat ha-yom* (the sanctity of the day).

The service follows the same format as any evening festival service:

the *Shema* and its surrounding blessings;
the *Amidah,* the central prayer;
Kiddush, the sanctification of the day with wine;

Aleinu, the proclamation of God's sovereignty and of a hope for the future recognition of God's kingship by all humankind;

Psalm 27, the penitential psalm;

Yigdal, the closing hymn.

The *Arvit* service contains fewer additional prayers and poems than the other services. The reason for this absence is twofold: the evening service is considered to be somewhat less important than the morning and afternoon services, and there was a general sense among the prayer-going populace that it was dangerous to remain outside after dark—thus encouraging short and simple evening prayers. Additionally, consideration had to be given to the custom of eating the festive evening meal after the *Arvit* service. All in all, *Arvit* was designed as a quick and concise service.

The Shema. The *Shema* is traditionally recited at the center of a series of blessings:

the *Barekhu,* the call to recite the *Shema;*

the blessing of creation;

the blessing of the Torah;

the first paragraph of the *Shema* (Deut. 6:4–9), on the theme of Israel's love for God (the acceptance of God's kingship);

the second paragraph of the *Shema* (Deut. 11:13–21), on the theme of reward and punishment (the acceptance of God's commandments);

the third paragraph of the *Shema* (Num. 15:37–41), on the theme of redemption;

the first blessing after the *Shema,* an affirmation of the truth in the doctrines of the *Shema* and a declaration of the hope for redemption;

the second blessing after the *Shema,* a declaration of faith in God's protection.

In some European communities, additions were made to the *Shema* in the Rosh Hashanah *Arvit* service; in France, for exam-

ple, *piyyutim* elaborating on the sovereignty of God were added.
Other changes include additions made to the blessings before the
Shema that mention the sounding of the shofar. Since this central act of Rosh Hashanah is not actually performed until the
morning, there was an attempt to make up for its absence by
speaking about it, as this *piyyut* does:

Sound the shofar before your King
And you will be saved from your enemies
He will find merit in you
The Merciful One will utter "I love you."[4]

According to the *piyyut,* the purpose of the shofar is to remind God, as it were, of our merit. This poem thus articulates
the idea of God's mercy and pardon and suggests that, as the day
of judgment begins, we are already assured of our vindication.[5]
It is, perhaps, unfortunate that these sentiments do not appear in
our commonly-used *Mahzorim.*

The Rosh Hashanah Amidah *for* Arvit.   The *Amidah* is the
main prayer of Jewish liturgy. Essentially a prayer in which Israel
asks God for redemption, the *Amidah* may be divided into three
sections: the first consists of three blessings that praise God and
affirm our belief in God; the middle section is a series of petitions that changes according to the occasion; and the final section consists of three concluding blessings—a prayer for acceptance, acknowledgment of God, and a prayer for peace.[6]
     The last blessing of the first section, the sanctification of God's
name (*Kedushah*), and the first blessing of the middle section, the
sanctification of the day (*Kedushat ha-yom*), are of particular importance on Rosh Hashanah. The paragraphs that make up the
Kedushah are known collectively as *U-vekhen,* since each paragraph begins with that word.[7] The three paragraphs that constitute *Kedushat ha-yom* are called *Ata vehartanu, Ya'aleh Ve-yavo,* and
Melokh al kol ha-olam. The first two are recited on all festivals.
The third is unique to Rosh Hashanah.
     The first paragraph of *U-vekhen* implores God to cause the

entire world to revere Him. This is clearly another "kingship" prayer, no different in essence from that of the second half of *Aleinu.* The next paragraph discusses not the universal, but the particular: "Grant glory to Your people and praise to those who fear You." It discusses the return of Israel to its land and specifically to Jerusalem, the kingship of David, and the coming of the Messiah. The third paragraph describes the rejoicing that will come to the righteous "when the kingdom of wickedness is dispelled from the earth" and God will rule alone over the entire world from Zion and Jerusalem.[8]

Following this third and final paragraph is the concluding blessing of the *Kedushah,* which incorporates the verse recited in daily prayers—"The Lord shall reign forever, your God, O Zion, for all generations. Hallelujah" (Ps. 146:10)—with the ancient *Kedushah* formula used daily in the Land of Israel: "You are holy and Your Name is awesome. There is no God aside from You." The final verse, "The Lord of Hosts is exalted by judgment, the Holy God proved Holy by retribution" (Isa. 5:16), connects the holiness of God with the idea of judgment, one of the primary themes of Rosh Hashanah.[9]

Ata veḥartanu (You have chosen us) emphasizes God's love for Israel, a love demonstrated through God granting us the opportunity to perform His commandments and to observe the High Holy Days. In this prayer, Rosh Hashanah—which is referred to here as *yom teru'ah,* or the day of the sounding of the shofar (a biblical designation found in Num. 29:1)—is represented as a gift given by God to Israel in love.

Yu'aleh Ve-yavo (may our remembrance arise and come before You) asks God to remember, that is, to act in favor of Israel by bringing the Messiah and by restoring the Temple, the city of Jerusalem, and the house of David. Remembrance, as we have noted, is one of the major themes of the day. Indeed, the key word in this paragraph is "remember," from the Hebrew root *z-kh-r;* it appears eight times and includes the reference to Rosh Hashanah as *Yom Ha-zikaron,* the Day of Remembrance. Notice the emphasis that is placed here on the idea of God's remembering (or visiting) us for our good:

Remember us, O Lord our God, on this day for good.
Visit us on this day for blessing.
Save us upon this day for life.
Have mercy, pity and show grace unto us according to Your word of
salvation.

These words are most appropriate for Rosh Hashanah, the day
when God judges us and is asked to be merciful toward us.[10] Although this prayer is recited on all holy days, it was most likely
written specifically for Rosh Hashanah and only later came to be
used for other occasions.

   Melokh al kol ha-olam (rule over the entire world) implores
God to assume His kingship over all humankind.[11] Reminiscent
of the *Malkhuyot* section of *Musaf* and the *Aleinu*, this prayer
stresses the universal aspect of the day. If the theme of the previous paragraph is remembrance, here it is kingship, another of
the motifs of Rosh Hashanah. This paragraph concludes with the
formulaic signature blessing (*hatimah*), "King of the entire world
who sanctifies Israel and the Day of Remembrance." This formula
appears in every Rosh Hashanah service, in the blessing for the
prophetic reading and in the *Kiddush,* and so has become a refrain of the Rosh Hashanah liturgy.[12]

   Much briefer, but no less important than the prayers of sanctification, are the four insertions into the *Amidah* made by the
Geonim. These were first inserted into the Rosh Hashanah *Amidah* and eventually were incorporated into the prayers for the Ten
Days of Penitence:

> The insertion for the first blessing is, "Remember us for life, King
> who delights in life, and inscribe us in the Book of Life for Your
> sake God of life."
> The insertion for the second blessing is, "Who is like You, Father
> of Mercy, who remembers His creatures for life in mercy."
> The insertion for the sixth blessing is, "Inscribe all the members of
> Your covenant for a good life."
> The insertion for the last blessing is, "In the Book of Life, blessing,
> peace and good sustenance may we be remembered and inscribed
> before You, we and all Your people, the House of Israel, for life
> and peace. . . ."

These insertions may be seen as one unit with one theme: the Book of Life. They appeared originally in the *Siddur* of Rav Amram Gaon and were adopted by the various traditions. Whatever opposition they may have evoked at first was based on the fact that these are supplications yet they are recited in the paragraphs of the *Amidah* that are not petitions but prayers of praise or thanksgiving. This opposition was overcome, however, because of the feeling that on these special days the need of the congregation for God's favor is urgent.

The evening service is relatively simple in structure and easy to follow. It introduces the major themes of the day: God as king, God as judge, and remembrance. In the morning, however, the services of Rosh Hashanah grow in length and intensity.

The Shaḥarit *Service: A Coronation Ceremony*

The *Shaḥarit* service contains more poetry than the *Arvit* service and includes the Torah and shofar services. The *piyyutim* in the *Shaḥarit* service concentrate on the theme of kingship; because of these elaborate poems, the service emerges as Judaism's great coronation ceremony for God. Indeed, if we were to single out the one word that recurs most often in the service, it would undoubtedly be *melekh* (king). This focus on God's coronation and kingship is signaled by the fact that the first word uttered by the leader of the main morning service is *ha-melekh* (the king). Just as a herald announces the entrance of a royal figure with a trumpet blast or by striking the floor with a mace, so does the *Shaḥarit* service begin with the elaborate chanting of *ha-melekh*. It is customary for the leader of the service to chant a wordless, haunting melody, leading up to the strongly uttered word itself. This melody is repeated in the chants that follow as well, establishing a kind of leitmotif for the morning service.

The pattern of the Rosh Hashanah *Shaḥarit* service is the same as that of any holiday service, with a number of exceptions: alterations to the text of the *Amidah*, the addition of *Avinu Malkeinu*, the sounding of the shofar, and perhaps most importantly, numerous *piyyutim* added both to the blessings of the *Shema* and to the repetition of the *Amidah*. The format for the service is as follows:

the morning blessings *(Birkot Ha-shahar)*;
verses of Psalms *(Pesukei De-zimrah)*;
the *Shema* and its surrounding blessings;
the *Amidah*,
Avinu Malkeinu (our Father, our King);
the Torah reading, including the Haftarah (reading from the Prophets);
sounding the shofar;
returning the Torah to the ark.[13]

It is customary for the preliminary service—the morning blessings and the verses of Psalms—to be led by one person, while the main morning service is chanted by someone else. On Rosh Hashanah, the proclamation *ha-melekh* is the first word uttered by this new leader. The word *ha-melekh* is not a special addition to the Rosh Hashanah service, but is present in the text used in all Sabbath and holiday services, where it is one of the closing words of the preliminary service:

The God—in the vastness of Your might;
The Great One—in the glory of Your Name;
The Mighty One—forever;
The Awesome One—in Your awesomeness;
The King—seated upon a high and exalted throne.

On Rosh Hashanah, *ha-melekh* becomes the first word of the main service, setting the tone for the rest of the day with its dramatic, wordless melody.

The Piyyutim: *A Centerpiece of the Holiday Service.*   The institution of the *piyyut* (from the Greek *poietes*, poem) is an ancient one dating to early liturgical poets such as Yose ben Yose, Eleazar Kalir, and Yannai, all of whom lived in the Land of Israel sometime between the third and sixth centuries. Their work was emulated by the *payytanim* of Spain, Italy, France, and Germany during the Middle Ages. These poems were composed to add variety to the service and were intended for the use of the leader of the service, rather than for the congregation (except for refrains which the congregation could repeat). Worshippers would often come to a service expecting to hear a new poetic work of devotion that would enhance the experience of worship.

Just as English poetry developed a canon of different types of poems—such as the sonnet, the ballad, and the ode—specific forms developed for the *piyyut:* the *Yotzer* for the first blessing, the *Zulat* after the *Shema,* the circulare with two lines, the *siluk* before the *Kedushah,* and so on.[14] *Piyyutim* that were particularly popular became staples of the service. In the 1920s, Israel Davidson collected some 35,000 poems written by 2,836 poets, which were incorporated into the Sabbath and Holy Day prayers.[15] The serious tone of the *Yamim Nora'im* and their unique place in the Jewish year made them a particularly appropriate time for reciting *piyyutim.* Today, only a few of the most popular *piyyutim* remain in printed *Maḥzorim,* and the variety and novelty they were meant to introduce have been lost. Unfortunately, even these remaining *piyyutim* may be difficult for us to appreciate today, as they require a thorough knowledge of Hebrew, rabbinic interpretations, and biblical allusions.

The *piyyutim* have gained such importance in the holiday services that the practice developed of opening the ark and standing while some of the *piyyutim* are recited. Interestingly enough, this practice is not a matter of Jewish law, but rather of local custom. Paradoxically, it is because the *piyyutim* are *not* part of the ancient, mandatory liturgy that many communities sought to enhance their status by having the ark of the Torah opened while they were recited.[16]

MAJOR PIYYUTIM IN SHAḤARIT. The following are some of the major *piyyutim* found in the *Shaḥarit* service for Rosh Hashanah:

Or olam (everlasting light) is a *piyyut* that follows the blessing of the light, "who forms light and creates darkness, makes peace and creates everything" (recited toward the beginning of the *Shaḥarit* service), and is a one-line fragment of an ancient *piyyut:*

Everlasting light in the treasury of life
Lights emerged from darkness. He spoke and it was so.

"Everlasting light" is a reference to the light that, according to rabbinic tradition, God created during the six days of creation and then hid away in order to shine it upon the righteous in the afterlife. It is not known whether this poem was intended as a general meditation on the theme of light, which would be appropriate for any Sabbath or Holy Day, or whether it was written specifically for Rosh Hashanah, to indicate that the righteous would attain eternal life and the divine light; in either case, the placement of this *piyyut* at the beginning of the main service gives a special cast to the liturgy of the day, making us aware that it will be different from the usual liturgy.

Melekh azur gevurah (King girt with glory) is a *piyyut* by Eleazar Kalir, an early poet who lived in the Land of Israel. Since it is inserted into the blessing of light and creation, it should follow the usual pattern and expound on those themes. But since this poem was written specifically for Rosh Hashanah, it is more concerned with the particular themes of the day, especially the one with which the morning prayers begin: God as king. Even the structure of the poem emphasizes this theme: the poem is an alphabetical acrostic in which each verse opens with the word *melekh* (king), followed by a line that begins with a letter of the alphabet, in order.

The emphasis of this *piyyut* on the theme of kingship is revealed in its refrain, "King garbed in ten different garbs. Adorn Yourself in holiness. God who is adored in the midst of the holy ones. Holy One." The reference here is to a rabbinic teaching in which God is described as donning certain garments on ten different occasions in the Bible. The first is when God created the world, and the last is in the messianic era during the apocalyptic war of Gog and Magog (Pesikta derav kahana 22.5). The poet has chosen this lesson since Rosh Hashanah is both the commemoration of the day of creation and the day on which the nations are judged. The conclusion of the *piyyut* emphasizes the concept of *malkhuyot* (kingship): "King, eternal God, proclaimed king by the eternal people, the Lord will reign eternally" (Exod. 15:16).

On the second day of Rosh Hashanah, it is customary to recite *Melekh amon* (faithful king), a different *piyyut* composed in the same style as *Melekh azur gevurah*—where the word *melekh* (king) begins each verse, followed by an alphabetical acrostic. In *Melekh amon*, however, the word *melekh* appears only at the beginning of three stanzas, after which the word *zekhor* (remember) takes its place. Three stanzas later, *zekhor* is replaced by *shofar*. These words continue to alternate in the same pattern throughout the poem. The theme, then, is the Rosh Hashanah triad: *malkhuyot, zikhronot, shofrot*—kingship, remembrance, and shofar. Since the poem lacks any connection to the idea of light or creation, it may well have been intended originally for another spot in the service and somehow ended up here. The poet, who very cleverly signed his name in an acrostic, was Rabbi Simeon bar Isaac of Mainz who was born around 950 and is one of the earliest German *payytanim*.[17]

Kevodo iḥel ke-hayom (on this day He stretched His glory) is a *piyyut* attached to the section of the blessing that describes the proclamation of God's kingship by the angels. This form of *piyyut* is called an *ofen*—from the Hebrew word *ofanim*, the name for one of the types of angels. It is a relatively short and simple *piyyut* thought to have been written by Kalir and consisting of a single acrostic, where each line concludes with the word *melekh*. The first line alludes to the idea that on "this day," that is, Rosh Hashanah, the world was created, as stated in the Talmud in the name of Rabbi Eliezer (B. Rosh Hashanah 10b). More importantly, it stresses the idea that mercy was built into the creation: "This day He stretched His glory like a tent in mercy—King!"

Rabbinic Judaism speaks of the two attributes of God, *midat ha-din*, the attribute of justice, and *midat ha-raḥamim*, the attribute of mercy. While there is always a tension between the two—we expe-

rience God in justice and punishment, but also in love and forgiveness—Judaism has always stressed mercy above justice. This *piyyut*
and most of the Rosh Hashanah liturgy make it clear that although
both attributes exist and this is *Yom Ha-din* (the Day of Justice and
Judgment) it is mercy upon which we confidently depend. As the
piyyut puts it: "Arouse mercy for those who wait upon You—King!"

In an attempt to heighten the mystic sense of awe aroused
by the description of the heavenly choir, on the High Holy Days
a more poetic depiction of the angels is substituted for the usual
brief description of the singing of the angels found in the prayers
at this point:

The heavenly creatures sing,
The cherubim praise
The serafim chant in joy
The erelim bless—
All creatures, ofanim and cherubim face the serafim—
Opposite them do they praise and recite:
　　Blessed is the glory of the Lord from its place!

Although beautiful *piyyutim* were written by Kalir and others to enhance the blessing after the *Shema,* none of them appear
in the Mahzorim most in use today.

PIYYUTIM IN THE AMIDAH. Since the *Amidah* is the central
prayer of any service, it is important to address the *piyyutim* added
to it for Rosh Hashanah.[18] During the opening blessing of the
Amidah the leader—called the *shali'ah tzibur* (the representative of
the congregation)—recites a *reshut*, a poem asking permission to
interrupt the standard prayer with special additions: *Mi-sod
hakhamim* (from the teachings of the Sages) asserts that whatever
the *shali'ah tzibur* will insert is based on traditional teachings,
midrashim, and talmudic statements.

On the first day of Rosh Hashanah, the leader continues with
Yareiti (I am in awe), a *piyyut* expressing one's feelings of trepi-
dation at the task of being the *shali'ah tzibur* on this awesome day.
Yareiti was written by the eleventh-century poet Yekutiel ben

Moses of Speyer and is similar to other, more elaborate *piyyutim* such as the *Hineni,* which introduces the *Musaf* service. These *piyyutim* stress the inadequacy often felt by the *shali'aḥ tzibur,* who recites them to request God's guidance in the task of leading the prayers, and forgiveness for any mistakes that he or she might make in the process. The leader asks God to grant these requests based on the merits of his or her parents and ancestors and of the people he or she represents.

On the second day we recite a different *piyyut, Atiti le-ḥane-nakh* (I have come to implore), on the same theme. Written by Simeon bar Isaac of Mainz (whose *piyyut Melekh amon* is re-cited earlier in the *Shaḥarit* service), *Atiti le-ḥanenakh* allows the *shali'aḥ tzibur* to question his or her worth in even more vivid terms and to plead for God's mercy upon His people.

The weight of responsibility upon the leader of the service is very great; it is for this reason that these heartfelt pleas are ut-tered by the *shali'aḥ tzibur* at the beginning of each repetition of the *Amidah.* But what is the status of the "representative of the congregation"? In the earliest references to prayer, we find that there was always a leader for the service whose responsibility it was to guide the participants in the liturgy.[19] The official status of *shali'aḥ tzibur,* however, ultimately came to apply to the indi-vidual who recites the *Amidah.* Since the *Amidah* is the central prayer of each service, it is the obligation of each person to re-cite it; but because of the prohibition by Jewish law during the early centuries of committing prayers to writing, a problem arose for those individuals who did not know the prayer by heart and therefore could not recite it. Because of this problem, some au-thorities felt that it was sufficient for a person to recite a brief and abbreviated version of the *Amidah.*[20] The ultimate solution, however, was to have the *Amidah* recited aloud by one who rep-resented the congregation, the *shali'aḥ,* or messenger. Since the prayer of the *shali'aḥ tzibur* is thought to represent that of the in-dividual, it is important for the messenger to perform perfectly. As the Mishnah puts it: "If one recites the *Amidah* and errs, it is a bad omen for him. If he is the 'representative of the congre-gation,' it is a bad omen for those who sent him, since a person's messenger is considered to be the person himself" (M. Berahot 5.5).

Several additional *piyyutim* are inserted into the third blessing of the *Amidah,* the *Kedushah.* This blessing calls on Israel to imitate the mystic utterances of the angels in their praise of God[21] and was an inspiration for further poetic exegesis:

Ata hu eloheinu (You are our God) is attributed to Kalir and is a clear example of his simple, concise poetic style. The *piyyut* goes through the alphabet quoting short biblical phrases that describe and praise God. Interestingly enough, this poem is not specific to the New Year and mentions none of the special themes of the Rosh Hashanah liturgy. In fact, it would be equally suitable for any *Kedushah.*

The following *piyyut, Ta'ir ve-tari'a* (rouse Yourself and sound the shofar), was also written by Kalir and is in the form of an acrostic that spells out his name. Although the theme of kingship is prominent here, this *piyyut* introduces a new idea: this is the moment for God to sound the shofar, the signal for freedom, and to overthrow the enemies of Israel, who destroyed Jerusalem and Judea and exiled the people of Israel. This nationalistic tone is a departure from the older, more basic concepts embodied in the Rosh Hashanah liturgy; it expresses a preoccupation with the status of the Jewish people following the destruction of the Second Temple. For Kalir, a poet living in the Land of Israel, this issue must have been particularly pressing, and he writes about the destruction of Jerusalem and the adversaries whose hands were all powerful, calling upon God to respond: "Rouse Yourself and sound the shofar to destroy all the forces of evil. Be sanctified by those who know how to sound the shofar. Holy One."

On the second day of Rosh Hashanah, the poem *U-vekhen va-Adonai pakad et Sarah* (and the Lord visited Sarah) is recited instead.[22] It was written by Rabbi Simeon of Mainz and is based on the biblical reading for Rosh Hashanah concerning Sarah's miraculous conception of Isaac (Gen. 21:1). The poet asks that, just as God visited Sarah, so should God visit her descendants for good. Each line contains a biblical quotation and ends with the word *kadosh* (holy). This *piyyut* contains allusions to many Rosh

Hashanah themes—the Book of Life, remembrance, repentance, observance of the covenant ("The Thirteen Attributes of Mercy"), and kingship—and also addresses the theme of the previous *piyyut,* the destruction of Israel by the nations and the call for national restoration and redemption.

The next *piyyut, Eten le-fo'ali tzedek* (I will proclaim my master's justice), is also by Rabbi Simeon of Mainz. An alphabetical acrostic composed of many biblical quotations, this poem discusses the justice God will show on the Day of Judgment. The main subject is Rosh Hashanah as *Yom Ha-din,* the Day of Judgment. God is described here as the perfect and merciful judge who calls upon all to search their hearts. The refrain originally was recited throughout the poem:

He judges the world with righteousness and the peoples with equity (Ps. 9:9).
He is one; who can dissuade Him? Whatever He desires, He does (Job 23:13). Awesome and holy!

Like many of the *piyyutim, Eten le-fo'ali tzedek* draws on verses from the Book of Job. The story of Job—the righteous man who demands justice of God and, after considerable suffering, is finally vindicated—is an appropriate subtext for these days of heavenly judgment. Rabbi Simeon and others who lived in a European society in which the Jew seldom triumphed may have found inspiration in the figure of Job and his ultimate triumph over suffering.

Several *piyyutim* are centered around the idea of God's kingship: *Adirei ayumah* (those mighty and awesome) is recited on the first day of Rosh Hashanah. Like many other *piyyutim,* this poem forms an alphabetical acrostic; here, each line concludes with the Hebrew word *be-kol* (aloud), which refers to the way the heavenly choirs and the people, Sages, and singers of Israel all give praise to God. The verses are written in sets of three. After the leader recites the first verse, the congregation responds, "The Lord is King"; after the second verse, "The Lord was King"; and after the third, "The Lord will be King." The refrain, repeated after each set of triplets, is, "The Lord is King, the Lord was King, the Lord will be King for ever and ever." The idea expressed in the *piyyut*— that the praise of God is made both on earth and in heaven—is the very essence of the *Kedushah,* which this poem is meant to introduce.

On the second day of Rosh Hashanah it is customary to substitute a different *piyyut* on the theme of God's kingship, *Melekh elyon* (most high king). Written by Rabbi Simeon of Mainz, this *piyyut* (an alphabetical acrostic) describes and praises God as king. Originally, the stanzas praising God alternated with parallel verses describing "the inferior king," that is human monarchs, but only one such stanza remains today.

Another *piyyut, Kol shinanei shaḥak* (all the hosts of heaven), recited on the second day uses the same refrain as the earlier *Adirei ayumah,* "The Lord is King, the Lord was King, the Lord will be King for ever and ever." Each verse consists of three lines each. The first line describes those in heaven who praise God, the second line describes those on earth who do so, and the third line speaks of *eilu ve-eilu*—both of these praising God together. The poem was written by Rabbi Simeon of Mainz and contains acrostics of his name.

The *piyyut* that brings this series to a conclusion and leads immediately to the *Kedushah* is perhaps the most famous of them all: *Le-el orekh din* (God who arranges judgment). In this short, classical *piyyut* by Eleazar Kalir, each stich begins with the letter *lamed* (used in its sense of "to"), followed by the letters of the alphabet in order. The first part of each line concludes with the word *din,* judgment, and the second part concludes with *be-yom din,* on the day of judgment, that is, Rosh Hashanah.

Although this magnificent poem precedes the *Kedushah,* it is not thematically connected to it. Rather, it stands alone as an expression of judgment, a major theme of Rosh Hashanah that has not yet been expressed in such blatant terms. The *piyyutim* up to this point in the service are concerned with God as King; the gaonic additions focus on the Book of Life. This poem, however, details the process of the trial and the judgment itself and thus adds a solemn note to the liturgy.

Rosh Hashanah, as the Mishnah teaches, is the day when all human beings are judged.[23] *Le-el orekh din* describes the God of justice, emphasizing God's quality of justice *(midat ha-din)* and reiterating that God judges mercifully: "He forgives sins . . . He exercises mercy . . . He is merciful to His people." Justice, according to the poet, is performed with the quality of mercy. This idea is reminiscent of the midrash concerning Abraham's dispute with God over the destruction of the cities of Sodom and Gomorrah. In this midrash, Rabbi Levi comments on the biblical verse, "Shall not the Judge of all the earth do justice?" (Gen. 18:25), which he reads not as a question but as a statement addressed by Abraham to God:

> The Judge of all the earth shall not do justice: if You want a world, there can be no justice. If You want justice, there can be no world. You are trying to grasp the rope at both ends. You want the world and You want justice. If You do not let go of justice, there will be no world (Genesis Rabba 49.25).

Were God to judge the world by absolute standards, it would not survive. God's justice, we believe, is, in fact, mercy.

Avinu Malkeinu.   *Avinu malkeinu* (Our Father, our King) is a penitential prayer that originated on fast days as a plea for rain. It has been included in an expanded version in the services during the period from Rosh Hashanah through Yom Kippur with the exception of the Sabbath, when such penitential prayers are never recited. They are inappropriate for the Sabbath, a day of joy. It is recited standing, before the open Ark, following the repetition of the Amidah.

The Talmud ascribes the origin of this prayer to Rabbi Akiba:

> Once Rabbi Eliezer came before the Ark and recited the twenty-four blessings (said on fast days) but his prayer was not answered. Rabbi Akiba then came before the Ark and exclaimed, "Our Father, our King, we have no king but you; our Father, our King, have mercy upon us for Your own sake!" whereupon the rain fell (B. Taanit 25b).

The Talmud ascribes the efficacy of the prayer to the forgiving nature of Rabbi Akiba. The formula is a unique one, combining what are usually seen as two contradictory features, that of a parent who is loving and accepting, and that of a sovereign who is usually seen as stern and demanding. God, however, is both. God is our ruler, but also our parent. Therefore we can appeal to Him for love, understanding, and forgiveness. It is as if we say to God, "We acknowledge You as sovereign, as all powerful, but we also know that we are Your children and can depend upon Your love and forgiveness." The specific list of prayers that now appears has undergone many changes over the centuries, but it retains the core, the beautiful formula devised by Akiba for addressing God.

The Torah Service.   The reading of selections from the Torah and the Prophets is a practice that stems from ancient times.[24] In fact, synagogues originally were places designated for reading the Torah and expounding upon it. Prayer played only a secondary role.[25]

In addition to the verses usually recited when the Torah is taken from the ark, the passage of "The Thirteen Attributes of God" (Exod. 34:6–7) is recited here three times on the festivals and on the Days of Awe. This kabbalistic practice began sometime in the sixteenth century under the influence of the Ari, the well-known Isaac Luria of Safed. Though the appropriateness of this passage on the festivals is questionable, one can easily understand why it should be said on the Days of Awe: these attributes, according to rabbinic interpretation, are God's assurance of His mercy and readiness to forgive. They bring to a conclusion the biblical story of the Golden Calf and mark the reconciliation of God with the people of Israel. They also form the basis of the *Selihot* prayers, the prayers of penitence that are recited before the High Holy Days, and that are so integral to Yom Kippur.

The Shofar Service.   Before the scrolls of the Torah are returned to the ark, the shofar service is performed. The placement of the shofar service is particularly appropriate, since there is a close tie between the significance of the shofar and the Torah readings on Rosh Hashanah, which describe the binding of Isaac and the substitution of a ram whose horn, in rabbinic tradition, became the shofar. We have hardly finished listening to the biblical stories connected with the sounding of the shofar, when the mitzvah itself is performed.

THE ORIGINS OF THE SHOFAR. Most holy days have some specific action-symbol connected to them. On Passover it is the Pascal Lamb and the unleavened bread that we eat; on Sukkot it is the four species—the *lulav* (composed of the palm branch, the myrtle, and the willow) and the *etrog* (citron)—that we wave, along with the sukkah, the booth, in which we sit; and on Rosh Hashanah it is the shofar—the ram's horn—that we sound and heed.

The commandment to sound the shofar is found in Leviticus: "In the seventh month, on the first day of the month, you shall observe complete rest, a sacred occasion commemorated with loud blasts" (Lev. 23:24), and in Numbers: "You shall observe it as a day when the horn is sounded" (Num. 29:1). Although it may have been the practice to sound the shofar on every new moon, the specific commandment applies only to the seventh new moon. Aside from cessation of work and the bringing of specific sacrifices, this is the only biblical commandment connected with Rosh Hashanah.

Anthropologists and historians of religion have argued that this symbol was not born de novo when Judaism came into being. Long before the inception of the religion of Israel, there existed religions in which the sounding of the horn was part of ritual practice. Judaism, then, did not invent this ritual, but rather reinvented it, divesting it of all former pagan meaning and incorporating it into the framework of monotheism. Some scholars have suggested that the making of loud noises on the New Year (a common practice even in the modern world) originally was connected with an attempt to frighten demons away so that the forces of good would triumph and the New Year would be a happy one.[26] There is no evidence that this approach informed the act of blowing the shofar in the religion of ancient Israel; nonetheless, it is interesting to note that the Talmud ascribes to the shofar the power "to confuse the accuser,"[27] suggesting that the sound of the shofar would destroy the power of Satan to speak against Israel on these holy days. Latter-day mystics, following this talmudic tradition, added a collection of verses from psalms to be read before the blowing of the shofar; one of them, *Min ha-meitzar* (out of the depths), is composed of an acrostic that reads, *kera satan* (destroy Satan).

Another ancient use of the horn on the New Year was to proclaim the coronation of the victorious gods. We can see how this practice has been reinterpreted in Jewish tradition, which sees Rosh Hashanah as the day when God, having completed the work of creation, is crowned king. In the words of the psalmist: "With trumpets and the blast of the horn, raise a shout before the Lord, the king" (Ps. 98:6).

Over the course of time, other meanings were ascribed to the action-symbol of the shofar. The most important is the connection made between the horn of the New Year and the horn of the ram in the story of the binding of Isaac.[28] According to the Midrash, God instructed Abraham that whenever his children were in danger of punishment because of sin, they were to blow the shofar—the horn of the ram caught in the thicket. That act would "remind God," as it were, of the merits earned by the binding of Isaac, and the people would therefore be forgiven.[29] The biblical idea of "remembrance" is thus enhanced with another meaning: God recalls the merit of Isaac and so redeems us from punishment for sin. The blowing of the shofar, then, serves to signify not only the coronation of God, but a means of arousing God to mercy.

The ninth-century master Saadiah Gaon offered his own interpretation, listing ten reasons for sounding the ram's horn:

1. accepting the kingship of God over creation;

2. announcing the beginning of the period of repentance, to warn people against transgression;

3. reminding us of the covenant at Sinai, when the ram's horn was heard;

4. reminding us of the warning words of the prophets (Ezek. 33:4–5);

5. reminding us of the destruction of the Temple and the alarms of battle;

6. reminding us of the binding of Isaac;

7. causing us to tremble and do the will of God;

8. reminding us of the great day of judgment when the horn will be sounded (Zeph. 1:14–16);

9. reminding us of the in-gathering of the exiles (Isa. 27:13);

10. reminding us of the revival of the dead (Isa. 18:3).[30]

Maimonides, a later scholar, suggested that the act of blowing the shofar was intended not for God but for human beings. He saw it as a means of compelling people to reconsider their actions and to repent or, as he put it, to "abandon evil ways and wicked thoughts."[31]

These interpretations (as well as others) are incorporated, in one way or another, into the Rosh Hashanah liturgy.[32] But for the listener, the sound of the shofar evokes a visceral, rather than intellectual, response: it conjures feelings of ancient times and sacred beginnings, and of one's place in the universe and one's relationship to the past, to Judaism, and to God.

WHEN IS THE SHOFAR SOUNDED?   The Torah prescribes the sounding of the horn but does not say when or how this ritual act is to be performed. It is rabbinic Judaism that supplies these details, as outlined in the Mishnah:

The following is the order of the blessings: One recites the Patriarchs, the Might of God, the Sanctity of the Name, including Kingship verses in it, and does not sound the shofar; the Sanctity of the Day and sounds the shofar, remembrance and sounds the shofar, *shofrot* and sounds the shofar . . . so taught Rabbi Yohanan ben Nuri. Rabbi Akiba said: If he does not sound the shofar with the saying of the kingship verses, why say them? Rather . . . he includes the kingship verses with the sanctification of the day and sounds the shofar, remembrance and sounds the shofar, *shofrot* and sounds the shofar . . . (M. Rosh Hashanah 4:5).

The reference here is to the main service of Rosh Hashanah, which was, in the rabbinic period, the morning *(Shaḥarit)* service. At some later time, this practice was changed, so that the sounding of the shofar and the reading of biblical verses connected with it were postponed until quite late in the day.[33] The Rabbis explained this postponement as follows:

> It once happened that they sounded the shofar at the beginning [of the day]. The enemy [the Romans] assumed that this was the signal for an uprising against them so they attacked and killed them.[34]

Although the historicity of this specific event is not verifiable, what is clear is that the shofar, like the trumpet of the Romans, was an instrument used in biblical times to signal battle—as exemplified in the story of Joshua and the walls of Jericho. Sounding it later, to avoid any misunderstanding, when it was obviously a part of the ritual of the day, was therefore plausible and indeed advisable.

Yet, moving the sounding of the shofar from *Shaḥarit* to *Musaf* was not completely appropriate. Indeed, the talmudic Rabbis found it problematic that the main mitzvah of the day was not performed until such a late time. An additional blowing of the shofar was therefore added at the conclusion of the Torah service (without the biblical verses that once accompanied the act), and the sounding of the shofar was never returned to its original place. Interestingly enough, then, what has come to be seen today as the main shofar service was originally a secondary service.

These two shofar services have specific names. The first is called "sitting" and the second (during the repetition of the *Musaf Amidah*) is called "standing." The latter refers to the *Amidah,* which means "standing." "Sitting" refers merely to a time other than the standing *Amidah.* Regardless of the name of the service, the custom is to stand whenever the shofar is sounded.

THE "SITTING" SHOFAR SERVICE.   The shofar service conducted after the Torah reading begins with the chanting of Psalm 47, which could well have been read on Rosh Hashanah in the Temple.[35] Its appropriateness to Rosh Hashanah is obvious:

God ascends midst acclamation:
the Lord, to the blasts of the shofar (47:6).
God reigns over the nations;
God is seated on His holy throne (47:9).

In some congregations, this psalm is recited seven times. This repetition is another of the many Lurianic mystical practices that have become part of the Rosh Hashanah service.[36]

The two blessings, "to hear the sound of the shofar" and *Sheheheyanu* (who has kept us in life), are recited by the person who sounds the shofar. While only one person blows the shofar, all the worshippers listen.

The Torah (Num. 10:6–8) mentions two different sounds, the *teki'ah,* one long blast, and the *teru'ah,* a shorter sound. Since the Rabbis were not certain exactly what the *teru'ah* was, two possibilities emerged: the *shevarim,* broken sounds resembling a moan, and the *teru'ah,* an outcry of nine staccato notes.[37] Both are used today.

Thus the blowing of the shofar follows a prescribed pattern; it is composed of three sets of blasts, each consisting of three repetitions of three notes. Each set is different from the other. The various notes of the shofar that are blown are:

teki'ah—one long blast,
shevarim—three broken sounds,
teru'ah—nine staccato notes.

The pattern of blasts is as follows:

teki'ah—shevarim teru'ah—teki'ah;
teki'ah—shevarim—teki'ah;
teki'ah—teru'ah—teki'ah.

The final *teki'ah* is prolonged (it is called *teki'ah gedolah*, a "great blast"). This last blast recalls the verse from Isaiah, "And on that day a great ram's horn shall be sounded" (27:13).

We conclude the service with a hopeful look toward the future, as the blowing of the shofar is followed by the reading of a verse from Psalm 89:

Happy is the people who know the teru'ah,
O Lord, they walk in the light of Your presence (89:16).

Since the first word of this verse in Hebrew is *ashrei,* this verse leads perfectly into the recitation of the next prayer, *Ashrei* (Psalm 145), after which the Torah is returned to the ark, concluding the morning service.

The Rosh Hashanah Liturgy II: From Musaf to Tashlikh

MUSAF FOR ROSH HASHANAH

From a logical point of view *Musaf*, the "additional service," should be just that—an addendum to the main service of the day. Yet *Musaf* actually *is* the main service of Rosh Hashanah. It is the longest and most complex service of the day, containing the most significant prayers and rituals. *Musaf* is so important that if the rest of the Rosh Hashanah liturgy were to be eliminated, and only the special inserts into the *Musaf Amidah* (the central prayer) remained, the essence of the Rosh Hashanah prayers would still be intact.

Musaf consists of the *Amidah* augmented by *piyyutim* and additional readings. It begins with *Hineni*, a special prayer recited by the *ḥazzan* (the leader of the service), who expresses feelings of trepidation and unworthiness and asks for God's assistance in the task of representing the congregation:

Here I stand, devoid of deeds, agitated and in awe of the Praised-One of Israel.

I have come to stand and plead before You for
Your people Israel who has sent me
even though I am unworthy.
Therefore I beseech You . . .
Help me succeed in my task . . .

The simple, sincere style of *Hineni,* combined with the beautiful melody with which it is chanted, makes this prayer one of the high points of the Rosh Hashanah service. In some communities, it is customary for the *hazzan* to begin this plea from the back of the synagogue and gradually come forward to the front of the congregation. This gesture emphasizes the *hazzan's* humility and reluctance to assume the sacred position of leading the people in the *Musaf* and stresses the fact that he or she is only a representative of the congregation and of no personal importance. Some *hazzanim* have made this gesture even more dramatic by having someone ask, "Where is the *hazzan?*" to which the *hazzan* would reply from the back, "*Hineni*—here I am!"[1]

Hineni is followed immediately by the *Kaddish,* the sanctification of God's name, sung in a special melody that is used only on the Days of Awe. The majestic tone of this melody captures the solemnity of the moment when we proclaim God's sovereignty. It also reflects the trepidation of human beings who know they are to be held accountable for their actions, and indeed for their lives.

The Musaf Amidah: Malkhuyot, Zikhronot, Shofrot

We have learned that the *Amidah* always begins and ends with the same paragraphs, while the middle section—the most important part of the prayer—changes to suit the occasion. In the case of the Rosh Hashanah *Musaf Amidah,* there are three blessings in this middle section: *Malkhuyot* (kingship), *Zikhronot* (remembrance), and *Shofrot* (shofar). These blessings represent the basic themes of the day. They were, at one time, part of the morning service and were only later transferred to *Musaf.*[2]

In ancient times the core of these three blessings existed as an independent prayer for Rosh Hashanah that was connected to the sounding of the shofar. They may have been created even prior to the destruction of the Temple and only later were incorporated into the framework of the *Amidah*.[3] The blowing of the shofar, as we have seen, was the main ritual performed on Rosh Hashanah and the only one mandated by the Torah for this day. During the Second Temple period, the sounding of the shofar was introduced by a series of biblical verses that conveyed the purpose and intent of the act. As the Mishnah teaches,

> No less than ten kingship verses, ten remembrance verses and ten shofar verses must be recited. . . . We do not recite remembrance, kingship and shofar verses that are punitive in nature. We begin with verses from the Torah and conclude with a prophetic verse (M. Rosh Hashanah 4.6).

While the Mishnah (compiled around 200 C.E.) does not describe a fixed list of verses to be recited, this text does insist that any verses read on this day contain the proper theme and be positive in nature. Even after the *Malkhuyot, Zikhronot,* and *Shofrot* sections were incorporated into the *Amidah,* it remained the prerogative of the individual to choose the verses to be recited. Eventually, specific verses were chosen and became a fixed part of the service.

Why these three themes of kingship, remembrance, and shofar? In the case of *Zikhronot* and *Shofrot* the origin may be traced to two biblical verses: ". . . a sacred occasion commemorated [*zikhron*] with loud blasts [*teru'ah*]" (Lev. 23:23), and "You shall observe it as a day when the horn is sounded [*teru'ah*]" (Num. 29:1). The third theme, that of kingship, is not explicitly mentioned in connection with the first of Tishre. Nonetheless, rabbinic interpretations attempted to find it in various verses:

> And on your joyous occasions, your fixed festivals and new moon days, you shall sound the trumpets over your burnt offerings and your sacrifices of well-being. They shall be a reminder of you before the Lord your God: I the Lord am your God (Num. 10:10).

According to Rabbi Nathan, "you shall sound the trumpets" refers to the shofar; "they shall be a reminder of you" refers to remembrance, and "I the Lord am your God" refers to kingship.[4]

The meaning of "remembrance" in the verse "a sacred occasion commemorated with loud blasts" (Lev. 23:23) is not entirely clear. The biblical scholar Baruch Levine suggests that it literally means "commemoration by blasting the shofar. . . . The horn was blasted to announce the forthcoming pilgrimage festival."[5] Leon J. Liebreich argues that "the first day of the seventh month is a day of arousal of God's mindfulness by means of the sounding of the ram's horn."[6] M. M. Kalisch, on the other hand, states that "the loud notes . . . were meant to rouse God's mercy in [the people's] favor, who would remember His people and grant them His blessing and protection in the coming year."[7]

The notion of remembrance is also connected with war, in the biblical text: "You shall sound short blasts on the trumpets, that you may be remembered before the Lord your God and be delivered from your enemies" (Num. 10:9). God's "remembrance" here indicates that God will not abandon His people but will help them. The text continues, "And on your joyous occasions, your fixed festivals and new moon days, you shall sound the trumpets . . . they shall be a reminder of you before your God" (Num. 10:10). The juxtaposition of these two verses suggests that Israel evokes God's remembrance to achieve success and to remind God to fulfill His promises to them.[8]

Whatever "remembrance" may have meant in the original biblical context, the Sages interpreted it, along with "kingship" and "shofar," in their own way:

> First proclaim Him "king" over you, then ask mercy from Him so that you will be remembered by Him. How? By the shofar of freedom. "Shofar" always indicates freedom, as it is said: "And on that day, a great ram's horn shall be sounded; and the strayed who are in the land of Assyria and the expelled who are in the land of Egypt shall come and worship the Lord on the holy mount, in Jerusalem" (Isa. 27:13).[9]

The order of the three themes, and the relationship between them, are therefore explained as follows: we accept God as our ruler, we ask to be "remembered" by God (that is, we ask that God fulfill His assurances and help us), and we declare our desire for redemption—for individual and national freedom—symbolized by the sounding of the shofar.

The Structure of the Three Blessings.   Three is an important number in the Rosh Hashanah liturgy: we sound three shofar blasts three times; we recite three special blessings (*Malkhuyot, Zikhronot, Shofrot*) with verses from three sections of the Bible; and we divide each of these blessings into three sections:

> an introduction or prologue affirming a quality of God,
> ten biblical verses,
> an epilogue with a concluding blessing.

The oldest part of each blessing is the middle part, consisting of the biblical verses. The concluding section was composed in order to allow the verses to fit properly into the framework of the *Amidah*. Last to be inserted was the prologue that introduces each of them.

KINGSHIP.   The introduction to *Malkhuyot* consists of the *Aleinu* prayer. *Aleinu* is a proclamation of monotheism as distinguished from paganism, possibly stemming from as early as Macabbean times.[10] Its vocabulary and literary framework are radically different from the prologues to the other two sections, which were composed specifically for them. It is one of the most exalted proclamations in Jewish liturgy. *Aleinu* consists of two separate prayers. The first, popularly known by its first word, *Aleinu* (it is our duty), calls upon Israel to adore and proclaim God. It focuses on the God of creation, who showed love for the people of Israel by making Himself known to them so they could worship Him while the other nations were steeped in paganism and idolatry:

It is our duty to praise the Lord of all,
To ascribe greatness to the creator of everything,
For He has not made us like the nations of the world
Nor like the families of the earth.

He has not made our portion like theirs
Nor our fate like that of their multitudes,
For they bow down to nothingness and vanity
And pray to an impotent god,[11]
While we prostrate ourselves and bow and kneel in thanksgiving
Before the king of kings of kings. . . .

The prayer continues with an affirmation that God created the world and is the sole God who exists.

The second part of the *Aleinu* is addressed directly to God and asks God to manifest Himself so that all the nations will come to acknowledge God and accept His kingship. The world will then be transformed, all human beings will have the privilege now afforded only to Israel, and the oneness of God will be completely realized:

Therefore do we place our hope in You, O Lord our God,
That we may speedily witness Your glorious might
As idols are eradicated from the earth
And false gods are totally destroyed. . . .
Every knee must bow to You.
Every tongue vow loyalty. . . .
For the kingship is Yours. . . .

This prayer is so powerful that it has become an integral part of each daily service, a fitting conclusion to every act of formal worship. When recited aloud on the Days of Awe, *Aleinu* (usually accompanied by a slight bending of the knees and bowing of the head) is often accompanied by a complete prostration (bowing down onto the floor) before God, physically demonstrating total obeisance to the Almighty.

Following this introduction, ten sovereignty verses are recited, the first of which is representative of the remainder: "The Lord will reign *[yimlokh]* for ever and ever" (Exod. 15:18). This verse was Israel's first proclamation of God's kingship after they passed through the Sea of Reeds. After reciting two additional verses from the Torah, we recite three from Psalms, three from the Prophets, and then the concluding verse from the Torah. With the exception of the last verse, all of them include some form of the Hebrew root *m-l-kh,* king. The last verse is the most famous of all: "Hear O Israel *[Shema Yisra'el],* the Lord is our God, the Lord is One" (Deut. 6:4). This is the verse that came to be used as the daily recitation of our acceptance of God's kingship, in the *Shema.*

The third section, the conclusion, begins with the phrase "Our God and God of our ancestors." The purpose of this section is to ask God to fulfill what has been described in the verses. We ask that God "rule *[melokh]* over the entire world in Your glory" so that "every creature shall know that You created him." This passage essentially restates the second paragraph of the *Aleinu,* which expresses a hope for worldwide recognition of the God of Israel as the sole creator and a hope for the acceptance of God as the sole ruler of the world.

REMEMBRANCE. The introductions to the Remembrance and the *Shofrot* sections were composed by the Amora Rav, the third-century head of the Babylonian academy in Sura.[12] Since paragraphs of the *Amidah* always begin with some sort of affirmation, he wanted these two, which had been added to the *Amidah* during the tannaitic period, to follow the same pattern. He took as his theme the idea of Rosh Hashanah as the day of the creation of the world and cleverly combined it with the concept of the day of judgment:

You remember the ancient deeds and visit all the creatures of old.
Before You are revealed all the secrets and the hidden matters from
   the beginning of creation.
For there is no forgetfulness before Your throne of glory, and nothing
   hidden from Your eyes.
You remember all that has been done, and no creature is hidden from
   You.
Everything is revealed and known unto You, O Lord our God. You look
   and gaze upon everything until the end of all generations.
For You have set a time for remembrance
to visit the spirit of all living things,

To be reminded of many deeds and the multitudes of creatures with-
    out end.
From the very beginning You let this be known, and from of yore You
    revealed this:
This day is the beginning of Your deeds, a remembrance of the first
    day.
It is a law unto Israel, an ordinance of the God of Jacob:
Concerning the nations on this day it is declared which are destined
    for the sword and which for peace,
Which for hunger and which for plenty.
All creatures will be visited on this day, to remember them for life or
    death.
Who will not be counted on this day, for the remembrance of every
    creature comes before You,
The deeds of each person and his works, the consequences of a per-
    son's steps,
The thoughts of each person and his devising, the inclinations of the
    plans of each person.
Happy the person who does not forget You and the human being who
    strives toward You.
For those who seek You shall never stumble and those who hope in You
    will never be ashamed.
For the remembrance of all deeds comes before You and You seek out
    the deeds of all.
You remembered Noah in love and visited him with news of salvation
    and mercy
When You brought the waters of the flood to destroy all flesh because
    of the evil of their deeds.
Therefore his remembrance came before You O Lord our God,
To increase his seed as the birds of the earth and his offspring as the
    sand of the sea.

This poetic prologue, which has been termed an "affirmation"[13] in that it affirms God and His deeds, is based on the rabbinic concept that the first of Tishre was the day when creation
was completed and the time when Adam was judged. It is also

based on the mishnaic teaching that Rosh Hashanah is the day of judgment for all humankind.

Remembrance here has multiple meanings: it refers to God's knowledge of all that we do and think and to God's positive actions (visiting or remembering) toward the righteous. Examples of this action are God's remembrance of Noah and of the Israelites in Egypt and God's recalling the merit of our ancestors. But it also means remembering in the sense of judging. Rav's contribution to the liturgy was to broaden the meaning of the remembrance section to include all of these and to emphasize one of the major themes of the day otherwise missing from the *Amidah*: this is the day of God's judgment of all human beings and nations. The positive and festive side of remembrance is darkened by the somber hues of judgment.

Like the verses that follow the introduction to *Malkhuyot,* the biblical verses that follow Rav's introduction to *Zikhronot* consist of three verses from the Torah, three from Psalms, and three from the Prophets. A tenth, concluding verse from the Torah is added in the paragraph that follows. In contrast to the introduction, however, all of these verses concern "remembering" in the sense of visiting for good and remembering merits earned and promises made. The other meanings of remembrance, so central to the rabbinic approach to Rosh Hashanah, are not found in the biblical texts.

The epilogue, the concluding paragraph, "Our God and God of our ancestors," also concentrates on the original biblical themes of remembrance as connected with merits and promises. A major theme that is mentioned neither in the prologue nor in the biblical verses, but that is featured in the concluding paragraph is that of the binding of Isaac. Using words that also appear in midrashim about the *Akeidah,* this prayer asks God to "let Your mercy overcome Your anger against us as Abraham overcame his mercy in order to do Your will." God is to remember the agreement that He made with Abraham following the binding of Isaac, as interpreted by the Sages, and to "annul Your anger against us. . . ." *Zikhronot* concludes with the words, "Blessed are You O Lord who remembers the covenant."

Shofrot.   What is the meaning of the section concerning the shofar? Certainly, there are as many meanings as there are interpretations of the purpose for sounding the shofar. When Rav wrote his prologue, his "affirmation" of one of God's actions, he had a very specific idea in mind: the revelation at Sinai. This revelation was not simply God's manifestation, but God "giving" the Torah to the people Israel:

You revealed Yourself in a cloud of glory
To Your holy people to speak unto them.
From the heavens You made Your voice heard
And revealed Yourself to them in a bright mist.
The entire world also quaked before You
And the creatures You had created trembled before You.
When You revealed Yourself, our King, upon Mount Sinai
To instruct Your people in Torah and mitzvot
You let them hear the glory of Your voice
And Your holy Pronouncements from flames of fire.
In thunder and lightning You were revealed unto them
And appeared to them with the sound of the Shofar.

This prologue leads directly to the biblical verses from the Torah, all of which (Exod. 19:16, 19 and Exod. 20:15) describe the revelation at Sinai. Next are four verses from the Psalms that describe the kingship of God as proclaimed by the sound of the shofar. Three verses from the Prophets express visions of the future when God will appear again accompanied by the sound of the shofar: "And on that day, a great ram's horn shall be sounded; and the strayed who are in the land of Assyria and the expelled who are in the land of Egypt shall come and worship the Lord on the holy mount, in Jerusalem" (Isa. 27:13). Unlike the prologue, then, these biblical verses speak of the shofar in various contexts, recalling the past, emphasizing the kingship of God, and looking forward to a time when the shofar will herald freedom and redemption.

The conclusion of *Shofrot* emphasizes this last concept, echoing a prayer recited in the daily *Amidah:* "Sound the great shofar proclaiming our freedom and unfurl the banner to gather in our exiles. Bring close the dispersed of our people from exile among the nations and gather our scattered people from the ends of the earth." *Shofrot* then ends by asking that all Israel be brought to Jerusalem to celebrate the holy days, sounding the trumpets as prescribed, over the sacrifices. The concluding blessing is: "Blessed are You O Lord who heeds the sound of the blast of His people Israel in mercy." Thus we return to the original purpose of the shofar as outlined by the Torah: to rouse God to remember and visit His people mercifully.

When the *Amidah* is recited aloud the shofar is sounded at the conclusion of each of the three sections, except on the Sabbath. Indeed, the original purpose of these verses and their accompanying introductions and conclusions was to provide a framework for sounding the shofar on Rosh Hashanah.

Piyyutim *in the* Musaf Amidah.   In addition to the sounding of the shofar, the other important feature of the reader's repetition of the *Amidah* is the *piyyutim,* the many poems that are added. The following is a description of the most well known of these *piyyutim.*

Mi-sod ḥakhamim (from the teachings of our Sages): once again the leader asks permission to interrupt the fixed prayers with *piyyutim* based upon the teaching of the Sages.

Upad me-az (this day was designated from of old): this alphabetical *piyyut* by the great Eleazar Kalir is added to the first blessing, the blessing of the patriarchs. It is based on the idea that Adam, the first human being, was judged and acquitted on Rosh Hashanah. It says, "The books are open before You and all pass before You in judgment." The *piyyut* concludes with a reference to the shofar: "Let the shofar ascend with a plea for mercy, to persuade You, Almighty, to freely pardon them."

Tefen be-makhon (turn from Your place): Kalir's reverse alphabetical *piyyut* for the second blessing of the *Amidah,* that of God's powers, is based on the midrash that God has a throne upon which Jacob's visage is engraved.[14] God is asked to seat Himself upon this throne and to be mindful of and merciful to

Jacob, that is, to the people Israel. Further reference is made to
two thrones, that of mercy and that of justice. God is asked to
judge the world He has created from His throne of mercy. The
plea of Abraham that God offer not justice but mercy, as the
midrash phrases it, in the case of Sodom becomes a plea for all
Israel. The theme of the binding of Isaac is also included as a reason for granting mercy; "The Thirteen Attributes," so important
in the *Seliḥot* prayers, are invoked here, too.

El dar ba-marom (God who dwells on high): this *piyyut*, of
unknown authorship, is similar to others we have already seen,
dwelling on the theme of God as king. Using alphabetical order,
it begins each line with "Most high God" and then describes God's
qualities using biblical phrases. The original *piyyut* alternated each
line with one that began "lowly king," a reference to human rulers
who lack power and dependability. With the exception of one
verse toward the end of the *piyyut*, these verses are not repro-
duced in *Maḥzorim* used today.

In most congregations these *piyyutim* are recited only on the
first day of Rosh Hashanah. On both days, however, the magnificent *U-netanah tokef* (we shall ascribe holiness to this day) is
chanted prior to the *Kedushah*. Although there are popular legends concerning the origin of this *piyyut*, we do not know who
wrote it. What is certain is that the poet was extremely gifted.
The structure of the poem and its language suggest that it was
composed during the Byzantine period.[15] The concepts on
which it is based come from Jewish apocalyptic literature and
parallel Christian writings based on similar sources, the most
famous of which is the *Dies Irae* (day of wrath)—found in the
requiem mass—which offers a vivid description of the day of
judgment for all humankind. In *U-netanah tokef*, however, the
subject is not the final judgment but the much more immedi-
ate, yearly day of judgment—Rosh Hashanah. The text of this
piyyut follows:

We shall ascribe holiness to this day
For it is awesome and terrible.
Your kingship is exalted upon it.

Your throne is established in mercy.
You are enthroned upon it in truth.
In truth You are the judge,
The exhorter, the all-knowing, the witness,
He who inscribes and seals,
Remembering all that is forgotten.
You open the book of remembrance
Which proclaims itself,
And the seal of each person is there.
The great shofar is sounded,
A still small voice is heard.
The angels are dismayed,
They are seized by fear and trembling
As they proclaim: Behold the Day of Judgment!
For all the hosts of heaven are brought for judgment.
They shall not be guiltless in Your eyes
And all creatures shall parade before You as a troop.
As a shepherd herds his flock,
Causing his sheep to pass beneath his staff,
So do You cause to pass, count and record,
Visiting the souls of all living,
Decreeing the length of their days,
Inscribing their judgment.
On Rosh Hashanah it is inscribed,
And on Yom Kippur it is sealed.
How many shall pass away and how many shall be born,
Who shall live and who shall die,
Who shall reach the end of his days and who shall not,
Who shall perish by water and who by fire,
Who by sword and who by wild beast,
Who by famine and who by thirst,
Who by earthquake and who by plague,
Who by strangulation and who by stoning,
Who shall have rest and who shall wander,
Who shall be at peace and who shall be pursued,
Who shall be at rest and who shall be tormented,
Who shall be exalted and who shall be brought low,

Who shall become rich and who shall be impoverished.
But repentance, prayer and righteousness avert the severe decree.

For Your praise is in accordance with Your name.
You are difficult to anger and easy to appease.
For You do not desire the death of the condemned,
But that he turn from his path and live.
Until the day of his death You wait for him,
Should he turn You will receive him at once.
In truth You are their Creator
And You understand their inclination for they are but flesh and blood.
The origin of man is dust
His end is dust.
He earns his bread by exertion,
And is like a broken shard,
Like dry grass, a withered flower,
Like a passing shadow and a vanishing cloud,
Like a breeze that blows away and dust that scatters,
Like a dream that flies away.
But You are King,
God who lives for all eternity!
There is no limit to Your years,
No end to the length of Your days,
No measure to the hosts of Your glory,
No understanding the meaning of Your Name.
Your Name is fitting unto You
And You are fitting unto it,
And our name has been called by Your Name.
Act for the sake of Your Name
And sanctify Your Name
Through those who sanctity Your Name.

These words lead directly into the *Kedushah,* the prayer of the sanctification of God's name.

Many consider this poem to be the pinnacle of the Rosh Hashanah liturgy. The poet has painted a picture of the most solemn day of the year, which to him is Rosh Hashanah, not Yom

Kippur. All other concepts associated with the day have been stripped away. "Awesome and terrible" are the only fitting words to describe it. The poet's primary concern is with the Mishnah's description of the first of Tishre as the day when humanity is judged. And he fills in the details that the Mishnah only hints at to spread before us a terrifying spectacle of heaven and earth called to judgment.

But this is not a day of suffering without hope; no matter what one has done, says the poet, the severe decree—the penalty of death—can be averted. Indeed, one need only follow the advice of the Sages: "Three things cancel the decree, and they are: prayer, charity and repentance" (Genesis Rabba 44:12). This rabbinic teaching is not confined to Rosh Hashanah but speaks in general terms of what one must do to avert the consequences of sin. The poet has set it correctly in the context of the day of judgment, focusing on the ten-day period from the beginning of Rosh Hashanah until the end of Yom Kippur as a time when these three actions must be undertaken to change the outcome of the trial.

There is a further note of hope expressed in this poem: God is depicted as a merciful judge who understands the frail nature of human beings. The pathetic description of the transitory nature of life and the heart-rending comparison between eternal God and human beings who are no more than "a dream that flies away" or a speck of dust that is gone with the wind are not intended to depress us but to impress God, as it were, and make Him incline toward forgiving us.

It is little wonder that this poem gave birth to legend. It is said that it was recited by Rabbi Amnon (Mainz, c. eleventh century) who had failed to reject a proposal of apostasy immediately and instead asked for three days to consider it. When he did not agree to give up his faith, he was taken away and tortured brutally. It was Rosh Hashanah, and he asked his disciples to take him to the synagogue, where he interrupted the service and recited this prayer in order to sanctify the name of God. Upon completing the recitation, he died. Later, the legend continues, he appeared to Rabbi Kalonymus in a dream and asked that this prayer be recited each year.[16] Moving as this legend is, it should not dis-

tract us from the *piyyut* itself, the subject of which is not martyrdom but human responsibility and the possibility for change,
as we face the judgment of our creator.

  Ve-khol ma'aminim (all believe) is the next major *piyyut*. It too
is part of the *Kedushah,* the third blessing of the *Amidah.* Probably written by the early poet Yannai, this poem is a double acrostic: the second letter of the first word of each line begins with a
letter of the alphabet in order (the first letter is always a *hey*). The
line is followed by the chorus: "And all believe that He is . . ."
which is, in turn, followed by a description of God that begins
with that same letter of the alphabet. The theme here is judgment:

He holds in His hand the quality of justice
And all believe that He is a faithful God.
He tries and searches the hidden secrets
And all believe that He judges that which is within.

The poet also speaks of God's remembrance of the covenant, of
God's kingship, and of God's forgiveness.

  Another alphabetical acrostic recited in some communities is
V'ye'etayu (they shall come), written by an unknown poet. In brief,
three- or four-word verses, the poet describes his vision of the
day when all human beings, whom he terms "Your servants," will
come to bless God and acknowledge His righteousness and sovereignty. Echoing Isaiah's theme that "many peoples shall go and
shall say: 'Come, let us go up to the Mount of the Lord, to the
House of the God of Jacob; that He may instruct us in His ways
and that we may walk in His paths'" (Isa. 2:3), the poet envisions
a time when all human beings will accept the kingship of God
and will present to God "the crown of majesty." Unlike
U-netanah tokef, this *piyyut* is an optimistic, universal recognition
of God, an expression of Rosh Hashanah as the day of *malkhuyot,*
the proclamation of God as King.

  Heyeh im pifiyot (be on the lips of the messengers of Your
people) is a prayer recited by the congregation before the leader
of the service begins the repetition of the most important part of

the *Amidah:* the sections of Kingship, Remembrance, and *Shofrot.* Here, the congregation asks God to assist the leader of the service so that all the prayers will be proper and acceptable. The poem is followed by a brief meditation by the leader himself, *Oḥilah la-el* (I will hope in God). These few lines are not directed to God, as prayer is, but to the *ḥazzan's* own heart and soul. The *ḥazzan* uses these words to strengthen himself or herself and to overcome his or her trepidation, placing hope in God, who will grant the gift of speech.

After each of these three special sections is recited, accompanied by the sounding of the shofar, two additional paragraphs are recited. The first is *Ha-yom harat olam* (today the world was born), a brief prayer expressing the idea that on the first of Tishre the world was created and on the same day all human beings are judged[17]:

Today the world was born; today stand in judgment
All the creatures of the world; either as children or as servants.
If as children, pity us, as a father pities his children.
If as servants, our eyes are directed to You until You pity us
And decide the trial in our favor, Holy One!

The second addition is *Areshet sefateinu* (may the prayers of our lips be sweet unto You). Here, God is asked to heed the sound of the shofar blasts "and accept with mercy and favor our order of . . ." and then the name of the specific section is mentioned: either Kingship, Remembrance, or *Shofrot.* This prayer dates back at least as far as the *Siddur Rav Amram,* compiled in the ninth century. Since it specifically speaks of the sounding of the shofar, it is omitted on the Sabbath, when the shofar is not sounded.

The *piyyut Ha-yom* (today) is commonly recited during the very last blessing of the *Amidah,* the blessing of peace. Again using an alphabetical framework, the poem asks God to bestow various blessings upon us "today." These include strengthening us, enhancing us, looking out for our good. The original poem went through the entire alphabet; the version in common use omits most of the central portion.

The *Musaf* concludes with the recitations of the usual prayers of any *Musaf* service: *Ein Keloheinu* and *Aleinu*. The only unusual feature is that in some congregations the full *Kaddish* at the end of the *Amidah* includes a sounding of the shofar, one of the methods found of coming to a total of one hundred blasts.

MINḤAH: THE AFTERNOON SERVICE

The afternoon service for Rosh Hashanah is similar to that of Sabbath or any festival day. It begins with *Ashrei* (Psalm 145 and additional verses) and continues with the *Amidah*, the text of which is the same as that of the evening service.

THE *TASHLIKH* CEREMONY

Since at least the fifteenth century a ceremony known as *Tashlikh* (literally, "casting forth") has been held among Ashkenazi Jews on Rosh Hashanah afternoon. In the sixteenth century it was adopted by Sephardi communities as well. *Tashlikh* is conducted near a body of water—a stream, an ocean, or a well—and commonly includes the recitation of passages from the Psalms and the Prophets.

The name *Tashlikh* derives from the prophet Micah's description of casting forth sins into the depth of the sea. Like the Yom Kippur ceremony of the scapegoat, the *Tashlikh* ceremony is a way of alleviating sins and casting away evil. And like another Yom Kippur ceremony, *Kaparot*, *Tashlikh* is not a rite devised by the Sages, but rather a popular practice eventually accepted by religious authorities. In fact, this ceremony, whose origins are unknown, may even have been a superstitious practice common to many peoples. As one scholar speculates, there was a "common custom of throwing sops to the spirits of rivers on critical days of the year."[18] This practice may explain why some of the customs originally associated with *Tashlikh,* such as feeding crumbs to fish, were opposed by religious authorities.

The significance of water as a purifying element in Judaism is well-known and serves an important function in the *Tashlikh* ceremony, too. Water was connected with the primal waters of creation. It is also associated with the story of the binding of Isaac, which plays an important role in the Rosh Hashanah services. According to rabbinic interpretation, Satan turned himself into a stream to prevent Isaac and Abraham from reaching their goal, but they did not let it stop them. Water is also the breeding ground for fish, which present us with an important metaphor for the *Tashlikh* ceremony: Ecclesiastes teaches that, just as fish may become enmeshed in a net, and birds may be trapped in a snare, so human beings may be caught by calamity when it comes upon them without warning (Eccles. 9:12). And so we can see how the basic themes of Rosh Hashanah—asking for God's protection and compassion, cleansing ourselves, and casting off our sins—are woven into the folk customs that became *Tashlikh.*

Whatever the origins of this rite, folk-wisdom was correct in seeing it as another opportunity to strengthen the positive feelings that Rosh Hashanah is designed to engender. Moving out of the synagogue into nature, where there is nothing but ourselves and our texts, can invest the afternoon with serenity and meaning. The readings for the *Tashlikh* ceremony are as follows:

I.
Who is a God like You,
Forgiving iniquity
And remitting transgression;
Who has not maintained His wrath forever
Against the remnant of His own people,
Because He loves graciousness.
He will take us back in love;
He will cover up our iniquities,
You will cast forth all their sins
Into the depth of the sea.
You will keep faith with Jacob,

Loyalty to Abraham,
As you promised on oath to our father
In days gone by (Mic. 7:18–20).

II.
In distress I called on the Lord;
the Lord answered me and brought me relief. . . (Ps. 118:5–9).

III.
Sing forth, O you righteous, to the Lord. . . (Ps. 33).

IV.
Out of the depths I call You, O Lord.
O Lord, listen to my cry, listen to my pleas (Ps. 130).

V.
In all of My sacred mount
Nothing evil or vile shall be done;
For the land shall be filled with devotion to the Lord
As water covers the sea (Isa. 11:9).

Some traditions include other prayers as well. At the conclusion, the practice is to shake out one's garments or pockets three times into the water.[19]

These readings convey a feeling of unrest and distress. We are disturbed by all that sullies our lives, and we turn to God to save us. Some of us may come to the service feeling troubled, wondering if we can indeed rid ourselves of what burdens us. But the biblical texts offer us hope: the final passage from Isaiah refers to the sea and proclaims that "nothing evil or vile shall be done." And so we may leave the *Tashlikh* ceremony feeling that we have been cleansed and healed and that the purity of the water can indeed wash away the guilt for our misdeeds and shake evil from the world.

What are these prayers of Rosh Hashanah meant to accomplish for us? What mood, what emotions might be evoked? Rosh

Hashanah produces a complex mixture of feelings: we may be excited at the thought of God's creation of the world and of God's kingship, and of the potential for a more complete kingship in the future. On the other hand, we may also be apprehensive of the trial that is now taking place, even though the prospects for a favorable decision are good. We should be considering our actions and character seriously and thinking of ways to change. We should be prepared now to enter a period characterized by repentance, good deeds, prayer, and meditation. We should feel that just as Adam was created at this time, so we are reborn and renewed. "Since you came for judgment on Rosh Hashanah and emerged exonerated, I consider it as if you have been created again as a new creature!" (J. Rosh Hashanah 4:8, 59c).

6

Opportunities for Change: The Ten Days of Penitence

Rosh Hashanah marks the beginning of the Days of Awe, the period of time designed to bring about both personal and collective change and renewal. At this time we are filled with optimism about the coming year, and we embrace the idea of a universe ruled by a compassionate God. We are also aware that we are in need of growth and improvement. The holy days spent in prayer and family celebration set the stage for what happens in the real world—the world of day-to-day existence, where we are sometimes confronted with difficult moral dilemmas. The days that lead up to Yom Kippur are the true test of the future and therefore determine how our decree will be sealed.

The period of time from Rosh Hashanah to Yom Kippur is known as the Ten Days of Penitence. This name appears in sources from the Land of Israel, including the Jerusalem Talmud.[1] The concept of these days as a special unit of time in the Jewish year dates at least to the third century B.C.E.[2] Rabbi Yohanan, who lived in the Land of Israel during that period, describes his conception of divine judgment and inscription in this season:

Three books are opened in heaven on Rosh Hashanah, one for the completely wicked, one for the completely righteous and one for those in between. The completely righteous are immediately inscribed in the book of life. The completely wicked are immediately inscribed in the book of death. The fate of those in between is suspended until Yom Kippur. If they do well, they are inscribed in the book of life. If not, in the book of death (B. Rosh Hashanah 16b).

The Ten Days of Penitence are seen as an opportunity for change. And since the extremes of complete righteousness and complete wickedness are few and far between, Rosh Hashanah functions, for the majority of people, as the opening of a trial that extends until Yom Kippur. It is an unusual trial. Most trials are intended to determine responsibility for past deeds. This one, however, has an added dimension: determining what can be done about future deeds. The Ten Days of Penitence are crucial to the outcome of the trial, since our verdict is determined both by our attitude toward our misdeeds and by our attempts to rectify them by changing ourselves.

The famous ancient *piyyut U-netanah tokef* discusses the fact that between Rosh Hashanah and Yom Kippur there is an opportunity "to avert the severe decree" through three actions: repentance, prayer, and charity. The requirements for repentance include a change of mind, a feeling of regret, and a determination to change, along with an effort to repair the effects of one's misdeed.

The efficacy of repentance and prayer were the subject of a debate between Rabbi Judah and Rabbi Joshua ben Levi, two early third-century Sages from the Land of Israel. Rabbi Judah teaches that "repentance cancels half the punishment for sin while prayer cancels all the punishment," while Rabbi Joshua takes the opposite viewpoint.[3] Another early Amora, Rabbi Hanana bar Yitzhak, recounted a legend of a meeting between Adam and Cain:

Adam said to him, "What happened regarding your punishment?" Cain replied, "I repented and it was mitigated." When Primal Adam heard this he banged his head and said, "So great is the power of repentance and I did not know about it!"[4]

The extremes to which rabbinic Judaism has gone to convince people of the possibility of repentance is illustrated in the Talmud by the story of Elazar ben Durdaya, a man who "sought out every harlot in the world":

> Once he traveled far just to enjoy the favors of one particular woman who spit in his face and said to him, "Just as this spittle will never return whence it came, so will Elazar ben Durdaya never achieve repentance!" He was so startled and troubled by this that he immediately attempted to repent: He went and sat between two mountains and hills and said, "Mountains and hills, beg mercy for me!" They replied, "Before we can do this for you, we must beg mercy for ourselves, as it is said: 'For the mountains may move and the hills be shaken'" (Isa. 54:10). He said, "Heaven and earth, beg mercy for me!" They replied, "Before we can do this for you, we must beg mercy for ourselves, as it is said: 'Though the heavens should melt away like smoke, and the earth wear out like a garment'" (Isa. 51:6). He said, "Sun and moon, beg mercy for me!" They replied, "Before we can do this for you we must beg mercy for ourselves, as it is said: 'Then the moon shall be ashamed and the sun shall be abashed'" (Isa. 24:23). He said, "Stars and planets, beg mercy for me!" They replied, "Before we can do this for you we must beg mercy for ourselves, as it is said: 'All the host of heaven shall molder'" (Isa. 34:4). He said, "This is dependent upon me alone!" He placed his head between his knees and cried bitterly until he expired. At that moment a voice from heaven declared, "Rabbi Elazar ben Durdaya has been received in the world to come." (B. Avodah Zarah 17a).

Another important rabbinic tale about repentance concerns the famous apostate Elisha ben Abuya (of the first to second century C.E.), who was urged by his pupil Rabbi Meir to repent, but replied that he could not. When asked why that was so, he explained that he had once ridden by the Holy of Holies on Yom Kippur and had heard a voice proclaim, "Return, O rebellious children, I will heal your afflictions [Jer. 3:22], except for Elisha ben Abuya who knew My power and rebelled against Me" (J. Hagigah 2.1, 77b). Saul Lieberman once remarked that this was Elisha's greatest apostasy, since repentance is always open to everyone.[5]

While repentance is the primary act to be performed during the Ten Days of Penitence, charity and prayer are no less important. *Tzedakah,* charity or acts of righteousness, requires that we look outside ourselves and see the needs of others. What can we do to help those who need us, financially or otherwise? In many synagogues charity plates are put at the door before Yom Kippur so that people can make donations at that time if they have not yet done so. It is important to point out that the emphasis placed on *tzedakah* during this crucial time in the Jewish year merely serves to impress upon us the need to make charity a part of our lives in general. Prayer, the other action that can mitigate our sentence, as it were, is a further method of introspection and change of character. The daily prayers and the special Sabbath between Rosh Hashanah and Yom Kippur intensify the usual services in a special way.

LITURGY FOR THE TEN DAYS OF PENITENCE

During the ten days between Rosh Hashanah and Yom Kippur, certain changes occur in the liturgy of daily and Sabbath prayers. These changes are recorded in the Talmud in the name of Rav, a third-century Babylonian Amora:

> In the *Amidah,* one says "King who loves righteousness and justice." But during the ten days between Rosh Hashanah and Yom Kippur one says "The holy King" and "The King of Judgment."[6]

"The holy King" is recited at the end of the third paragraph of the *Amidah* and "the King of Judgment" at the end of the tenth paragraph. This wording was based on the idea that during these ten days God is exalted in justice, as mentioned in the verse: "And the Lord of Hosts is exalted by judgment" (Isa. 5:16).[7] Although all scholars and teachers did not agree that this change was obligatory, it eventually was accepted as an expression of the belief that these ten days, and not merely Rosh Hashanah, were all days of judgment.

Other changes in the liturgy made somewhat later by the Geonim are references to being inscribed in the Book of Life, which were inserted into the first and last two blessings of the *Amidah:* "Inscribe us in the book of life, King who delights in life. . . . Who is like You, Father of Mercy, who remembers His creatures for life in mercy. . . ." Originally said only on the holy days themselves, these references eventually were carried into the period of the ten days.[8] Additionally, *Avinu Malkeinu* is recited daily, as are special *Selihot* (penitential) prayers. The special penitential Psalm 27 is recited.

In a sense, the language of the Rosh Hashanah liturgy is extended so that we may grasp the importance of the Ten Days of Penitence, which lead to the climactic moment of Yom Kippur. As the Talmud puts it, the ten days between Rosh Hashanah and Yom Kippur are a time to "Seek the Lord while He can be found, call to Him while He is near" (Isa. 55:6).[9]

SHABBAT SHUVAH

The Sabbath that falls during this time period also takes on a special character. The Sabbath prayers contain the additions outlined above, but the main feature of the day is the reading from the Prophets; regardless of what the Torah portion may be, the Haftarah for Shabbat Shuvah is always Hosea 14:2–10,[10] which begins with the words:

Return, O Israel, to the Lord your God,
For you have fallen because of your sin.
Take words with you
And return to the Lord.
Say to Him:
Forgive all guilt

And accept what is good;
Instead of bulls we will pay
[The offering of] our lips.[11]

The opening word of the reading in Hebrew is *Shuvah*—
return. The designation Shabbat Shuvah (the Sabbath of return)
comes from that word, although in gaonic literature it is called
Shabbat Teshuvah (the Sabbath of repentance).[12]

In a highly unusual move (since the prophetic reading usually comes from one single source), the Sages decreed that passages from two other prophets should be added to the Haftarah
reading. The first stresses God's forgiving nature:

Who is a God like You,
Forgiving iniquity
And remitting transgression (Mic. 7:18–20).

And the second passage looks forward to the conclusion of
this period by describing a day like Yom Kippur:

Blow a horn in Zion,
Solemnize a fast,
Proclaim an assembly (Joel 2:15–27).

The tripartite message is: repent, God will forgive, prepare
for the fast-day (the day of judgment).

Because of the importance of this Sabbath, rabbis have cus-
tomarily delivered a special, often lengthy sermon on Shabbat
Shuvah, even in places where it was not or is not customary for
rabbis to preach each week.[13] The objective of these sermons is
to move people to repentance.

YOM KIPPUR EVE: *KAPAROT*

Over the centuries, many customs have sprung up to enhance
the way in which we enter Yom Kippur, the final day of this sea-

son. Some of these customs, such as flogging oneself to atone for sin, happily have been forgotten. Others, such as immersion in a *mikveh* to indicate a state of purity, are still practiced by some. The most well-known and yet most controversial of these customs is the practice of *Kaparot*, which literally means "atonements," but in the sense of "ransom." Traditionally, a rooster is swung around one's head and is then slaughtered while being declared a "substitute" for the individual, as an atonement for his or her sins. Like the *Tashlikh* ceremony of Rosh Hashanah,[14] *Kaparot* is a folk-ceremony that may have had superstitious, pagan origins. Rabbinic opposition to *Kaparot* has been strong and remains so today.

Kaparot begins with the recitation of biblical verses, starting with the Book of Psalms:

Some lived in deepest darkness,
bound in cruel irons . . . (Ps. 107:10).
He brought them out of deepest darkness,
broke their bonds asunder . . . (107:14).
There were fools who suffered for their sinful way,
and for their iniquities.
All food was loathsome to them:
They reached the gates of death.
In their adversity they cried to the Lord
and He saved them from their troubles.
He gave an order and healed them;
He delivered them from the pits.
Let them praise the Lord for His steadfast love,
His wondrous deeds for mankind (107:17–21).

These verses are followed by an additional excerpt from the Book of Job:

Then He has mercy on him and decreed,
"Redeem him from descending to the Pit,
For I have obtained his ransom" (33:24).
To this is added the words:
Life for life.

Prayers are then recited, indicating the function of the rooster as a substitute for the individual. The rooster is twirled three times around the head of each man; a hen is used for women. Both birds are then slaughtered and given to the poor.[15] Some people have substituted money, in this ceremony, for the rooster or hen.[16]

One need not go as far as those scholars who see the *Kaparot* as originating in an offering to Satan[17] in order to understand the many objections to this ritual. *Kaparot* follows the pattern of the scapegoat, a ritual of riddance, but comes too close to superstition in indicating that one may substitute the death of an animal for one's own life. Among those who objected to the ceremony were the thirteenth-century Moses ben Nahman (the Ramban) and the sixteenth-century Rabbi Joseph Karo, who wrote in his great work the Shulhan Arukh: "The custom of *Kaparot* . . . is a practice that ought to be prevented."[18] Needless to say, the objections of great authorities were not sufficient to prevent this ritual from becoming an accepted custom among the people.

THE LAST MEAL

The meal eaten before the beginning of the Yom Kippur fast has special significance. The talmudic Sages were puzzled by the verse, "[Y]ou shall practice denial on the ninth day of the month at evening". . . (Lev. 23:32). Since Yom Kippur begins on the tenth day, why mention the ninth day at all? The Sages understood this verse as teaching that our meal at the end of the ninth day, the day before Yom Kippur, is as important as our affliction on the tenth day itself: "If one eats and drinks on the ninth day, Scripture considers him as if he had fasted on the ninth and the tenth" (B. Yoma 81b).[19]

Since this meal must be eaten before sunset, it is obviously not a holiday meal and there is no *Kiddush* to recite. Nevertheless, it is considered a festive meal, and the blessing after meals begins with the recitation of Psalm 126, *Shir Ha-ma'alot,* usually said only on the Sabbath, holidays, and festive occasions.[20]

Following the meal, candles are lit with the blessing, "to kindle the lights of Yom Kippur," followed by the *She-heheyanu* blessing, "who has kept us in life." Memorial lights are kindled for departed members of the family.

It is customary to give money to charity before the evening begins and to ask forgiveness of everyone for any wrong or slight, however inadvertent, that we may have committed in the past year. At the same time, we indicate our forgiveness of others. What a splendid time this is to bring to an end all feelings of rancor and bitterness that have accumulated, to eliminate petty quarrels that have sullied our relationships, and to begin the holiday with a clean slate. In this manner, we prepare ourselves to enter the most sacred and solemn day of the year free of hostility toward others, at peace with ourselves and with our fellow human beings. Peace with God remains to be attained through the observances of Yom Kippur, for that is the deepest meaning of "atonement."

7

The Yom Kippur Liturgy I: Kol Nidre

Yom Kippur, the Day of Atonement, has long been considered the most sacred day in the Jewish year. The idea of atonement, the central theme of Yom Kippur, affects us in a profound manner. Most of us are aware of our own faults and of things we have said or done that fall short of our own criteria for appropriate behavior. Yom Kippur offers us an opportunity to redress these wrongs, and many of us feel an urgency to do so during this time of judgment. The liturgy of Yom Kippur may inspire us to look within ourselves and to feel cleansed as we begin a new year and as we approach anew our relationship with God and with our fellow human beings.

The best-known of all the Yom Kippur services is the very first one: *Kol Nidre* (literally, "all vows"). Even though *Kol Nidre* refers only to the opening prayer of the Yom Kippur evening service, the entire service is commonly referred to by that name. For many people, *Kol Nidre* is the most important of all the High Holy Day services; indeed, it has attained a degree of unprecedented popularity among the masses of Jews for hundreds of years and still holds that distinction today. If a Jew attends only one service a year, it is usually *Kol Nidre*. Through the ages, *Kol Nidre* has become the time and place where Jews express their solidarity with other Jews and reaffirm their membership in the community of Israel. Today in Israel, for example, it is common for crowds of secular Jews to stand outside synagogues when *Kol Nidre* is being chanted, even if they do not go inside.

The effect of the Yom Kippur services, especially the opening *Kol Nidre* prayer, is so profound that, on occasion, it has irrevocably changed people's lives. A famous incident of this sort concerns the German-Jewish modern philosopher Franz Rosenzweig, who had decided to become a Christian but recanted after attending the *Kol Nidre* service on the eve of Yom Kippur in the year 1913:

> ... [Rosenzweig] ... wished to enter Christianity as did its founders, as a Jew, not as a "pagan." [He] attended the synagogue services of the New Year's Days and the Day of Atonement in preparation for the church. . . . He was stopped on his way and called back into Judaism. This event came about with the suddenness and in that spirit of absolute finality reported in great conversions. . . . What he had thought he could find in the church only—faith that gives one an orientation in the world—he found on that day in the synagogue.[1]

Psychoanalyst Theodore Reik relates that upon hearing the melody of *Kol Nidre* played on a cello, he was gripped by an intense emotion:

> ... [A] distinct association grew with the recurrence of the melody. I saw myself as a child and remembered that my holidays over a period of years had been spent in a little Hungarian town. . . . During my visits . . . I had often heard the ancient melody of the *Kol Nidre,* and there grew into my mind a picture of the primitive synagogue; of long-bearded men in white robes, moving their bodies rhythmically in prayer; and of my grandfather at my side. I remembered the mysterious trembling that possessed the congregation when the cantor began the *Kol Nidre.* I remembered the visible signs of deep contrition exhibited by all these serious men, and their emotional participation in the text, and, how I, child as I was, had been carried away by that irresistible wave of feeling.[2]

Both of these personal accounts describe the powerful effect that *Kol Nidre* has on people's lives. But what is it about this service that creates such a profound impact? Why is it that of all the days in the Jewish year, Yom Kippur is the one with such overriding importance? The answer may be sought in the liturgy of Yom Kippur and the feelings and ideas it transmits.

The *Kol Nidre* service precedes and introduces the evening service of Yom Kippur; it is not actually a part of it. It consists of the following components:

a declaration of permission to pray with transgressors;
Kol Nidre;
biblical verses concerning divine forgiveness;
the *She-heheyanu* blessing.

Elements of daily life fade away as we prepare for this service, in which we attempt to transcend ourselves. Before all else, we must achieve a state of forgiveness from others; it is therefore customary to express contrition for whatever wrongs we may have committed during the past year and to ask others for forgiveness before going to the service.[3] We strive to feel no enmity toward others as we enter the *Kol Nidre* service, no sense of division between ourselves and those dear to us.

The transcendence of *Kol Nidre* is marked not only by asking for and granting forgiveness, but by the wearing of the *tallit* (prayer shawl). *Kol Nidre* is the only evening service during the year when the *tallit* is worn; it is otherwise worn only during the day. The biblical verse concerning the *tallit* speaks of *seeing* the fringes (Num. 15:39); this phrase is taken to mean that the fringes of the *tallit* are to be worn only when they can be seen, that is, during the day when it is light. Why, then, do we wear the *tallit* for *Kol Nidre?* Although it leads directly into the evening service, *Kol Nidre* is always begun and the *tallit* donned while it is still daylight. This timing is most likely due to the fact that *Kol Nidre* is viewed as an act of canceling vows, an act that according to Jewish law may not be performed on a sacred day, such as Yom Kippur. Therefore it must be recited before nightfall, i.e., prior to Yom Kippur.[4] Since the service begins during daytime, it is therefore proper for the *hazzan*, the leader of the service who repre-

sents the congregation, to wear a *tallit*. Gradually, it became customary for all those in the congregation who wear a *tallit* to do
so for *Kol Nidre* as well.[5]

One might have expected that the *tallit* would be removed
after *Kol Nidre* before reciting the evening service. The fact that
it is not makes it clear that the wearing of the *tallit* must not be
seen only as a legalistic interpretation of a biblical verse, but also
as an opportunity to differentiate Yom Kippur further from other
days and to mark *Kol Nidre* as a time more sacred than any other.
Rabbinic teaching indicates that, on Yom Kippur, human beings
take on attributes of celestial beings. Like them, we have no need
for food, drink, or other material goods on this day. Entering Yom
Kippur at the *Kol Nidre* service, we take upon ourselves aspects
of eternity and feel ourselves more than merely human. It is no
mere coincidence that the dead are buried in a *tallit* and that on
Yom Kippur it is customary to wear white, the color of the Jewish burial shroud. The *tallit* therefore represents a connection between *Kol Nidre* and the ideas of eternity and separation from the
world of the living.

PERMISSION TO PRAY WITH TRANSGRESSORS

The solemnity of the occasion is emphasized by the opening
of the ark. Two scrolls of the Torah are removed and held by
members of the congregation, who stand next to the *ḥazzan*. They
serve, as it were, as witnesses to the ceremony about to take place
and are reminiscent of Aaron and Hur, who stood on either side
of Moses and stayed his hands during the battle with the
Amalekites (Exod. 17:12).[6]

Following the opening of the ark, the *Kol Nidre* service begins with a declaration granting permission to pray with transgressors. It points to the importance of including all Jews in the
Yom Kippur ritual; on this day, even the barriers between the
righteous and sinners are broken down.[7] The declaration is
couched in solemn, legalistic terminology:

By the Heavenly tribunal, and by the earthly tribunal
With the consent of God, and with the consent of the congregation,
We permit prayer with those who have transgressed.

This reading was instituted by the noted talmudist Rabbi Meir ben Barukh of Rothenburg (1220–1293), who made other changes in the service as well.

The idea of praying with sinners dates to an ancient talmudic teaching by the Babylonian Amora Rabbi Hisda the Pious (c. 217–309): noting that one of the spices included in the list of those used in the Temple worship has an unpleasant odor, Rabbi Hisda explains its presence by suggesting that it represents sinners and proclaims that "a fast in which no sinners of Israel participate is no fast."[8] Many scholars, however, interpret this declaration as intended specifically to lift the ban on those who had transgressed the regulations of the community and therefore had been excommunicated.[9] Viewed in this way, the declaration is not merely a general permission to pray with all sinners, but refers specifically to those who had defied particular regulations adopted by a self-governing medieval Jewish community and were consequently excommunicated. On Yom Kippur these "transgressors" were permitted to join the general community in prayer. The opening declaration of *Kol Nidre* therefore adds another extraordinary aspect to the service, creating an atmosphere different from that of any other occasion.

THE TEXT OF *KOL NIDRE*

We now come to *Kol Nidre,* the most unusual part of the service. The text exists in many different versions and in two different languages, Hebrew and Aramaic. The following is a literal translation of the text as it appears in most Ashkenazic *Mahzorim.*

Every vow, renunciation, declaration, pledge, promise, obligation, oath, which we have vowed, sworn, declared, and renounced upon ourselves from this Yom Kippur until the next Yom Kippur—may it come upon us for our good!—we renounce them all, we are released from them all, they are erased and abolished, they have no binding force or obligation. Our vows are not vows, our renunciations are not renunciations, our oaths are not oaths.

The text then continues with the biblical verse that refers to the forgiveness granted the Israelites after their initial refusal to enter the Promised Land: "All the congregation of Israel shall be forgiven, as shall the stranger who dwells in their midst, for the entire people has sinned unwittingly" (Num. 15:26). This is repeated three times, first by the leader and then by the congregation.[10]

Two additional verses are then recited. The leader says: "Pardon, I pray the iniquity of this people according to Your great kindness, as You have forgiven this people ever since Egypt, as it is said," and the congregation responds: "And the Lord said, 'I pardon, as you have asked'" (Num. 14:19–20).

These verses are followed by the *She-heheyanu* blessing, which thanks God for keeping us alive and for permitting us to reach this season, a blessing usually said at the beginning of a festival when the *Kiddush* is recited over wine.

THE MEANING OF *KOL NIDRE*

Kol Nidre is the most controversial prayer in Jewish liturgy; it has been denounced by many great Jewish religious authorities of the past and rejected by modern liberal religious leaders. It also has been a source of embarrassment to Jews because Christians misinterpreted its message as proof that Jews could not be trusted: a Jew's word was not his bond. In fact, when Manasseh ben Israel tried to persuade Oliver Cromwell to readmit the Jews to England in the seventeenth century, he had to demonstrate that *Kol Nidre* did not mean that Jews could not be trusted.[11] Furthermore, an article printed on September 3, 1910 in the Berlin newspaper *Staatsburger-Zeitung* called the *Kol Nidre* prayer an insult to civilization:

Like the Talmud . . . it is a culpable deception of the Aryans by the Jews. A Jew can commit perjury in court; his religious convictions allow him to do it. He may brand truth a lie and ruin his fellow-men. . . . These moral views of Judaism are . . . criminal assaults on humanity and civilization.[12]

Despite the Jewish community's explanation that the *Kol Nidre* prayer applied only to vows between man and God or to impulsive vows, those who needed no excuse to defame Judaism paid no heed to such a defense.[13] Still, *Kol Nidre* triumphed over all objections, rabbinic and anti-Semitic alike, to become the most sacred moment of the Jewish year.

The *Kol Nidre* prayer is almost impossible to translate. The words with which it begins are synonyms for one another, describing varieties of vows; the tenses in the version we use make little sense, since we speak of what we have done in the past but then talk of annulment in the future—from now until next Yom Kippur. The text sounds like an archaic legal formulation that has little relevance to our lives today. Why recite it at all, much less three times,[14] and why set it to a magnificent melody, at that?

On the surface, the subject of *Kol Nidre* is clear: it is a renunciation of vows. But what vows, and made when—during the last year or in the year to come? And if the subject is vows, why do we then recite the verses from Numbers, which refer not to vows, but to the story of one of Israel's greatest sins: the slander against the Land of Canaan told by the Israelite spies and the subsequent rebellion and refusal of the people to enter the Land they had been promised?

Vows are a serious subject within Judaism. Specific laws in the Torah pertain to them, and the rabbinic writings devote whole tractates to them. The specific terminology of *Kol Nidre* is actually borrowed from a law in Numbers 30:14, which talks of "every vow and every sworn obligation," *kol neder ve-khol shevu'ah.*[15]

Why are vows regarded with such seriousness? The writer of Ecclesiastes felt that vows could be dangerous: "When you make a vow to God, do not delay to fulfill it. . . . It is better not to vow at all than to vow and not fulfill" (5:3–4). The Rabbis advised against making a habit of swearing vows (B. Nedarim 20a), and some, like the Amora Samuel, were of the opinion that making a vow, even if one fulfills it, is a sin (B. Nedarim 22a). Furthermore, certain vows were considered automatically void: "The Sages have invalidated four types of vows: incentive vows, exaggeration vows, erroneous vows and vows made under pressure" (M. Nedarim 3.1).[16] Rabbinic Judaism also evolved a specific method for annulling legitimate vows, requiring that they be declared void by an ordained teacher or by three laymen (Shulḥan Arukh Yoreh De'ah 228).

Although at first glance *Kol Nidre* appears to be a legal formula for such a nullification of vows, it does not, in fact, meet the criteria for doing so. It does not specify the vows that are to be annulled, nor is there any specific court convened for doing so. All in all, *Kol Nidre* is something of a paradox.[17] And before we can unravel it, we must look into its origins.

THE HISTORY OF *KOL NIDRE*

While numerous attempts have been made to trace the historical origins of *Kol Nidre,* they remain shrouded in mystery. Many of these theories—such as the idea that it originated with the Marranos, or that it dates to the seventh century when the Visigoths forcibly converted Jews[18]—are romantically fetching, but historically suspect. Only two suggestions warrant serious consideration. The first is that *Kol Nidre* is a later displacement of an ancient custom mentioned in the Talmud, a ceremony held to annul vows on the eve of Rosh Hashanah:

> He who wishes that none of his vows made during the year shall be valid should stand at the New Year and declare, "Every vow I may make in the future shall be void." His vows are invalid if he remembers this when he makes the vow (B. Nedarim 23b).

It should be noted, however, that the Talmud indicates (on the very same page, no less) that this idea was not to be taught publicly "so that vows would not be treated lightly." It would seem strange, then, to have this furtive teaching turned into a major public ceremony. It should also be noted that this practice refers to annulling vows for the coming year, while the ancient text of *Kol Nidre* speaks of vows already taken but not fulfilled.

The second credible explanation of the origins of the prayer derives from Aramaic texts (discovered during this century) containing formulas very similar to *Kol Nidre.* During the gaonic period in Babylonia (the ninth and tenth centuries C.E.), magic formulas were in common use among Jews and non-Jews alike. Many of these were written on bowls and used as spells for the exorcism of demons and evil spirits. These formulas contain many of the key-words that we find in *Kol Nidre,* such as "released," "abandoned," "inoperative," "null," and "nullified."[19] It has been suggested that *Kol Nidre* may have originated as a magical formula to eliminate demons, assuring that no evil spirits could interfere with the sacredness of Yom Kippur. This explanation would account for the vehement opposition to this popular custom on the part of many of the Geonim because it strayed so far from the non-magical beliefs of normative Judaism.[20] Whatever its origin, scholars generally agree that *Kol Nidre* was not an official prayer formulated by the Tannaim or even by the Geonim, but was the popular creation of the masses, who overcame official opposition to make *Kol Nidre* the most sacred of all prayers.[21]

Excepting its origin, the history of *Kol Nidre* is well-documented. We can date its first appearance to eighth-century Babylonia, where it was opposed vehemently by the Geonim: in 879 C.E. Amram Gaon cites a Hebrew text of *Kol Nidre,* but disapproves of it, calling it a "foolish custom." Saadiah Gaon (882–942) accepted the text, and in 1000 C.E. Hai, another of the Geonim, approved a revised text, making it clear that it was to be understood as a plea for mercy rather than a legal annulment of vows.[22] Gradually, the custom of reciting *Kol Nidre* spread both to the Land of Israel and to Europe. There, too, it encountered opposition and was regarded as an invalid practice that made light of vows. This opposition was overcome when Rabbi Meir ben Rabbi Samuel (the son-in-law of Rashi) implemented the talmudic concept of permitting the cancellation of vows in advance and changed the tenses in the prayer to the future. This change was endorsed by the great authority Rabbenu Tam, but the required changes were never officially made in the generally accepted text. The traditional text of *Kol Nidre* therefore speaks of annulling vows from now until next Yom Kippur but uses the past tense in speaking about them. The final changes were made in the thirteenth century by Rabbi Meir of Rothenburg, who introduced the opening formula ("By authority of the Heavenly court") and turned the verses at the end of the prayer into a congregational response.[23]

THE *KOL NIDRE* MELODY

One cannot speak about *Kol Nidre* without noting its famous and haunting melody, a melody as profoundly affecting as the words of the prayer are prosaic. The poet Nikolaus Lenau, in comparing the melody to Rakoczy's "March" and to the "Marseillaise," calls it

> a song draped with the veil of grief; a night song dying away in the innermost recesses of penitent, contrite, repentant human hearts. . . . Years ago I heard it [on the] Day of Atonement . . . the cantor began to chant that profoundly solemn and heart-rending song of absolution, so fraught with terror, and yet so rich in mercy. I struggled with an inexplicable emotion. I sobbed convulsively while hot tears poured from my eyes. Then I ran out into the night; my spirit torn and purified.[24]

Although the melody we now associate with *Kol Nidre* was first written down and published only in 1765 by Cantor Ahron Beer of Berlin,[25] it undoubtedly is much older than that. A *Kol Nidre* melody is referred to in the twelfth century by the Karaite Judah Hadassi; the Maharil (the fifteenth-century Rabbi Jacob Moelin) had his own tune for it.[26] The eleventh-century work on prayer known as the *Mahzor Vitry* provides some details concerning the singing of *Kol Nidre:*

On the eve of Yom Kippur one should don his *tallit* without saying a blessing and recite "vows" *[Kol Nidre].* The first time, he should
say it more quietly than normal, like a person who approaches the
palace of the king with temerity, hoping to enter and ask the king
for a boon, but fearful of approaching him. He therefore speaks
softly like one who is fearful. The second time, he raises his voice
a bit more. The third time, he raises it yet higher like someone who
feels at home and therefore is accustomed to being with the king
and feels familiar with him, knowing that the king is ready to listen to his request.[27]

In the seventeenth century, Mordecai Jaffe of Prague (known
as the Levush) mentions a tune so well-established that it was a
stumbling block to any attempt to change the text.[28] It has been
suggested that the famous Ashkenazic melody may be related to
Gregorian chants that were familiar to the Rhenish Jews prior to
the eleventh century.[29] Another familiar strain in the melody is
the German "Minnesong" that was popular from the eleventh to
the fifteenth centuries and was itself based upon the Gregorian
chant and folk songs. Some elements of the music are rooted in
biblical musical forms, especially the melody for reading the
prophetic books.[30] The popularity of this melody has spread even
beyond Jewish prayer circles, into classical music composition:
part or all of the melody may be found in Beethoven's C minor
quartet, in Max Bruch's *Kol Nidre* for cello, and in Schoenberg's
Kol Nidre.

It cannot escape our notice that the melody, which Tolstoy
called "one that echoes the story of the great martyrdom of a grief
stricken nation,"[31] does not seem connected to the words of the
Kol Nidre prayer. As A. Z. Idelsohn puts it, the melody tries to
give expression "to the emotions of the Jew as he approaches God
on the most solemn Day of Atonement. In the first part of the
tune he expresses his contrition and his plea for forgiveness. In
the second part he voices his hope in the mercy of God; and fin-
ishes in the third part with strong confidence that God will pardon him and inscribe him in the Book of Life."[32]

The emotional experience of hearing *Kol Nidre,* then, over-
whelms any intellectual attempt to understand what is being said.

And yet, although the melody accounts for part of that emotional experience, it does not account for all of it. For, even before the music made its appearance, Jews were insistent upon reciting these words despite the opposition of well-respected rabbinic leaders. Similarly, when modern reformers have attempted to keep the melody but substitute more contemporary words,[33] they have been rebuffed.

INTERPRETIVE READINGS OF *KOL NIDRE*

In an attempt to understand the tenacious persistence of the text and melody of this ancient formula, numerous modern scholars and other thinkers have offered various interpretive approaches. One view points to the power of guilt caused by unfulfilled vows: "The religious consciousness, which felt oppressed at the thought of the non-fulfillment of its solemn vows, accordingly devised a general and comprehensive formula of dispensation which was repeated by the *ḥazzan* in the name of the assembled congregation at the beginning of the fast of Atonement."[34]

Theodore Reik, unsatisfied with scholarly explanations, sought what he saw as a deeper reading, a "psychological explanation supported by historical fact."[35] Basing his theory in psychoanalytic method, he suggests that there is "an unconscious root of all temptation to break prohibitions,"[36] which must be exorcised before the solemn day begins. Breaking our vows is symbolic of the desire to break the Covenant itself. To illustrate this point, Reik tells the story of a child who breaks some crockery. When his mother asks him to promise not to do it in the future and asks, "Will you be a good boy?" he answers, "Bubi wants to be good, but Bubi can't be good." Reik's commentary on this statement: "Is not this sincere admission like an infantile counterpart of the *Kol Nidre* formula with its naive and unnatural antithesis of two tendencies?"[37]

Shlomo Deshen, who writes from an anthropological viewpoint, attempts to understand *Kol Nidre* better by placing it within the context of the entire religious experience of Yom Kippur. This is a day when the world is left behind, when all barriers between human beings are eradicated, even those between the righteous and the sinners, as are barriers between human beings and God, and between life and death. On this day we enter a new dimension, the realm of holiness where the self is negated and we are all equal before God. As *Kol Nidre* frees us from the bonds we have taken upon ourselves, we take yet one more step away from this worldly life.[38]

What began as a magical incantation to free us from demons who would subvert the holiness of the day[39] gradually became, in the popular mind, a means to abolish all our unfulfilled obligations—a source of guilt—and a necessary prelude to God's forgiveness ("I pardon, as you have asked"). The biblical verses referring to the request and granting of God's forgiveness, which we recite after *Kol Nidre* (Num. 14:19–20), are therefore completely appropriate. The release we have obtained from our human imperfections and failings leads directly to the possibility of forgiveness. *Kol Nidre* is indeed a release, but from much more than technical vows: it releases us from all that binds us to our imperfect selves—the limitations that keep us from fulfilling our ideals of who we would like to be. When Ismar Elbogen writes that *Kol Nidre* "has nothing at all to do with the themes and the liturgy of the Day of Atonement; only with great difficulty can a connection between them be found,"[40] he could not be further from the truth. Those who created the profoundly moving melody instinctively understood that the words themselves, dry as legal tomes, are but the inspiration for powerful feelings that can only be released in a deeply emotional setting: the eve of the year's most sacred occasion.

8

The Yom Kippur Liturgy II: Arvit

The unique *Kol Nidre* service is a powerful prelude to the unusual evening service, *Arvit,* or *Ma'ariv,* which follows it. Most evening services are brief affairs; even that of Rosh Hashanah is very short, with few special features. Yom Kippur, however, is different. As the Rabbis remarked, "there is a time to shorten prayer and a time to lengthen it."[1] Yom Kippur is a time to lengthen prayer. With no evening meal to follow, time is plentiful. But there is much more to it than that: if we really want to divorce ourselves from the outside world and enter a realm of holiness, we must isolate and weave a cocoon about ourselves in order to emerge as different creatures. We begin this process in the evening, by introducing the themes that will occupy our thoughts for the next twenty-five hours or so.

THE STRUCTURE OF THE EVENING SERVICE

Every evening service consists of two major sections: the *Shema* and its blessings, and the *Amidah,* followed by *Aleinu.*[2] The

Arvit service for Yom Kippur retains these components and adds others as well:

> the *Shema;*
> the *Amidah;*
> concluding with an individual silent confession;
> *Seliḥot* (penitential prayers);
> *Vidui* (communal confession);
> verses and prayers concerning confession and repentance;
> *Avinu Malkeinu* (our Father, our King);
> *Aleinu.*

The Shema

Although the words of the *Shema* are the same on Yom Kippur as on all other days, there is one significant change in practice. The first line of the *Shema,* "Hear O Israel, the Lord is our God, the Lord is One" (Deut. 6:4), is usually followed by the recitation of a rabbinic response, "Blessed be the name of His glorious majesty forever and ever," which is said in a whisper; on the evening and again on the morning of Yom Kippur, however, this response is said aloud. The historical reason that the response is usually said quietly is known: originally, the *Shema* was recited by having the leader of the service proclaim the first line aloud for all to hear. The congregation, upon hearing this important declaration, would respond by saying "Blessed be the name," which was the equivalent of saying, "Amen," that is, "I believe and accept this declaration." Thus, the worshippers blessed the name of the Lord, which had just been recited, a gesture similar to the current practice of saying, "Blessed is He and blessed is His name" when one hears the name of God. When this practice of saying *Shema Yisra'el* aloud was changed and everyone said the *Shema* individually (possibly because of the Roman prohibition against reciting the *Shema* during second-century persecutions), the response seemed out of place and merely interrupted the flow of the biblical passage. Therefore, it became the practice to say it silently and consequently to print it in smaller type in prayer books.[3]

Legends grew up to explain this anomaly. According to the midrash, the line "Blessed be the name" was the response of the angels when they heard Israel proclaim, "Hear O Israel, the Lord is our God, the Lord is one." The midrash asks, "Why is it said in a whisper?" and an answer is proffered:

> When Moses went up to heaven [to receive the Torah] he stole it from the angels and taught it to Israel. . . . It may be likened to the son of the king's daughter who had a maiden daughter. When [the maiden daughter] would see lovely garments, she would say to [her father], "Get me these lovely garments" and he would do so. Once he entered the king's palace and saw a magnificent jewel belonging to a noblewoman. He stole it and gave it to his daughter. He commanded her, "All the garments which I have brought you, you may wear in public. But this jewel is stolen. Only wear it indoors." Thus Moses said to Israel, "All the mitzvot I have given you I received from the Torah, but this verse is something which I overheard the angels say when they praise the Holy One. I took it from them, therefore say it in a whisper." Why then is it said aloud on Yom Kippur? Because then they are like angels, wearing white, not eating or drinking; nor do they have any sins or transgressions for the Holy One has forgiven all their transgressions.[4]

This midrash reflects the common Ashkenazi practice of saying the verse aloud on Yom Kippur. It has been suggested that the real reason for saying this response aloud in the synagogue service is to imitate the Second Temple practice of responding, "Blessed be the name of His glorious majesty forever and ever" aloud whenever God's name was mentioned on Yom Kippur.[5] Whatever the original reason, this gesture serves to highlight the special holiness of the occasion. There is a different tenor to this night, and so our proclamation of belief in God is greater and fuller than usual. We are on a different plane of existence, closer to angelic beings than to humans, and this difference is expressed in a simple but noticeable change in the recitation of the *Shema*.

The Evening Amidah

The *Amidah* for Yom Kippur contains special sections that are unique to this holiday. As discussed above,[6] there is a fixed formula for the *Amidah,* the central prayer of all services; part of that formula—the opening and closing blessings—remains the same on Yom Kippur. The third blessing, the *Kedushah* (the sanctity of God), has the same special additions on Yom Kippur that it has on Rosh Hashanah. During the Ten Days of Penitence, the last day of which is Yom Kippur, additional lines concerning the Book of Life are inserted into the opening and closing blessings.

It is in the fourth, or middle paragraph (which is always changed to suit the occasion) that we find the special liturgical formulations for Yom Kippur. The standard pattern for the fourth blessing of the *Amidah* for festivals is followed by insertions that stress the nature of Yom Kippur as a day of forgiveness; these additions include biblical verses suggesting that God forgives and pardons Israel on this day.[7] Whereas the main theme for Rosh Hashanah was God's kingship, that of Yom Kippur is God's forgiveness:

> In love, O Lord our God, You have given us this Day of Atonement for pardon and forgiveness, for atonement and for pardoning all our transgressions. . . . Our God and God of our ancestors, pardon our iniquities on this Day of Atonement. Wipe out and erase our transgressions from before Your eyes, as it is said, "It is I, I who, for My own sake, wipe your transgressions away and remember your sins no more" (Isa. 43:25). And it is said, "I wipe away your sins like a cloud, your transgressions like mist. Come back to Me, for I redeem you" (Isa. 44:22). And it is said, "For on this day atonement shall be made for you to cleanse you of all your sins; you shall be clean before the Lord" (Lev. 16:30). . . . You are a forgiving and pardoning [God] unto Israel and the tribes of Jeshuran throughout all generations. We have no king who forgives and pardons other than You. . . . Blessed are You, King who forgives and pardons our transgressions and the transgressions of His people the House of Israel, who causes our trespasses to pass away year by year, King of the entire world who sanctifies Israel and the Day of Atonement.

This closing blessing (the *hatimah*) points to the central theme of Yom Kippur, as articulated in the biblical quotations: God forgives our sins on this day. Since this paragraph is the "blessing of the sanctity of the day," it concludes with a proclamation of that sanctity. It is the notion of God as one "who forgives and pardons"[8] that expresses the essence of the prayer.[9] According to the talmudic text *Masekhet Sofrim,* the day should be referred to as "this day of forgiveness of transgressions" and the conclusion should read, "King of the entire world who sanctifies Israel, this fast day of Atonement, the seasons and the holy days of assembly."[10] It is likely that the blessing originally read something like this: "Blessed are You, O Lord, who forgives and pardons His people Israel with mercy, and sanctifies His people Israel and the Day of Atonement."[11]

Forgiveness and Confession

The most important ideas of Yom Kippur are introduced in two special sections that appear for the first time in the evening service: *Selihot* (forgiveness) and *Vidui* (confession). These two sections are repeated in each of the five Yom Kippur services (*Arvit, Shaharit, Musaf, Minhah,* and *Ne'ilah*).

Rabbinic theology teaches that confession is the sine qua non of atonement. Without confession of wrongdoing, repentance cannot be achieved. There would be no point in confessing, however, without the assurance that forgiveness is possible. Judaism teaches that God is a God of forgiveness and mercy. Of the two qualities that the Sages ascribed to God—justice and mercy— mercy is predominant.[12] The entire liturgy of Yom Kippur rests upon these two pillars: God is merciful and forgiving, and confession brings forgiveness and atonement.

Selihot. Selihot and *Vidui* stand in a complementary relationship to one another. *Vidui,* confession, is the human response to a divine imperative; *Selihot* is the divine assurance that confession is met with forgiveness. *Selihot* prayers are not, however, unique to Yom Kippur. They are recited on all fast days and during the preparatory period preceding the High Holy Days.

The core of *Seliḥot* is the rabbinic interpretation of the biblical passage known as "The Thirteen Attributes":

> The Lord came down in a cloud; He stood with [Moses] there, and proclaimed the name "Lord." The Lord passed before [Moses] and proclaimed: "The Lord! the Lord! A God compassionate and gracious, slow to anger, rich in steadfast kindness, extending kindness to the thousandth generation, forgiving iniquity, transgression, and sin; and remitting all punishment" (Exod. 34:5–7).

In the Torah, the last verse reads:

> ". . . forgiving iniquity, transgression, and sin; yet He does not remit all punishment, but visits the iniquity of fathers upon children and children's children, upon the third and fourth generations."

The Hebrew phrase for "yet He does not remit all punishment" is *venakeh lo yenakeh*—literally "remits He does not remit," a common biblical grammatical form that by repetition stresses the action. By cutting off the verse after the first word of the phrase *venakeh* the rabbis changed the meaning so that it indicates that indeed He does remit or cleanse all sins! This remarkable midrashic transformation became the accepted usage whenever this verse is quoted in the liturgy. Although it may do violence to the simple meaning of the particular verse, it is well in keeping with the general tenor of the passage, which stresses the merciful nature of God.

This passage can best be understood in the context in which it appears in the Torah—the incident of the Golden Calf. God's initial reaction to that sin is an impulse to destroy, rather than to forgive the people of Israel (Exod. 32:10). But Moses conducts a dialogue with God in which he argues the case for the people and brings about a reconciliation between God and Israel. At the conclusion of this dialogue, Moses asks to "behold [God's] Presence" (Exod. 33:18), as an assurance that Israel indeed has been forgiven. When God, in response, causes His Presence to pass before Moses, God proclaims the words in the verse above, describing the attributes of His nature. It is this description that the Sages called "The Thirteen Attributes." Their essence is to assure Moses that God is indeed forgiving.

These "Thirteen Attributes" are an expansion and reworking of the description of God in the Decalogue. There, God describes Himself this way:

> For I the Lord your God am an impassioned God, visiting the guilt of the fathers upon the children, upon the third and fourth generation of those who reject Me, but showing kindness to the thousandth generation of those who love Me and keep My commandments (Exod. 20:5–6).

A comparison between the two passages indicates quite clearly that the new description emphasizes the compassionate nature of God to an even greater extent. The Sinai covenant hinted at God's forgiveness but mentioned it only after describing God's impassioned nature as a punishing divinity. The later revelation of God to Moses makes God's merciful nature explicit. There is no biblical passage more appropriate than this for describing the merciful, forgiving nature of God.[13]

The Talmud says, "This verse indicates that the Holy One drew His robe around Him like the leader of the service and showed Moses how to pray. He said to him, 'Whenever Israel sins, let them recite [the thirteen attributes] before Me and I will forgive them'. . . . A covenant has been made concerning the thirteen attributes that [the people] will not be turned away empty handed" (B. Rosh Hashanah 17b).

The individual who sins is compared to the people of Israel at the time of the Golden Calf. Just as that incident concluded with God's forgiveness, so too the individual who confesses can expect the forgiveness of God. By reciting this passage over and over again, we are both reminding God, as it were, of His assurance of forgiveness and receiving assurance from God, thus prompting us to repent.

In addition to the recitation of these specific verses, the *Selihot* section contains prayers of forgiveness, mostly in the form of *piyyutim* (liturgical poems), calling upon God to exercise His attribute of mercy and forgive us.

THE HISTORY OF SELIḤOT.   The combination of confession and supplication for forgiveness is already found in the Book of Nehemiah where a great national day of fasting is described: "Standing in their places, they read from the scroll of the Teaching of the Lord their God for one-fourth of the day, and for another fourth they confessed and prostrated themselves before the Lord their God" (Neh. 9:3). The practice described here took place in the fifth century B.C.E. Based on this incident, the Talmud specifies that for one quarter of any fast day we must "offer up supplications" (B. Megillah 30b). The nature of these supplications, however, remained fluid for centuries and varied greatly from one community to another.

Amram Gaon (a ninth-century thinker) declared that *Seliḥot* must be recited at all the Yom Kippur services.[14] The original format consisted of the recitation of various biblical verses on the theme of forgiveness, followed by the verses describing "The Thirteen Attributes." Eventually, *piyyutim* were added between the biblical verses. The leader of the service would vary the *piyyutim* to suit his taste, but the verses remained constant.[15] Ultimately, most of the verses were discarded, and today the service consists primarily of *piyyutim* and the recitation of "The Thirteen Attributes," together with an introductory passage that begins with a fifth- or sixth-century poem:[16]

God, the King enthroned upon the throne of mercy,
Who acts graciously, forgiving the sins of His people. . . .
God, You instructed us to recite the Thirteen Attributes.
Remember for us today the covenant of the Thirteen Attributes,
As you informed the humble one [Moses] long ago. . . .

The passage of "The Thirteen Attributes" is then recited, after which the following lines are added:

. . . pardon our iniquity and our sin, and take us for Your own (Exod. 34:9);

*Forgive us our Father for we have sinned; pardon us our King for we
have transgressed (from the* Amidah);

*For You, Lord, are good and forgiving, abounding in steadfast love to
all who call on You* (Ps. 86:5).

Originally, these lines were repeated several times; today,
many *Mahzorim* have reduced the number of times they are recited.

THE PRESENT FORMAT OF *SELIHOT.* The *Selihot* section for the
evening of Yom Kippur consists of the following components:

> *Ya'aleh* (an introductory *piyyut*);
> verses of mercy;
> *piyyutim* leading to the recitation of "The Thirteen Attributes";
> *Darkekha*
> *Selah na*
> *Amnam ken*
> *Ki hinei ka-homer;*
> Verses of remembrance (concluding with *Shema koleinu*);
> *Ki anu amekha.*

YA'ALEH. In most Ashkenazi *Mahzorim* in use today, the
Selihot prayers are introduced by the *piyyut Ya'aleh.* The anony-
mous poet takes as his point of departure the holiday prayer
that begins with the words, *Ya'aleh ve-yavo ve-yagi'a ve-yera'eh*
(May our remembrance arise, come, reach, and appear unto You
. . . for good . . . on this day . . .). The *piyyut* is in the form of
an inverse alphabetical acrostic, in which three of these words
("arise," "come," and "appear") are rotated at the beginning of
each line, and in which the times of day—evening, morning,
and evening—are rotated at the conclusion of each line. Thus,
the first verse reads:

*Let our supplication arise from evening
And our prayer come from morning
And our songs appear until evening.*

The *piyyut* thus emphasizes the fact that on this day we send our prayers to God in the evening and then again all the following day, from daylight until dark. Unlike the everyday cycle of prayer (with services in the evening, morning, and afternoon), it is only on Yom Kippur that is there a continuity of prayer from evening to evening.

VERSES OF MERCY.   *Ya'aleh* is followed by a collection of biblical verses known as "verses of mercy." These are strung together by having each verse pick up a word or phrase that appeared in the previous one,[17] as in this example:

You who hear prayer, all flesh comes to You (Ps. 65:3).
All flesh shall come to bow down before You, O Lord (Isa. 66:23).[18]
They will all come to bow down before You, O Lord and they will pay
    honor to Your name (Ps. 86:9).

Although the exact verses and their order differ in various rites, the ideological structure is similar: verses stating that the soul of every being belongs to God are followed by verses that stress the need for all human beings to come and worship the Lord. An example follows:

The soul is Yours; the body is Your handiwork. Pity the fruit of Your
    labor.
The soul is Yours; the body is also Yours. O Lord, do this for the sake
    of Your name.
We have come unto You, do this for the sake of Your name.
For the honor of Your name, for Your name is "God, gracious
and merciful."
For the sake of Your name, O Lord, pardon our iniquity though it be
    great (Ps. 25:11).[19]

Through this collection of verses, we address God as the creator of all human beings; we praise God, His greatness, glory, and mercy and ask that God pity our bodies and souls, both of which are God's creations.

PIYYUTIM.   The "Verses of Mercy" prepare us for the main part of the *Seliḥot:* four recitations of "The Thirteen Attributes," each of which is preceded by an introductory *piyyut.*[20] The first of these poems, *Darkekha* (your way), is an ancient composition by Yose ben Yose, who flourished in the Land of Israel around the early fifth century. It expresses the idea that the ways of God are the ways of mercy:

It is Your way [Darkekha], O our God, to be slow to anger, both to
  the wicked and to the good. That is your praise!
Do it for Your sake, O Lord, not for ours. Behold, we stand here poor
  and empty.

The Rabbis interpreted the phrase "slow to anger" as indicating that God is slow to anger toward two groups: the righteous and the wicked.[21] This *piyyut* is long and elaborate: a quadruple alphabetical acrostic in which the lines quoted above serve as the refrain. Replete with biblical quotations, it emphasizes the unworthiness of Israel and its many sins and betrayals, as opposed to God's mercy and righteousness.[22]

The second *piyyut* emphasizes the word "forgive." Known as *Selaḥ na* (please forgive), the poem was written by the thirteenth-century Rabbi Meir ben Barukh of Rothenburg. Like Moses, the first to ask God for forgiveness for His people, Rabbi Meir admits the faults of his people, but reminds God, as it were, that Israel belongs to Him. Israel is "Your children," "Your beloved," "Your servants," "Your flock."

The next *piyyut, Amnam ken* (indeed it is so), was written by Rabbi Yom Tov of York, who was martyred in the York massacre of 1189, and reflects the troubles of English Jewry at the time of the Third Crusade (1189–1192). In September, 1189, anti-Jewish riots swept the town of London; six months later, the bloodbath in York took place.[23] The poem is an alphabetical acrostic, and each line is divided into three parts: the last words of the first and second parts rhyme, and the third words of each line of each couplet rhyme. Each couplet concludes with the refrain *salaḥti* (I pardon).

A few lines from Israel Zangwill's archaic translation, which manages to capture the poetic scheme, will illustrate:

A y, 'tis thus	Evil us	hath in bond;
B y Thy grace	guilt efface	and respond, "Forgiven."
C ast score o're	and abhor	th' informer's word;
D ear God, deign	this refrain	to make heard, "Forgiven."

Salaḥti (I pardon) is the word uttered by God in response to Moses' plea following the sin of the spies:

> "Pardon, I pray, the iniquity of this people according to Your great kindness, as You have forgiven this people ever since Egypt." And the Lord said, "I pardon (*salaḥti*) as you have asked." (Num. 14:19–20).

Since these same verses were quoted at the conclusion of *Kol Nidre,* this *piyyut* forms a connecting thread between *Kol Nidre* and the *Seliḥot* prayers.

The fourth and last of the *Seliḥot* poems to have found a permanent place in most Yom Kippur *Arvit* services is the touching *Ki hinei ka-ḥomer* (behold like clay). This is an alphabetical *piyyut* of unknown authorship, based on the verse from Jeremiah, "Just like clay in the hands of the potter, so are you in My hands, O House of Israel" (Jer. 18:6). God, having brought Jeremiah to a potter's workshop, proclaims that He has the ability to do with nations what a potter does with clay, that is, to mold, destroy, or create. The poet takes up this theme and compares God with various types of craftspersons—masons, carpenters, glaziers, and weavers. The poet then compares human beings with the materials craftspersons use—stone, wood, glass, or cloth. He pleads with God to use us creatively, not destructively. In a direct reference to "The Thirteen Attributes," the poet implores God at the conclusion of each couplet, "Look to the covenant and do not regard our [evil] inclination."

Although each of these *piyyutim* was written by different people at different times, taken together they represent the core concepts of the Forgiveness prayers: God's ways are ways of mercy. We are fragile and helpless when standing before God, but we are confident that God recognizes both our inherent weakness and the covenant He made to forgive the people of Israel.

VERSES OF REMEMBRANCE.   The central section of *piyyutim* and "The Thirteen Attributes" is followed by another collection of verses reminiscent of the Remembrance section of the Rosh Hashanah service. These verses ask God to "remember" His mercy, that is, to act according to His quality of mercy, and to forgive us. As we approach the conclusion of these biblical verses, we call upon God to hear our voice *(Shema koleinu)* and accept our prayers. We then add a few more verses emphasizing our dependence upon the mercies of God:

Do not cast us out of Your presence
or take Your holy spirit away from us (Ps. 51:13).
Do not cast us off in old age;
when our strength fails, do not forsake us (Ps. 71:9).
Do not abandon us, O Lord;
our God do not be far from us (Ps. 38:22).[24]

We repeat many of these verses of Remembrance and ask God to be with us and to forgive us, re-emphasizing the idea of *Selihot* by quoting again the verse, "Pardon my iniquity though it be great (Ps. 25:11) This section of the service is chanted with great fervor and pathos, as it embodies an innate, collective fear that we will find ourselves alone and abandoned, with no one to help us.

WE ARE YOUR PEOPLE.   We have now reached the transition point between the *Selihot* prayers and the confession. This transition is made by reciting the simple, yet beloved *piyyut Ki anu amekhah* (for we are Your people), in which the close relationship between God and Israel is paralleled with other close relationships: children and parents, servants and masters, sheep and shepherds, vineyards and their keepers, lover and beloved. The *piyyut* is based on a midrash to the verse, "I am my beloved's and my beloved is mine." (Song 2:16). The Sages consistently interpreted the Song of Songs as a love poem expressing the relationship between God and Israel.[25] The "beloved," according to the midrash, refers to God:

He is God to me and I am a people to Him.
He is a father to me and I am a child to Him.
He is a shepherd to me and I am a sheep to Him.
He is a watchman to me and I am a vineyard to Him (Song of Songs
     Rabba 2.34).

Unlike this midrash, however, the poem turns sharply toward the end from a description of intimacy and closeness and takes on a darker tone, contrasting God and Israel:

We are brazen and You are gracious and merciful
We are stubborn and You are patient;
We are imbued with iniquity and You are imbued with mercy
We are of fleeting duration, as a shadow and You are He whose years
     are endless.

We plead with God not to turn away from our prayers, because in spite of our faults, we are capable of admitting to them: "We are not so brazen and stubborn as to claim . . . that we are righteous and have not sinned, for indeed we have sinned." This admission of sin, which is the core of confession, is followed immediately by the short confession, *Ashamnu.*

Vidui: *The Confession.*   In addition to fasting and otherwise afflicting oneself, the central mitzvah that must be performed on Yom Kippur is the *Vidui*, confession. The commandment to confess is to be performed on the eve of Yom Kippur (T. Kippurim 4.14). This rabbinic requirement is based on the biblical passage that describes the confession of the High Priest when performing the ceremony of the scapegoat: "and [he shall] confess over it all the iniquities and transgressions of the Israelites . . ." (Lev. 16:21). During the days of the Second Temple, this rite was expanded into a more elaborate one in which the High Priest recited a confession first for himself (M. Yoma 3.8), then for the entire priesthood (M. Yoma 4.2), and finally for the entire people of Israel (M. Yoma 6.2).[26]

Confession was an integral part of ceremonies designed to clear one from sin: "When he realizes his guilt in any of these matters, he shall confess that wherein he had sinned" (Lev. 5:5).[27] Following the destruction of the Temple, when greater emphasis was placed on synagogue ritual and individual prayer, it fell upon each person to make his or her own confession on Yom Kippur. Without this admission of guilt, atonement and forgiveness could not be expected. As Maimonides put it,

> Concerning any commandment of the Torah, positive or negative, if one transgresses it either wittingly or unwittingly, when one repents and returns from his sin, he must make confession before God, blessed is He, as it is said, "When a man or a woman commits any wrong toward a fellow man, thus breaking faith with the Lord, and that person realizes his guilt, he shall confess the wrong he has done" (Num. 5:6–7). This refers to a verbal confession. This confession is a positive commandment.[28]

THE DEVELOPMENT OF THE *VIDUI*.   Originally, only one confession was required at the beginning of Yom Kippur so that the sacred day would be begun free of the burden of sin. The Sages soon increased the requirement. First, they added a confession in the afternoon prior to the final meal before the fast, lest one's mind not be clear enough after eating and drinking to make proper confession. Later, the Sages specified that additional confessions be said at every service—evening, morning, *Musaf*, afternoon, and *Ne'ilah*. Since the confession was to be recited at each service both by the individual during silent prayer and then aloud by the leader of the service, the Sages determined that ten confessions were to be recited during the Day of Atonement itself, in addition to those recited before it.[29]

According to Rabbi Yehudah ben Beterah (second century)

it was necessary to specify exactly what sins one had committed.
His contemporary, Rabbi Akiba, disagreed. A general confession
was sufficient. All agreed that if one confessed specific sins one
year, they need not be confessed the next Yom Kippur unless one
had committtted them again.[30]

As the quantity of confessions expanded, the text of the confession became more elaborate. The formula uttered by the High
Priest is an example of a complex confession text. Interestingly
enough, although the Torah gives no specific formula for confession, not even for that of the High Priest, the Mishnah specifies
precisely what the High Priest is to say:

> Please, Lord, I have transgressed, I have done wrong, I have sinned
> before you. . . . Please, Lord! Atone for the transgressions, the wrongs
> and the sins that I have transgressed, done wrong and sinned before
> You . . . as it is written in the Torah of Moses Your servant, "For on
> this day atonement shall be made for you to cleanse you of all your
> sins; you shall be clean before the Lord" (Lev. 16:30).[31]

CONFESSION IN THE TALMUD.   The first reference to a specific
formula for individual confession is found in the Talmud, where
third-century Amoraim and their successors offer suggested wording for the *Vidui*. The Amoraim asked themselves, "What should
one say?" The texts they offer in response incorporate references
to prayers that were certainly well-known at the time:

> Rav: You know the secrets of the universe. . . .
> Samuel: Out of the depths of [my] heart. . . .
> Rabbi Yohanan: Lord of the universe. . . .
> Rabbi Judah: For our transgressions are too numerous to count and
> our sins greater than can be listed. . . .
> Rav Hamnuna: My God, before I was created I was not worthy,
> and now that I have been created, it is as if I had not been created.
> I am but dust in my life and even less in my death. . . . Behold I
> am but a vessel filled with shame. May it be Your will that I sin no
> more, and may You erase those sins I have committed in Your great
> mercy, but not through suffering.
> Mar Zutra: All of this applies only if one has not said, "But we have
> sinned." If one says, "But we have sinned," nothing more is re-
> quired.[32]

Another suggestion found in the midrash in the name of Rabbi Biva ben Avina is as follows: "I confess all that I have done. I stood in the path of evil, and all that I have done I shall do no more. May it be Your will, O Lord my God, to erase all my iniquities and forgive my transgressions and grant atonement for all my sins."[33]

The fact that there are so many varied suggestions indicates that no specific formula for confession had been adopted at the time of the Amoraim.

CONFESSION OF THE GEONIM. The ninth- and tenth-century Geonim formulated confession texts that serve as the basis of the *Vidui* we recite today.[34] Two forms of confession developed simultaneously: a brief listing of sins known as *Ashamnu* (we have trespassed), called "the lesser confession," and a longer, more complicated, and more specific list using the formula *Al ḥet* (for the sins we have sinned before You), known as "the great confession."[35]

In the ninth-century *Siddur Rav Amram Gaon, Ashamnu* appears in a version briefer even than what we recite today, and the *Al ḥet* consists of the following:

For the sin we have sinned before You unwittingly;
For the sin we have sinned before You willingly;
For the sin we have sinned before You deliberately;
For the sin we have sinned before You secretly;
For the sin we have sinned before You openly;
For the sin we have sinned before You knowingly;
For the sin we have sinned before You unknowingly.

This formulaic text is followed by a list of the sins that require various sacrifices and have specific punishments. The entire section concludes with the words, "We have sinned in all of these, as it is said, 'Concealed acts concern the Lord our God' (Deut. 29:28) . . . except for You, we have no one who pardons and forgives."[36]

There was a tension during this period between the desire to

create a fixed and elaborate liturgy and the need to encourage
people to confess sincerely, on a more personal level. Sherira Gaon
(a tenth-century Gaon) therefore insists that the first confession,
before the final meal prior to Yom Kippur, should be an individual one. As he put it, "The easiness with which one may make
confession should be explained to them, so that every single person will rise and confess with full comprehension in a language
he understands."[37]

Eventually, both the "lesser" and the "greater" confession for-
mats were expanded. *Ashamnu* became an alphabetical list of sins,
and *Al het* became first a single alphabetical list and then a double alphabetical list. By the time of the *Mahzor Vitry* (the eleventh
century), the confessions were similar to those we have today.
Rabbi David Abudarham of Seville (b. 1340) comments that "there
are *siddurim* that contain an alphabetical list of the sins specify-
ing what they are and that is the proper way."[38] He then provides
one such list of sins, which is a single alphabetical acrostic complete with biblical and rabbinic sources for the expressions used
and with explanations for each of them.

This process of expansion is common in liturgical development. The simple requirement is that one confess to personal misdeeds; the confession had to be recited before Yom Kippur, when
Yom Kippur began, and at every service of the day, and it had to
be said both by individuals and by the leader of the service. Spon-
taneity ultimately gave way to specific, more involved formulas,
which adopted the popular convention of alphabetical acrostic
and, in Ashkenazic lands, added the refrain: "For all of these, O
God of forgiveness, forgive us, pardon us, grant us atonement."[39]
At one point, there was even a special blessing recited at the conclusion of the confession, a *hatimah* (a concluding blessing). There
was some controversy among the Tannaim as to whether this
blessing was required or even permitted. Saadiah records that
some people said a blessing concluding with the words *ha-el ha-
salhan* (forgiving God), but he does not approve of this practice.[40]
The *Mahzor Vitry* records that it was used during the *Ne'ilah* (closing) service.[41] This practice did not persist, but the words of the
blessing (forgiving God) did enter the *Amidah* prayer of Yom Kippur: "Blessed are You, O Lord, King who pardons and forgives

our transgressions and the transgressions of His people, the house of Israel. . . ."[42]

THE FORM OF THE CONFESSION.　Today, the *Vidui* is an integral part of each Yom Kippur service. It is read individually and silently at the conclusion of the silent *Amidah.* In services where there is a reader's repetition of the *Amidah,* the *Vidui* is included in the fourth (middle) blessing, the blessing of the sanctity of the day. It was incorporated into that prayer rather than being recited by the reader after the *Amidah,* since technically the reader represents the congregation only during the repetition of the *Amidah.*[43] The two confessional forms are embedded in a larger text consisting of five parts:

I. An introduction beginning with "Our God and God of our ancestors" and quoting the psalms "Let my prayer reach You" (Ps. 88:3) and "Do not ignore my plea" (Ps. 55:2), both of which express the idea that "we are not so brazen and stubborn as to claim before You, Lord our God and God of our ancestors, that we are righteous and have not sinned, for we have sinned." These last words are themselves an ancient confession suggested in the Talmud by Mar Zutra.[44] It is the willingness to say "we have sinned" that constitutes the heart of confession, as noted by the Sages in their commentary to Numbers 21:7: "The people came to Moses and said, 'We sinned by speaking against the Lord and against you.' This teaches you the power of repentance. Since they said 'We sinned,' [Moses] was immediately reconciled to them."[45]

II. The *Ashamnu* (lesser confession).

III. "You know the secrets of the universe"—a passage affirming that we have strayed and that there is nothing we can say since all is known to God. This passage is based on Rav's confession and serves as an introduction to the "great confession."

IV. *Al ḥet* (the great confession).

V. A conclusion taken from Rav Hamnuna's confession: "My God, before I was created, I was not worthy. . . ."[46]

We can see how this five-part formula for specific confession incorporates the various confessions suggested earlier by the Amoraim.

THE CONTENTS OF THE CONFESSION.   The first thing one notices about the confessions is that they are written in the first person plural: "*We* have sinned," "*we* have transgressed." In keeping with the Jewish concept of communal responsibility, we confess not only those things we may have done personally, but everything done by anyone within the community. Each person shares in the responsibility for society as a whole. Although the use of the *aleph-bet* as the format for the confessions dictates the specific words used, the sins mentioned are not there simply because they fit the scheme, but because they are the ones that tradition considers most serious. Many stress the misuse of words to wrong others. The importance of expressing reverence for parents and teachers is mentioned, as are business ethics and the evils of haughtiness and vanity. The emphasis here is clearly on our relationship to others, including those acts that may not be seen outwardly but that lead to inner corruption. We confess to "causeless hatred," the sin the Rabbis believed to have led to the destruction of the Temple.[47] The entire gamut of human feelings is related here, and there is no one who cannot find him- or herself in these lines.

Rabbi Simon Greenberg was once asked if he did not find it repetitious to recite the same list over and over again. His reply was that he did not, because invariably he would begin the recitation, find one sin that spoke to him, contemplate it, and somehow never get any further. Since constant repetition can sometimes dull our senses or become a meaningless routine, it is worth following Rabbi Greenberg's example and pausing from time to time to think seriously about what we are saying. Perhaps we should return to the original form of the confession and do what the Amoraim did: make up our own confessions in our own words and add or substitute specific wrongs we know we have committed during the past year. The confessions are there not to enable us to escape looking into ourselves, but to provide a framework that will enable us to do so more meaningfully.

It is customary to beat one's breast as a symbol of contrition when reciting the confessions. Rabbi Meir explained that this was done "because the heart is the seat and the source of sin."[48] Since body language is sometimes more expressive than words, we add physical action to stress the severity of what we have done and the sincerity of our repentance.

In Judaism confession is both a public and a private act: we join together publicly to recite the same lists, indicating that no one is free from sin and that all must come to terms with wrong-doing, but we confess specific sins privately to God, and not to other human beings. No intermediary stands between us and God when we seek absolution and forgiveness.

God alone can wash away sin and cleanse us of it. This was the magnificent teaching of Rabbi Akiba, the first-century Sage, who expanded Jeremiah's pun on the word *mikveh*, which means both a ritual bath and hope:

> Happy are you, O Israel! Before whom are you cleansed and who is it that cleanses you? Your Father in Heaven, as it is said, *I will sprinkle clean water upon you, and you shall be clean* (Ezek. 36:25), and it says, *O Hope (mikveh) of Israel! O Lord!* (Jer. 17:13). Just as the *mikveh* cleanses the impure, so does the Holy One cleanse you! (M. Yoma 8:9).

THE SIGNIFICANCE OF YOM KIPPUR EVENING

Although for purposes of clarification we have separated *Kol Nidre* and *Arvit* and have discussed their individual components, it is important to consider them as an integrated experience, if we are to grasp the significance of this first service of Yom Kippur. The service represents the first step in our journey toward renewed life; it is the radical break between what is and has been, and what should and will be. Leaving behind what has been perceived as the essentials of life—food, drink, possessions, sexual activity, care of the body—we attempt to find what is truly important. We look toward the source of life and affirm that it is not of this world but resides in God, whom we cannot fathom, but whose concern for human beings is apparent to us. Layer by layer, we strip away the pretensions that "we are righteous and have not sinned" and admit to ourselves that "we have sinned." We wrap ourselves in the symbols of eternity, we divest ourselves of the symbols of authority and ownership, we feel ourselves closer to the angelic than to the human. We have gone far toward ridding ourselves of all that defiles us and separates us from the divine, but we have yet to reshape ourselves and to replace what we have eschewed with new content. That renewal, however, has only begun by the end of the evening service; we have participated only in Act One of a five-act drama. The long day of contemplation that constitutes Yom Kippur sets the stage for our more complete transformation, our entry into the realm of sanctity.

9

The Yom Kippur Liturgy III: Services of Yom Kippur Day

FROM THE OPENING TO THE CLOSING OF THE GATE

The services of Yom Kippur are designed deliberately to occupy the entire day from dawn until dark. As early as the time of Philo (the first century B.C.E.) Yom Kippur was described as a day spent entirely in prayer.[1] The Sages, too, describe it as a day when people come early to the synagogue and stay late.[2] Even today, the liturgy offers us the opportunity to experience the various moods of Yom Kippur, which may lead us deeper into ourselves and unite us with the past. The services take us on a journey that begins at a leisurely pace and becomes more urgent and profound as the day progresses.

Although the Yom Kippur services are similar in format to those of the Festivals, they are prolonged by the inclusion of special *piyyutim* (liturgical poems) and the addition of *Ne'ilah*, the service of "closing." We often use the term "service" informally to indicate a special section of readings and prayers such as "The

Avodah Service" or "The Martyrology Service,"[3] but technically a "service" refers to the recitation of the *Amidah*, the central prayer. Thus, on Yom Kippur day there are four services (one more than on any other holiday): *Shaḥarit* (morning), *Musaf* (additional), *Minḥah* (afternoon), and *Ne'ilah* (closing). At each of these services the *Amidah* is recited silently and then repeated by the leader of the service. The special sections and the *piyyutim* are added to the repetition. Since the *piyyutim* are so significant a part of the liturgy (literally thousands were written and many of these have been incorporated into the services in various communities throughout the world), we shall discuss them in some detail here. The focus, however, will be only on those *piyyutim* commonly found in the traditional Ashkenazi *Maḥzor* used by European, American, and Israeli Jewry.

Shaḥarit

Every *Shaḥarit* service, including that of Yom Kippur, has the following structure:

morning blessings;
verses of song;
the *Shema* and its blessings;
the *Amidah*.

As on all holidays (and on Mondays and Thursdays, in an abbreviated fashion), a Torah reading follows.

The morning blessings and the verses of song are introductions to the main prayers and are intended to help the worshipper attain concentration (*kavanah*) and the proper mood for meaningful worship.[4] In ancient prayerbooks, the verses of song on Yom Kippur were enhanced by including additional psalms such as this one, which is appropriate for the mood of penitence:

Happy is he whose transgression is forgiven,
whose sin is covered over.

Happy is the man whom the Lord does not hold guilty,
and in whose spirit there is no deceit (Ps. 32).[5]

Unfortunately, these additions seldom appear in *Mahzorim* today.

Additions to the Blessing of Light.   The unique status and special importance of Yom Kippur are indicated by the fact that the first of the morning blessings—the blessing of light, which celebrates creation—is changed by the insertion of a reference to the "gates of mercy": "who opens the gates of mercy unto us and enlightens the eyes of those who wait upon Him [for His pardon]." Thus, on Yom Kippur, the light we speak of in this daily blessing takes on the sense of the special spiritual light of forgiveness as well as the physical rays of the sun. The phrase "gates of mercy" anticipates the gates referred to in *Ne'ilah* at the conclusion of the day; the gates are opened now and are closed at the end of this long day of prayer. The image of open gates remains with us throughout the day, reinforcing the feeling that this day is our greatest opportunity to achieve closeness to the source of all.

Following the opening blessing is the remnant of another poem, *Or olam* (the complete version of which is now lost), which expands on the theme of light: "Everlasting light in the treasury of life, He spoke and light emerged from the gloom." Like all *piyyutim* inserted into this first blessing, this poem is termed a *yotzer,* from the first word of the blessing *Yotzer or,* creator of light. Such poems play on the concepts of light and creation. Here, the poet speaks of everlasting light and the creation of light. What the continuation of the theme might have been and how it was connected to Yom Kippur, we do not know.

The *piyyut* that follows, *Az be-yom kippur* (then on Yom Kippur) is preceded by a refrain in which the word *yotzer* (creator) is used, calling God "our Creator" but emphasizing His role as the forgiver of sin: "Forgive a holy nation, on a holy day, O exalted Holy One. We have sinned, O our Rock, forgive us our Creator." *Az be-yom kippur,* whose authorship is unknown, is a double acrostic. The author uses the word "light" eleven times and the word "forgiveness" sixteen times. The poem begins by connecting the Day of Atonement, the tenth of Tishre, with God's creation of the possibility of forgiveness:

Then, on the Day of Atonement, You decreed forgiveness,
You created light and pardon for this people,
For You forgive the transgressions and sins of the congregation
When they crowd together in the synagogue on the tenth.

According to rabbinic tradition, the tenth of Tishre—Yom Kippur—was the day when Moses returned from carving the second set of tablets and received God's assurance of forgiveness in the form of "The Thirteen Attributes" (Exod. 34:4–8). The day of the first forgiveness therefore became the time when, forever after, Israel would come together to receive forgiveness.[6]

The idea of the open gate of prayer is mentioned in this poem as well: "Open unto us the gate and let our prayer arise," as it is in the blessing itself: "Who opens the gates of mercy unto us." This theme becomes much more vivid at the close of the day, when the entire *Ne'ilah* service repeatedly expresses the idea of opening the gates and keeping them open even to the last moment before they are closed. It is worth noting that the phrase "gates of mercy" alludes to the gate by the same name in the eastern wall of the Temple compound and that, according to tradition, it is through this gate that the messiah will enter Jerusalem.

Later in this blessing, there is a section in which the verses proclaiming the holiness of God (the *Kedushah*) are inserted. Following the verse where Isaiah quotes the words of the angels, "Holy, holy holy! The Lord of Hosts! His presence fills all the earth!" (Isa. 6:3), the following phrase is recited: "Blessed be the name of His glorious Majesty." On Yom Kippur this phrase is followed by an explanatory poem, *Malkhuto bi-kehal adato:*

His Majesty I acknowledge in this assembly.
His glory is my faith.
Unto Him do I pray for atonement of my transgression and sin.

On the fast day of Yom Kippur He will grant pardon and say: I have pardoned.

This poetic insertion has two bases: the historical remembrance that "Blessed be the Name of His glorious Majesty" was the phrase uttered by the people when the High Priest proclaimed the Name of God on Yom Kippur (M. Yoma 6.2), and the legend that this phrase—usually recited in the *Shema* in a whisper—was stolen by Moses from the angels and could therefore only be recited aloud by Israel on Yom Kippur, when we are as pure as the angels.

This section serves as the introduction to the poem *Kadosh adir*, on the theme of God's holiness. Every line of this *piyyut* (another alphabetical acrostic) begins with the word *kadosh*, holy, and then addresses one of God's attributes or actions. In some versions, each line is followed by the recitation of the words "Blessed be the Name of His glorious Majesty." One stanza of the *piyyut* is particularly interesting:

The Holy One awards His forgiveness by means of repentance.

This is based on the words of the Talmud:

"They asked wisdom: 'What is the punishment of the sinner?'
Wisdom replied: 'Misfortune pursues sinners' (Prov. 13:21).
They asked prophecy: 'What is the punishment of the sinner?'
Prophecy replied: 'The person who sins, he shall die' (Ezek. 18:20).
They asked The Holy One: 'What is the punishment of the sinner?'
The Holy One replied: 'Let him repent and his sin will be atoned!' "[7]

The remainder of the *Shema* and its blessings are the same as in any holiday service with the following exception: as in the evening service, the second line of the *Shema*, "Blessed be the Name of His glorious Majesty for ever and ever," usually said quietly, is recited aloud.

These augmented morning blessings set the mood for the beginning of Yom Kippur day. Appropriately, it is a mood of optimism, a feeling of being encompassed by the light of creation, eternity, and forgiveness. If, on the eve of Yom Kippur, we were immersed in thoughts of sin and then emerged with a feeling of having our burden lightened, now we are presented with the opportunity to come closer to God. The gates are open, the light streams forth, and forgiveness bathes the morning.

The Shaharit Amidah.   The *Amidah* contains the major liturgical message of the day. As on the Sabbath and other major holidays, the *Amidah* consists of seven blessings.[8] The first three and last three of these are usually the same: "The Patriarchs," "The Wonders of God," and "The Sanctity of God"; "The Service," "Thanksgiving," and "Peace" (including the blessing of the Priests). These serve as the setting for the fourth blessing known as "The Sanctity of the Day," in which the unique features of the specific holiday are spelled out.

As we have noted,[9] on both Rosh Hashanah and Yom Kippur the third blessing, the *Kedushah* (sanctity of God), is expanded considerably: three paragraphs have been added, each beginning with the same Hebrew word, *u-vekhen* (therefore). The first paragraph discusses God as the sovereign of the entire world, the second His relationship to His people Israel, and the third His feelings for the righteous. These paragraphs originally were connected to the service for Rosh Hashanah—when the theme of God's sovereignty is paramount—but because of their beauty and the importance of their content, they came to be recited on Yom Kippur as well. This inclusion both establishes a tie between the beginning and end of the Days of Awe and blurs the differences between the two holy days.[10] We should not forget that the real theme of Yom Kippur is not sovereignty but forgiveness.

The fourth blessing, "The Sanctity of the Day" (which is identical to that of the evening service), is only one "blessing," that is, the entire section leads up to one *hatimah* (concluding blessing formula, or signature). But because it is a long and complex composition, it is best understood by breaking it up into two parts: the first is identical to the one recited on all festivals, and the second is unique to Yom Kippur.

The first part begins with the words *Ata vehartanu* (You have chosen us). The text suggests that God has demonstrated His love for Israel by giving us this sacred day. The specific holiday is then mentioned by name. The connection of "chosenness" and "love" is the same as that found in the blessing before the *Shema,* where the phrase "who chooses His people Israel in love" is used. This section then continues with *Ya'aleh Ve-yavo* (may this arise and come before You) asking God to remember our ancestors, the city of Jerusalem, and all the people of Israel for good and to bring about our salvation. These words also appear in the festival prayer. There was a dispute, however, concerning this paragraph. Should it be said, thereby emphasizing the similarity between Yom Kippur and all the festivals of the Jewish year, or should it not be said, thereby emphasizing the uniqueness of Yom Kippur as a solemn occasion, as distinct from the joyful festivals? Amram Gaon did not include it in his order of prayer,[11] nor was it always to be found in the order of prayer in the Land of Israel.[12] In some rites, biblical verses connected to the idea of repentance were inserted in this section, and in some versions the section was omitted altogether in favor of poems and prayers asking for forgiveness, such as this one:

Please forgive the sins of Your people.
Accept their repentance which they implore with all their heart.
On the tenth day eliminate the transgressions of those burdened with
  sin. . . .
For You have assured us concerning repentance and forgiveness. . . . [13]

The second section of "The Sanctity of the Day" is unique to Yom Kippur and expounds upon the idea of forgiveness. Citing biblical verses in which God promises to wipe out our sins, this part of the blessing implores God to do so now. The concept of the forgiving God is re-emphasized at the end of the section: "For You are forgiving unto Israel and pardon the tribes of Jeshurun throughout the generations. Besides You we have no king who pardons and forgives. Blessed are You O Lord, King who pardons and forgives our transgressions and the transgressions of His peo-

ple the house of Israel and cancels our wrongdoing every year,
King of the entire world who sanctifies Israel and Yom Kippur."

At the conclusion of the *Amidah*, each individual recites the
Vidui, the confession of sins.

The Repetition of the Amidah.   While the morning *Amidah* is
almost identical to that recited the evening before, it takes on a
new format now when repeated aloud because of the many *piyyutim* added to it. Just before the *ḥatimah* in the first paragraph of
the *Amidah* (the blessing of the Patriarchs), the reader recites a
personal prayer, *Mi-sod ḥakhamim,* requesting permission to in-
tersperse the prayer with poems based on the teachings of the
Sages: "Using the teachings and knowledge of the Sages and the
wise, I will open my mouth in prayer and supplication, beseech-
ing the presence of the king who pardons and forgives sins." In
this way, the reader declares that the *piyyutim* to be inserted have
the authority of the Sages. He or she also immediately states that
the purpose of these insertions is to help attain a pardon from
God, who is known to pardon.

The reader then recites a poem known as a *reshut* (permission) expressing his or her personal trepidation and fear at the
great task of leading the community in prayer. God is asked for
instruction so that the leader's prayers will be accepted. This is
the same pattern seen in the repetitions of the Rosh Hashanah
Amidah. The particular *piyyut* used on Yom Kippur, *Eimekha nasati*
(I am in awe of You), was composed by Meshullam ben Kalonymus, who lived in Rome in the tenth century. The first paragraph
of the *Amidah* is then concluded.

The second paragraph, *Gevurot*, on God's might and powers, is interrupted by a *piyyut* beginning with the refrain *Ad Yom
Moto:* "Until the day of his death You will wait for him to repent to direct him aright so that he may live." This theme is
appropriate here since the subject of death and resurrection is
one of the main concepts of this blessing, which ends with the
words "reviver of the dead." Although a few lines of the poem
are directed to God, as the One who understands all secrets and
who is the sole and undisputed judge, most of it is directed at
human beings. Indeed, it is a meditation whose theme is well-

stated in the opening line: "What is man that he can be cleared of guilt when the hosts of heaven themselves are not guiltless in Your eyes?"

The poem is based on the Book of Job (15:14–15), in which Eliphaz the Temanite contends that no one, neither Job nor any "righteous" person, can claim to be completely guiltless and pure, and so it has a dark vision of human beings:

". . . impure from his bodily emissions
impure from outside contact
rendering him impure when he dies
the days of his life are chaos
his nights confusion
all his deeds futility!"

Clearly echoing the pessimism of Kohelet, the poet sees human life as little more than a "dream surrounded by terrors." Still, this severe view of humanity ends in the *piyyut* with a single glimmer of light:

If one acts righteously, these deeds will accompany one to the grave.
If one studies the wisdom of Torah, it will accompany one to life's end. . . .
If one acquires a good name, it is to be preferred over any possible titles.
Thus the day of death is to be preferred to the day of birth.

Based on biblical quotations and rabbinic interpretations, this reflection rouses one to repentance by painting a dark picture of life and its worth and then pointing to good deeds and to Torah as all that is worthwhile. One is reminded of the more somber paintings of the medievalists, in which skulls and other signs of mortality appear, urging reformation of character by serving as a reminder of the brevity of life and its ultimate end.[14]

The third blessing, the *Kedushah* (holiness of God), contains many *piyyutim*. The first of these, *Ata hu eloheinu*, is also recited on Rosh Hashanah. The second, *Moreh hata'im* (You instruct sinners), was written by Meshullam ben Kalonymus and is based on

Psalm 145. The poet concludes each stanza with a quote from the first part of each of the verses of that psalm in order. Another plea for mercy, the poem describes the observances of the day, specifically the four services that take place during the day, and contains many allusions to the ancient Temple service for Yom Kippur.

Another *piyyut* in this section, *Ana elohim ḥayim* (please, living God), has an extremely sophisticated poetic scheme. Each line consists of three stiches: The first begins with the letters of the alphabet in order. The second begins with the reverse alphabet (*alef* is followed by *tav*, *bet* by *shin*, *gimel* by *resh*, and so forth). The third is a plea for God's mercy. In addition, the last word of each stitch rhymes: *teḥinati—rinati—shavati*. The poem begins and ends with the congregational refrain, "You are merciful. Forgive us." If the poetics are complicated, the theme is simple: the human being asks God's forgiveness. Written expressly for the morning service, this *piyyut* asks God to heed "the morning prayer" and, paraphrasing Isaiah, to "accept it and turn the crimson [sin] completely white" (Isa. 1:18). The feeling of this text is positive, and its emphasis is on purification, a theme first introduced in the evening service: "Cleanse me from the stain of my sin, the Lord is the purifying water [*mikveh*, which also means hope] of Israel." The poem is written almost entirely in the first person singular. In contrast to the *Amidah,* which is always in the first person plural, this *piyyut* and others like it individualize prayer. (Many of the psalms, our oldest liturgical creations, are also written in the singular.)

An urgent plea follows this personal prayer. The reader addresses the congregation and, like a prophet wishing to rouse the listener to change and repent, urges: "This day life and death are inscribed in the book of remembrance. Please, [God's] stock, please awake, arouse yourself, please, please stand, please attend, please get up, supplicate and plead for your soul before He who dwells on high!"[15]

Two additional *piyyutim* by the prolific Meshullam ben Kalonymus follow: *Imru l'elohim* (speak of God) and *Ma'aseh eloheinu* (the works of our God). Like many of his other works, these are alphabetical acrostics that quote extensively from biblical verses. Neither of these is a prayer in the sense of addressing God; they are, rather, proclamations of God's greatness. The first speaks of God, the second of God's creation. *Ma'aseh eloheinu* originally contained a contrasting set of verses in which "the works of humans" were described, emphasizing the superiority of what God has made and done to anything within the power of human beings. With one exception, these verses do not appear in most *Maḥzorim*. They may have been eliminated because of excessive length or because they interfered with the thrust of the service, which at this point is building toward the praise of God in the *Kedushah*, the responsive recitation of God's holiness.

The next few *piyyutim,* also by Meshullam ben Kalonymus, reach an even more exalted and feverish pitch in praising God and are similar to ancient mystic prayers that influenced the *Kedushah* and that produce an almost hypnotic effect through rhythmic repetition. The first of these, *Al yisra'el* (upon Israel), is constructed of short, three-word phrases (unlike the long and elaborate phrases of the previous *piyyutim*). Two words, "upon Israel," are followed by a single Hebrew word, in alphabetical order, describing a quality or gift God: "Upon Israel is His faithfulness/Upon Israel is His blessing. . . ." The repetition of "Israel" strengthens the idea of the unique relationship between God and Israel. As the Rabbis put it in the midrash, "His name rests in greater measure upon Israel."[16] The next *piyyut* in this set, *Ein Kamokhah* (there is none like You), speaks of the singularity of God's being and God's deeds. It, too, is brief and is similar in style to *Al yisra'el.*

Ha-aderet veha-emunah (might and faithfulness) is even closer in style to the ancient mystic hymns of praise.[17] This poem features two Hebrew words forming a double acrostic, followed by the phrase, "unto He who lives forever." This poem is taken from the twenty-eighth chapter of *Hekhalot rabbati,* a sixth-century mystical work. By means of piling praise upon praise, the mystic ascent is facilitated as a trance-like atmosphere is created.

Two brief *piyyutim* in a similar, though less-accomplished style, follow: *Na'amirakh be-eimah* (we will acknowledge You in

fear) and *Romemu el melekh ne'eman* (exalt God the faithful King).
The Rosh Hashanah *piyyut*, "God who orders judgment" is repeated, followed by the *Kedushah,* the mystic praise of God. Thus,
the brief *Kedushah* has a rather extended introduction, out of pro-
portion to its length. These additions, however, have enabled us
to dwell on some of the major themes of the day, to plead for
forgiveness, to be stirred to repentance, and to experience the Holiness of God.

The pace and urgency of the day has quickened. The light-
ness of mood with which we began has become both more somber
with its intimations of mortality and more intense with its staccato approaches to God's presence. All of this prepares us well
for the significant *Selihot* prayers and confessions, which are repeated once again.

Yizkor.   During the Torah service, before the Torahs are returned to the ark, it is customary in Ashkenazi synagogues to recite prayers in memory of the dead. These prayers are known collectively by the word that begins them: *yizkor* (may He [God]
remember). In many congregations this is one of the most solemn
moments of the entire day, if not of the entire year; it is a time
for remembering parents, children, siblings, grandparents,
friends, or spouses. It is as if on the day when we feel our own
mortality most keenly and have brought ourselves closest to leaving this world, we wish to experience again the closeness of those
who have already departed and whose presence is most sorely
missed.

The *Yizkor* prayer itself is very brief:

> May God remember the soul of . . . who has gone to eternity. May
> his/her soul be bound up in the bond of life. May his/her rest be
> honorable, basking in the radiance of Your Presence, pleasantly en-
> sconced in Your right hand forever. Amen.

"Remember" in this context does not mean to think about
and recall, but to act favorably toward someone. Thus, God is
asked to be favorable to the individual mentioned and to guard
that soul forever in God's presence.

In many congregations meditations upon life and death have been added to this simple request. Prayers are said in memory of martyrs, and in Israel fallen soldiers and victims of terrorism are recalled. Appropriate psalms are sometimes recited, and the mourners' *Kaddish* is said. Often, lists of congregational members who died during the year are read as well.

Yizkor originated when prayers were offered on Yom Kippur in memory of the martyrs of the Crusades. The terrible slaughter of Jews by Crusaders on their way to the Holy Land at the beginning of the second millennium affected Jewish communities in Europe much as the *Shoah* has affected us today. One of their ways of memorializing them was to recite their names and to utter this prayer. Such a list was recited, for example, in Nuremberg in 1295. The custom spread throughout the European Jewish world and was even extended to the three festivals. The Yom Kippur *Yizkor*, however, was the original prayer and so remains the most important one. Indeed, *Yizkor* is much more appropriate for this solemn day of awe than for the festivals, which are times of rejoicing and gladness.[18]

The Musaf Service

Unlike the morning service, which consists of many different components, *Musaf* has only one prayer, the *Amidah*. It is introduced by the reader's recitation of the personal prayer, *Hineni*, the same prayer that is recited prior to *Musaf* on Rosh Hashanah.

The *Musaf Amidah* is almost identical to the *Shaharit Amidah*. The only difference is that in the fourth, or middle blessing, the second half reads not *Ya'aleh ve-yavo* (arise and come forth), but *U-mipnei hata'einu* (because of our sins), which describes the sacrifices offered on this day and laments the fact that because of the exile imposed upon us we can no longer participate in the Temple ritual. We pray for the restoration of the Temple, the rebuilding of Jerusalem, and the ingathering of the exiles. This same prayer is recited at *Musaf* on the three pilgrim festivals. Once again, we can see how the pattern of Yom Kippur prayers has been taken from that of the ancient biblical festivals. Like the *Shaharit Amidah,* that of *Musaf* concludes with the double confession of sin.

Repetition of the Amidah.   The unique features of *Musaf* are all part of the repetition of the *Amidah.* These include two unusual services, the *Seder Avodah* and the Martyrology. These services are not only unique to the Yom Kippur *Musaf,* they are also liturgical masterpieces, each in its own way. The repetition of the *Amidah* also contains liturgical poems written throughout the ages. Some of these, such as *U-netanah tokef, Ve-khol ma'aminim,* and *Ohilah la-el,* are part of the Rosh Hashanah liturgy as well. Others, such as *Imru l'elohim* and *Ma'aseh eloheinu,* are alternate versions of *piyyutim* by Meshullam ben Kalonymus that appear in the morning service. The *Aleinu,* including the acceptance of God's kingship through the act of prostration, made such a powerful impact on the people that it too is inserted here, even though there is no recitation of the Kingship verses it was intended to introduce on Rosh Hashanah. The repetition also contains the penitential prayers and the confessions that are found in all the Yom Kippur services.

Seder Avodah.   Before the penitential prayers are recited, *Seder Avodah,* the description of the service in the Temple on Yom Kippur, is read. The recitation and re-enactment of that rite serve as a substitute for the ancient service itself, which cannot be performed because of the destruction of the Temple[19]. While the *Avodah* is similar to descriptions of the sacrifices inserted into the various *Musaf Amidah* prayers, it is much more elaborate and extensive. It may be the only instance in which the description of an ancient ritual constitutes a *seder* or "order of service." It is not a prayer in any sense of the term, but rather a poetic version of the description given in Mishnah Yoma of the Yom Kippur rite.

What purpose does *Avodah* serve? Perhaps it is intended to keep alive the ancient tradition in the most vivid way possible and to reassure us that what we are doing today can achieve the same result as the most sacred ancient rituals. The Yom Kippur rite of the High Priest in the Second Temple was without doubt the most impressive and important ritual of ancient Judaism. In the course of time, it became the most solemn moment of the Jewish year, the moment in which the key elements of holiness came together: the holiest individual, the holiest time, the holiest place. The result was that although Yom Kippur is not one of the festivals when Jews are commanded to attend the Temple in Jerusalem, multitudes thronged there to witness the ritual and to hear the words of the High Priest. It is no accident that an entire tractate of the Mishnah and later, page upon page of the Talmud, are devoted to a detailed description of the Yom Kippur rite. From a religious standpoint, it was of supreme importance as the time when forgiveness and atonement could be attained.

The destruction of the Temple in 70 C.E. produced a religious crisis among the people. Nothing was more important to them than atonement; this act was achieved through the *Avodah,* which was no now longer possible. Shortly after the destruction of the Temple, Rabbi Joshua ran after Rabban Yohanan ben Zakkai and cried to him, "Woe unto us that the Temple, the place where the transgressions of Israel are atoned for, has been destroyed!" Rabbi Yohanan ben Zakkai answered him, "Be not so dismayed, my son. We have an atonement just like it. What is it? Acts of loving-kindness *[gemilut ḥasadim],* as it is said: 'For I desire loving-kindness *[ḥesed],* not sacrifice.'"[20] Nevertheless, the feeling of loss and lack of purity and forgiveness remained deep within the psyche of the people. The recitation of the *Avodah* service helps to fill this void; it is a magnificent pageant that reenacts the Temple ritual, complete with prostration. Paradoxically, it also serves to increase the feeling of sin, for it was transgression, in some views, that caused the Temple to be destroyed.

The telling of the *Avodah* in poetic terms is an ancient practice. The version read in most synagogues today was written by Meshullam ben Kalonymus and is only one of many extant versions. *Piyyutim* describing the *Avodah* were written as far back as the fourth or fifth century C.E., the time of Yose ben Yose, the earliest liturgical poet. Meshullam himself wrote at least one more version, even more elaborate than the one we now read. Our version, *Amitz Koah*, is organized alphabetically, with each letter repeated four times at the beginning of a five-word stanza. The poem may be divided into two sections: the prologue describes the creation and history of humankind from Adam and Eve through Jacob and his sons, and the text that follows describes the actions of the High Priest on Yom Kippur.

The prologue is a magnificent achievement, a brief summary intended to demonstrate the cosmic importance of the *Avodah* and place it in proper context. It suggests that the *Avodah* can be understood only when one remembers the history of humanity, its descent into sin through Adam and Eve, Cain and the generation of the flood, and its subsequent ascent from Noah to Abraham to Jacob and his sons—from whom sprang the tribe of Levi, entrusted with the work of atonement:

> *Vast in power, mighty, great in strength,*
> *There is none to equal your powerful deeds.*
> *You made firm the vast heights upon the waters,*
> *You founded the earth upon emptiness.*
> *When the world was darkness, shadow and gloom,*
> *With Your shining garment You caused the morning light to shine forth.*
> *You divided the seething waters with awe-inspiring crystal,*
> *You gathered together the deeps so never to envelope the earth.*
> *You revealed the face of the earth and caused the vegetation to burst forth,*
> *You planted a garden in the east for the pleasure of those who exalt You.*
> *The great lights You placed in Your mighty firmament,*
> *The stars You commanded to accompany them.*
> *Fish and fowl, swooping birds, You created with the hollow of Your hand,*
> *The leviathan as feast for those who paradise inhabit.*
> *Clods that cling together brought forth those who creep and crawl,*
> *Dwellers of the marsh and swamp as a meal for those called unto You.*
> *You prepared food and drink, but there was as yet no one to feast*

You nipped a form from clay in the stamp of Your likeness.
Into his body You breathed the pure soul from Your heaven,
   As he slept You formed his intended partner.
You commanded him not to eat of the tree of knowledge;
   But like a fool he disobeyed Your command on the word of the
   slithering serpent.
He was punished, made to snatch his bread from the sweat of his brow,
   The woman—by pains of birth—and the devious one by making
   dust his diet.
The outpouring of his fluid You congealed within the tempting womb,
   She conceived and brought forth a farmer and a shepherd.
Together they offered sacrifice and gift;
   You were wrathful toward the elder and accepted the gift of the
   younger.
With no shred of pity, he slaughtered, killed a brother,
   He implored and You set a sign upon his brow.
The third generation called their idols by Your name,
   You called forth the sea, it flooded them and they perished.
The proud ones in their error commanded You to depart,
   You ensnared them in boiling water, they burned and disappeared.
He who was commanded to create the ark of gopher wood was saved
   when You closed him within,
   His children You made fertile and they populated the world.
They took counsel, banded together to rise to the heavens,
   They were caught and scattered by sweeping wind and tempest.
A friend from over the river[21] *spread Your fame in the world,*
   In old age he was fruitful bringing You praise.
Like an innocent lamb the simple man[22] *was chosen,*
   He loved to study and was drawn after You.
Worthy, lovely sons You brought forth from his loins,
   truthful seed entire with no defect.
You appointed Levi, Your pious one, to serve You,
   Separating his stock to be sanctified above all.
To wear the holy band upon his forehead, the breastplate to adorn,
   To dwell alone within for seven days.
For seven days before the tenth the elders
   instruct the priest upon his task. . . .

It is interesting to note the similarities between this prologue
and Milton's introduction to *Paradise Lost*:

Of Man's First Disobedience, and the Fruit
Of that Forbidden Tree, whose mortal taste
Brought Death into the World, and all our woe . . .
Sing Heav'nly Muse, that on the secret top
Of Oreb, or of Sinai, dids't inspire
That Shepherd, who first taught the chosen Seed,
In the Beginning how the Heav'ns and Earth
Rose out of Chaos. . . .
Instruct me, for Thou know'st; Thou from the first
Wast present, and with mighty wings outspread
Dove-like satst brooding on the vast Abyss
And mad'st it pregnant. . . .

In Milton's poem, the subject is original sin, that is, the taint-
ing of all human beings through the sin of Adam and Eve, and
eventual salvation through grace.[23] These concepts are not a part
of normative Judaism. The Jewish notion of sin revolves around
the idea that each individual, much like Adam and Eve, starts life
in purity but later becomes susceptible to temptation. Because of
the *yetzer,* the inclination or urges with which we are born, we
ultimately fall into error. Nevertheless, the sin of Adam and Eve
does figure as the beginning of human transgression, even in Jewish tradition. Kalonymus, following the biblical scheme, describes
Adam's sin as the first in a line of sins that eventually led God to
destroy humankind with the flood and to start anew. Later in the
biblical account, the figure of Abraham represents God's attempt
to create a people who would follow God's ways, since sin had
again taken hold. If humankind was not rescued from sin, it was,
at the very least, offered a means of cleansing itself by following
God's will. The message of Meshullam's *piyyut* is that, although
sin continues to exist, it may be expiated, and the *Avodah* service
of Yom Kippur is the symbolic means of enacting this ritual of
spiritual cleansing.

The description of the Yom Kippur ritual follows the prologue. It is based on the Mishnah's descriptions of the High Priest's
preparation, including the way in which the Sages taught him and
made him swear to follow their rules; the beginning of the sacrificial ritual; his donning of ritual garments with the first light of
dawn; and so forth. The ritual of the scapegoat is also described
in detail. The body of the poem is interrupted several times in
order to recite the Mishnah's description of the High Priest's confessions of sin and of the people's reaction upon hearing him pro-
nounce the Name of God; included as well is the description of
the priest counting the number of times he sprinkles the blood
of the sacrifice within the Holy of Holies and on the golden altar. These are the poetic highlights of the ritual re-enactment.

The *piyyut* concludes with an exalted description of the earth
rejoicing over the atonement that had been achieved and of the
people's delight in their newly-attained purity. The description of
this latter sentiment is a clear paraphrasing of Rabbi Akiba's
words, "to proclaim that He who purifies them is the source of
living water, the hope [mikveh] of Israel cleanses them, water
which can be depended upon!" The poet builds on this idea of
purity and joy and moves the poem to an end with the words:

The radiance of their light breaks forth as the dawn
They raise their voices in song, praising the greatness of the Rock of
     Eternity.

To this description, fittingly, the poet adds a verse from the
Psalms:

Happy the people who have it so;
Happy the people whose God is the Lord (144:15).

Appended to the end of the poem is the poet's description
of the High Priest's prayer for the people, including his blessing
for a good year. Beginning each line with the word *shenat* (a year
of), he goes through the alphabet describing what kind of year is

wanted: "A year of plenty, a year of blessing, a year of God's good decrees. . . ."

Various poems follow in different rites, some dwelling on the sins of the people and the consequences of sin (the destruction of the Temple and the end of Temple rites), and others describing the happiness of those who were permitted to participate in or witness the rites of the Temple when it stood. The mutual end of all the poetic readings is to return to the theme of our sins and our unworthiness—a fitting prelude to the prayer of penitence.

The Ten Martyrs.   The story of ten Sages who were martyred by the Romans has been a major feature of the penitential prayers of the Yom Kippur *Musaf* since the Middle Ages. It is, however, only one of many liturgical pieces written to enhance these prayers by expounding upon the troubles and sorrows that Jews have suffered, whether as individuals or as communities. These poems lend another dimension to the penitential prayers, intended to remind God, as it were, that He is merciful and has promised to forgive, and this added dimension is at least as appropriate for our time as it was for the Middle Ages. The message of the poems is this: We have suffered enough. Put an end to our torments and our tormentors. Show mercy not only by forgiving us, but by ending the black days of our suffering.

These poems can be divided into two categories: descriptions of historical events, such as the Crusades, and descriptions of ancient martyrdoms. A poem signed in acrostic by the twelfth-century David son of Meshullam Ha-katan (the younger or lesser) of Speyer falls into the first category:

O God, do not be silent; do not hold aloof; do not be quiet [Ps 83:2]
  to those who rise against me!
. . . Sons of the holy seed do not lie; "This is my God and I will glorify
  Him" they cry aloud. . . .
Children and women they bound up together; like lambs gathered for the
  sacrifice; O Unique and Exalted One! for Your sake are we slain. . . .
Can this be? Do we really hear or see this? Who can credit this—great
  is our astonishment!

They lead their children to the slaughter as to a lovely wedding canopy!
  Can You continue to hold back, O exalted One?!
. . . Credit their righteousness unto us and bring our sorrows to an
  end![24]

This poem, and others like it, reflect the tragic events of the Crusader period when whole communities of Jews were slaughtered and when fathers slew their children, their wives, and then themselves rather than submit to baptism or permit the enemy to torture and kill them.

Other poems commemorate specific tragedies; this text recounts the events in Blois in 1171 when all the Jews of the town were burned at the stake, as a result of a blood libel:

Those of perfect faith in the people Israel, their bodies like jewels,
You abandoned and neglected. You were like a warrior stunned
When You delivered Your people into the hand of the detestable
Tibalt. . . .[25]
On the twentieth of Sivan . . . in the year 1171 it was given into
his hand to decide.
All were to be offered as a burnt offering, the mandrakes yielded
their fragrance. . . .
It was decided to bring them to the stake; they rejoiced together
as a bride being brought to the canopy;
"We praise You," they chanted with willing souls, "Ah, you are
fair, my darling, Ah you are fair" [Song 4:1].

Using rhyming quatrains, the poet Hillel ben Ya'akov describes in detail the terrible story of this martyrdom and calls for justice and vengeance:

He will fight their fight forever for His name's sake;
Before our eyes let it be know among the nations. . . .

The only one of these many *piyyutim* that remains in our *Mahzorim* today is the story of the Ten Martyrs, which falls into the second category of poems—those written to commemorate

ancient martyrdoms. This particular text was composed to serve
as an example and a justification for those who had been martyred or who might be called upon to do so. This story demonstrated that martyrs were not alone, nor were they the first to die
in the name of God *(al kiddush ha-Shem)*; rather, they joined a
long list of individuals who had martyred themselves for God,
among them great Sages such as Rabbi Akiba and Rabbi Ishmael.
The story of the Ten Martyrs appears in the form of a medieval
poem, signed in acrostic by Yehudah Hazak and based on an older
midrash found in Jellinek's *Beit ha-midrash*.[26]

Told in stirring terms to arouse terror, pathos, and tears,
the story is of a Roman ruler who proclaims the Jews guilty of
the kidnapping of their ancestor Joseph, a capital crime according to the Torah. The Roman uses the biblical text as a justification, and he slays each of ten great Sages, amongst whom
are Rabbi Akiba, Rabbi Ishmael, and Rabban Simeon ben Gam-
liel. It is important to point out that the story is historiography,
not history; the Sages featured in it did not all live at the same
time and were therefore not martyred together.[27] The writer has
taken individual stories from various places in rabbinic literature, changed them, and suited them to his dramatic scheme.
The martyrdom of Akiba, for example, is movingly described in
the Talmud.[28] He was imprisoned by the Romans in Caesarea
for violating the ban on teaching Torah publicly and was martyred early in the morning. Though his flesh was raked with
iron combs, he retained enough strength to recite, "Hear O Israel, the Lord is our God, the Lord is one" as his dying words.
The martyrdom of Rabbi Ishmael and Rabban Simeon ben Gam-
liel is taken almost entirely from the account in *Avot derabbi
natan* 38. Thus, although the composite story of the Ten Martyrs is not literally true, it nonetheless reflects the events of the
Hadrianic persecutions of the Jews in the second century C.E.,
when loyalty to Judaism led all too easily to Roman executions.
To the Jewish communities of Europe at the beginning of the
second millennium, these stories were all too familiar. Retelling
them strengthened their own resolve to die rather than abandon Judaism. Their reflections on these events include the most

profound questions: Why was God silent? Why did He give the Jews into the hands of the wicked, in the second century, and in their own time? Why did the hands of Esau prevail over the voice of Jacob? In the words of Yehudah Hazak:

The hosts of heaven cried out bitterly:
Is this Torah and its reward, O He who is clothed in light?
The enemy blasphemes Your great and awesome name
And scorns the words of the Torah?!
A voice from heaven answered: if I hear one more such sound
I will turn the world into water, I will return the earth to chaos and
*   the void.*
Such is My decree. Accept it. . . .

Today, many congregations and some newer *Mahzorim* add poems and readings at this point concerning the Holocaust—the tragic martyrdom of our own age—thus carrying on the tradition of the Middle Ages, whose poets saw the tragedies of their time as a continuation of the sorrows of the past.

The experience of Yom Kippur up to this moment reaches a point of exhaustion. We began in the evening with a profound opening statement. We achieved a measure of uplift in feeling the possibility of forgiveness and the chance of being relieved of sin and guilt. In the morning we began refreshed and renewed, assured of God's everlasting light and mercy. It was a period of calm, ruffled only by the continued self-reflection that the confessions precipitate. As the day wears on, however, a note of sadness and nostalgia, almost of "world-weariness" creeps in. We remember the past and those we have lost (*Yizkor*). The spiritual uplifting effected by the *Avodah* ultimately is replaced with the sad realization that all this exists no more. The recollection of the martyrs causes us to question the foundations of the world, and when we come again to confession it is with a feeling that although we may be forgiven, we may not be worthy of forgiveness. We have reached the nadir of the day, the depths from which we must begin to climb upwards again to a triumphant conclusion.

Minḥah

The afternoon service, *Minḥah,* is the least complicated of the five services. It consists of an *Amidah* and a Torah reading, followed by the reading of the entire prophetic book of Jonah.[29] The usual prayers with which *Minḥah* begins at other times—the *Ashrei* and *U-va le-tziyon*—are not recited; they are postponed until *Ne'ilah,* the final service of the day. The *Minḥah Amidah* follows the pattern of the morning service, including the prayers of penitence and the confessions. *Piyyutim* are not added to the repetition of the *Amidah* in most *Minḥah* services today, although many have been written and were often recited in medieval times.

Minḥah begins our ascent from the depths of the Martyrology service, gradually lifting our spirits with the reading of Jonah. The story is profound, but delightful, and its message allows us to feel that there is hope for humankind and for ourselves. We see that the end is in sight. Only one more movement remains to be played in the symphony of Yom Kippur: *Ne'ilah.*

Ne'ilah

The last service of Yom Kippur, *Ne'ilah* (closing, or locking), is unique. There is no other day during the current Jewish year when this fifth service is recited, although there were such times when the Temple stood. Some scholars believe that a fourth sacrificial service was held daily at the Temple, and we know that one was added on public fast days.[30] As late as the talmudic period, the nature of the *Ne'ilah* service was a matter of debate among the Rabbis and different methods of observing it existed. Rav taught that *Ne'ilah* consisted of the recitation of an additional *Amidah.* The Amora Samuel thought that no *Amidah* was required, but that a special prayer should be recited, beginning with the words, "What are we, what is our life?" At least as early as the time of the great Sages of the second century, however, it was generally accepted that a special *Amidah* was recited.[31] Some thought that this recitation could even take the place of the evening service, *Ma'ariv*, recited immediately after the conclusion of Yom Kippur, but this opinion was rejected.[32]

What is the origin of the name of the service? Although all the authorities agreed that the reference was to *Ne'ilat she'arim* (the closing of the gates), there is a dispute as to whether the reference is to the gates of the Temple or the gates of heaven, that is, the gates that are open to receive our prayers and supplications.[33] If the first idea is correct, it constitutes a historical reference to the fact that the extra service was recited at the close of the day when the gates to the Temple were being closed. If the second, it is a theological concept of a more spiritual nature. The special *piyyutim* written for *Ne'ilah* generally favor the idea of the heavenly gates.

Ne'ilah is one of the most moving of all services, bringing this sacred day to a close with poetry of unusual beauty and with melodies reflecting a profound depth of spiritual feeling. It is a worthy twin to *Kol Nidre*, with which this journey began.

There is a sense of urgency about the *Ne'ilah* service. During the day, prayers are recited in leisurely fashion; there is time to add lengthy prayers and recitations, time for elaboration of liturgical music, time for contemplation and meditation. With nothing to do except pray, we have the luxury of being divorced from the world on Yom Kippur. With the beginning of *Ne'ilah*, however, the mood suddenly changes:

Open the gates for us at this time when the gates are closing—for the day wanes!
The day will wane, the sun will set and disappear—let us come into Your gates!

This feeling of urgency is found in almost every one of the insertions into the repetition of the *Amidah*, such as, "Quickly open for those who obey Your laws. Quickly. . . ."

We have had an entire day to achieve atonement. Indeed, we have had ten whole days of penitence, preceded by a month of preparation. Now we have barely an hour. What have we achieved? How have we changed? Can we close the day with a feeling that our sins have been purged and that a new year with a clean page awaits us? Quickly. . .

The time of day also plays a part in creating the last act of this drama: the waning sun, the lengthening shadows, the intense red colors that envelope the earth and slowly turn into darkness—all contribute to the feeling that the end is near. There is no more time. In addition, the physical weakness and weariness that result from a day of fasting intensify our emotions. But it often happens that by the end of the day the initial hunger has worn off and the individual feels a renewed surge of strength. This is the moment when people may achieve a kind of spiritual elation that stands in an inverse ratio to waning physical strength. We also feel a lingering sadness that this day during which we existed in another sphere is coming to an end. We must prepare ourselves to return to the world. Our hope is that we return transformed.

During the *Ne'ilah* service the motif of "opening the gates" is symbolized by keeping the ark of the Torah open. People therefore stand as they always do when the ark is open.[34] This act requires an additional effort and adds to the feeling of urgency and transformation.

The Order of the Ne'ilah *Service.*   The *Ne'ilah* service begins with *Ashrei* (Psalm 145) and *U-va le-tziyon* (may the redeemer come to Zion), which were postponed from *Minḥah.* They are chanted in a special, haunting melody reserved for this service alone.

The silent *Amidah* is recited next. It follows the same pattern as that of *Shaḥarit* and *Minḥah,* with one difference: only the short confession, *Ashamnu,* is recited, and not the longer *Al ḥet.* In place of it, we have an ancient prayer of penitence that includes the prayer referred to by the Amora Samuel as the *Ne'ilah* format: "What are we, what is our life?"

This prayer is composed of two sections—possibly alternate conceptions of what was to be recited—which were then amalgamated into one text. The first section begins with the words *Ata noten yad la-posh'im* (You extend Your hand to transgressors):

You extend Your hand to transgressors
And Your right hand is extended to receive the penitent.
Teach us, O Lord our God, to confess all our iniquities before You so
*   that our hands may refrain from unrighteousness*
And receive us in perfect repentance before You as You received the
*   offerings [in the Temple] for the sake of the words You have uttered.*
There is no end to the sacrifices we are obligated to bring
And to the offerings for our guilt.
You know that our destiny is worms and decay.
Therefore You have been generous in pardoning us.
What are we, what is our life, what are our good deeds, what is our
*   righteousness. . . .*

The prayer continues to expound on the unimportance of
our deeds and the meager nature of our goodness in comparison
with God. It concludes with the pessimistic words from Ecclesiastes, "man has no superiority over beast, since both amount to
nothing" (3:19).

As we have already noted,[35] Jewish ideology incorporates the
notion that the worth of human beings is, at times, to be depre-
ciated. While we exist on a plane only slightly lower than the angels, we are also only dust and ashes. Repentance and confession
therefore require us to recognize the vanity of life and the rela-
tive insignificance of our deeds. Looked at in this light, confession is a sobering and humbling experience.

But this idea represents only one aspect of the Jewish concept
of human life. The second prayer that follows *Ata noten* lifts us out
of this bleak mood with an affirmation of the value of our lives:
Ata hivdaltah enosh me-rosh (from the very beginning, You set humans apart and permitted them to stand before You). Whereas the
previous paragraph ended with the statement that humans and
beasts are identical, this one begins by asserting the very opposite:
in the very act of creation, humans were separated from the rest
of existence and given a special status before God. This approach
echoes the biblical story of creation in which God determines to
"make man in My image, after My likeness" (Gen. 1:26) and gives
humans dominion over all of creation (Gen. 1:28).

The prayer then goes on to discuss the purpose of Yom Kippur:

> In love You have given us, O Lord our God, this day of Yom Kippur, the conclusion of pardon and forgiveness for all our transgressions so that our hands may cease doing unrighteousness and we may return unto You to fulfill Your laws and perform Your will with a perfect heart.

Next, the prayer expounds upon the forgiving nature of God:

> Have mercy upon us in Your great mercy. For You do not desire the destruction of Your world. . . . You want the repentance of the wicked and You do not desire their death. . . . For You are forgiving unto Israel and pardoning to the tribes of Jeshurun in every generation. Aside from You we have no king, no pardoner and forgiver except You.

These concluding words are the same as those found at the conclusion of the middle blessing of every Yom Kippur *Amidah*.

The Repetition of the Amidah.   Although at one time the repetition of the *Ne'ilah Amidah* included all of the penitential prayers found in the other Yom Kippur services, the pressure of time has resulted in a curtailed version of these prayers and in the omission of the long *Al ḥet*. This change permits the insertion of *piyyutim* that are found nowhere else and that reflect the special mood of *Ne'ilah*. These *piyyutim* are artful and short—almost staccato— as opposed to the long, elaborate *piyyutim* of the other services; they add momentum to the prayer and contribute a sense of urgency to the end of the marathon that *Ne'ilah* signifies.

The first such *piyyut, Av yeda'akha* (the patriarch recognized You—a reference to Abraham, who came to know God while still a child), was written by the sixth-century Tiberian poet Eleazar Kalir and is one of the earliest poems retained in the current liturgy. It follows the alphabet and originally concluded with the poet's name in acrostic form. At one time, the poem also contained many biblical verses, which were interspersed throughout, but the version published in most *Maḥzorim* today is extremely abbreviated and does not even continue beyond the letter *lamed,* thus eliminating more than half of the *piyyut.*

The poem is divided among the first three paragraphs of the *Amidah,* commenting on each of them specifically. For the first paragraph, the blessing of the patriarchs, there is a discussion of Abraham's qualities, the tests he underwent, his faithfulness to God, and a plea that Abraham's descendants be allowed "to enter this gate." For the second blessing, known as "the powers of God," the poet follows a well-known tradition that each of the three paragraphs refers to one of the three patriarchs and discusses Isaac specifically. He refers to the midrash that Isaac perished on the altar, connecting it with the blessing that God revives the dead. He pleads that God save us just as he saved Isaac, "as evening comes." "Evening" here is a reference to the way in which Isaac "went out to meditate in the field toward evening" (Gen. 24:63), which the Sages took to mean that he was praying. The poetic segment before the third blessing, the *Kedushah* (sanctification), describes Jacob and his dream of the angels and leads to the *Kedushah* itself, in which the angelic praise of God is imitated by Israel.

The refrain of another *piyyut* is now recited: "Oh heed! Oh forgive this day! For the day wanes! We shall praise You awesome and imposing One! Holy One!" The body of the poem itself, missing in our versions of the prayerbook, is another alphabetical acrostic describing how we have pleaded with God and beseeched God "from evening to evening," asking His forgiveness.

The theme of "gates" predominates the next *piyyut, Sha'arei armon* (gates of the palace). The original *piyyut,* only the first part of which is recited today, begins each line with the word "gates," followed in alphabetical order by various descriptions of the gates of heaven. The second part of each verse begins with the words "quickly open" and then, in alphabetical order, a description of those to whom the gates should be opened: "those who believe," "Your people," "those who yearn for God," and so forth.

In the fourth blessing, penitential prayers are inserted and "The Thirteen Attributes" are recited, preceded by another brief exhortation:

Open the gates for us when the gates are closing, for the day wanes!
The day is waning, the sun is setting, let us come into Your gates!
Oh God, please! Please pardon! Please forgive! Please wipe out! Please
*   atone! Please have mercy! Please suppress anger, sin and trans-*
*   gression!*

Each of these lines is actually the refrain for another *piyyut;* the urgency of the day and the time has caused the elimination of these poems, but has utilized the almost staccato phrases of the refrains to urge the worshipper to compel himself or herself to greater repentance.

The next two *piyyutim* frequently are run together, although they are completely separate creations. The first, *U-mi ya'amod,* was written by the tenth-century Solomon ben Judah, who signed his name Shlomo Hakatan in the acrostic. The theme is the mercy of God as shown to all of us, since no human being is so free of sin as to be completely guiltless. All of us depend on God's merciful nature and not on our own merits alone.

The second of these *piyyutim, Merubim tzorkhei amkha* (Your people's needs are great) is by the twelfth-century Joseph ben Isaac of Orleans. The poet elaborates on the inverse ratio between our needs and our inability to express them; we are neither pious nor well-versed enough to plead before God properly. We therefore ask God to act as if everything we said was worthwhile and as if our prayers were worthy of God. Although both of these *piyyutim* are appropriate for this section of penitential prayers, neither is specific to the *Ne'ilah* theme and could easily be recited at any time on Yom Kippur.

Another *piyyut* appearing in this section of the services, *Zekhor brit Avraham* (remember the covenant of Abraham) was written by the famous eleventh-century Sage Rabbeinu Gershom of Metz, who is known as "the light of the exile." The poem is a double alphabetical acrostic followed by the name of the author. Unfortunately, only a portion of it appears in most *Mahzorim.* Not specific to Yom Kippur, this *piyyut* is similar to the martyrology poetry discussed above.[36] Beginning with the classic theme of this poetic genre, the binding of Isaac, the poem bemoans the fate of the Jewish people, describing in particular the destruction of the First Temple and the subsequent exile:

We were driven hastily from the goodly land. . . .
All of Judah has suffered one exile after the other. . . .
The holy city and its surroundings have become despoiled. . . .

What follows are descriptions of the destruction of Jerusalem, which could easily have been taken from a Tisha b'Av lament. The poem concludes by asking God to repent of His wrath and to "remember Your mercy. . . . Mighty Redeemer, rescue us for Your name's sake . . . remember the covenant of the patriarchs, matriarchs, and tribes. . . . Fight our cause, He who requites blood, return sevenfold justice upon our oppressors. We were sold for naught and not redeemed for silver. Restore our devastated Holy Temple before our very eyes!" This is not a plea for forgiveness, but rather a cry for salvation. While it is true that Yom Kippur is the most universal of all the holidays and the one least connected with the history of the Jewish people, the awareness of exile and suffering and the need for restoration are a constant element of Jewish consciousness. The final moments of Yom Kippur, when the people Israel has reached a state of purity as great as any that can be attained, are therefore certainly an appropriate time to pray for justice and redemption.

Enkat mesaldekha (the cry of those who beseech You) is one of the most well known of the *Ne'ilah piyyutim*. It consists of four paragraphs emanating from different *piyyutim* by different poets, some of whom have signed their names in the scheme of the poem. These include Shephatiah ben Amitai, Yitzhak ben Shmuel, and Shlomo ben Shmuel of France or Italy, all of whom lived between the ninth and thirteenth centuries. This amalgam of poems begins with a plea that God hear our prayers, followed by an assurance that Israel will indeed be saved by God, since He is merciful. The plea is then reiterated: "Arise and show Your strength, heed our cry!" Then, on a less urgent and more confident note, "Let us hear Your word, 'I have forgiven' . . . . O God, be our help." This *piyyut* leads to the recitation of "The Thirteen Attributes."

Another important *piyyut* is *Ezkerah elohim* by Amitai ben Shephatiah, a ninth-century Italian poet who signs his name through the first letter of each paragraph. A magnificent dirge for Jerusalem, this poem also mentions the thirteen attributes of God, which are invoked in these prayers of penitence. Like one of the previous *piyyutim*, *Zekhor brit Avraham*, this composition is more of a cry for salvation than a plea for forgiveness.

This *piyyut* is followed by yet another urgent plea for forgiveness as the day wanes:

O have mercy upon the Congregation of the Assembly of Jeshurun! Forgive and pardon their transgression and save us, O God of our salvation!

Open the gates of heaven! Open for us Your good treasury! Save and do not delay! Save us, O God of our salvation!

An important difference between Rosh Hashanah and Yom Kippur is articulated by a change in the wording of the *Ne'ilah Amidah*. The phrase we have been using since Rosh Hashanah, "inscribe us in the Book of Life," now becomes "*seal* us in the Book of Life." The image constantly before us has been that of the writing in the Books of Life and Death, which takes place during the entire period of the *Yamim Nora'im*. The books, however, are sealed only on Yom Kippur: "sealing" is the end of the process, and since *Ne'ilah* is the conclusion of Yom Kippur, it is the time when our fates are sealed. We conclude the process of confession and repentance and place the final imprint on our lives for the coming year.

At the end of the *Ne'ilah Amidah*, *Ashamnu* (the brief confession) is recited, along with the paragraphs that substitute for the longer confession. *Avinu Malkeinu* is then chanted for the last time, and *Ne'ilah* comes to an end. The curtains of the ark are closed, signifying the closing of the gates. The great effort we have made to complete the task of repentance is now over.

Still, something is lacking. The day that began so emotionally and powerfully with the *Kol Nidre* service must be brought to an end with an equally powerful statement. This climax of Yom Kippur is achieved through the confession of faith.

CONCLUDING THE DAY

How can such a day be brought to an appropriate conclusion? Can or should anything follow these five services? Originally, the services themselves constituted the whole of the Yom Kippur experience. But just as *Kol Nidre* emerged to raise the curtain on the day in the most powerful way possible, the "Confession of Faith" developed to bring down the curtain in a rousing finale. The final gesture of Yom Kippur consists of a confession of faith and the sounding of the shofar.

This confession is prescribed in the prayerbook of Rashi (the eleventh-century Bible commentator): it begins with a seven-fold recitation of the verse, "The Lord is God." This verse is taken from the story of Elijah's confrontation with the priests of Ba'al at Mount Carmel. When Elijah is vindicated and the people are convinced that the Lord is indeed the only God, they shout, "The Lord is God!" (1 Kings 18:39).

The sacredness of the number seven is well-known. It represents not only the days of creation but the entirety of creation. The eleventh-century *Maḥzor Vitry* offers the explanation that God ascends through the seven heavens following Yom Kippur and that the seven-fold repetition is our way of accompanying God on this journey. Interestingly enough, the author cautions that the verse should not be recited until after the evening service, lest God ascend while there are still prayers to recite.[37] Since the end of *Ne'ilah* may feel somewhat anti-climactic, the proclamation offers us a way of reassuring ourselves by affirming that there is indeed one God, who is with us at all times and in all places.

Sometime later, the *Shema*—the most basic Jewish confession of faith ("Hear, O Israel, the Lord is our God, the Lord is One" [Deut. 6:4])—and the line usually recited as a silent response to the *Shema* ("blessed is the name of His glorious majesty forever and ever") were added to the ceremony. Thus, the *Shema* is recited once, "blessed is the name" is said three times, and "the Lord is our God" is proclaimed seven times. The *Shema* can only be recited once; if said more than once, it could be taken to indicate belief in more than one God.[38] Twice each day, individu-

als pledge acceptance of God as the king to whom all allegiance
is due, by reciting the *Shema*. This pledge is even more powerful
when made as a collective act by the entire people Israel at the
conclusion of the most sacred day of the year.

Like the number seven, the number three holds significance
in Jewish tradition: it represents the three patriarchs, the threefold repetition of certain prayers (such as *Kol Nidre*), the tripartite blessing of the priests, and the three judges needed for trials.

The *Siddur* of Abudarham, written in Seville in 1340, suggests sounding the shofar at the conclusion of the Yom Kippur
services. This act is not a requirement, but is a custom, and it is
followed by the recitation of a most appropriate verse: "Go, eat
your bread in gladness, and drink your wine in joy; for your action was long ago approved by God" (Eccles. 9:7). If any of us
had the lingering feeling that perhaps we were still in disfavor
and that a return to the world is somehow a betrayal of piety,
this verse dispels it.

The blowing of the shofar at the conclusion of Yom Kippur
is an echo of an ancient practice, a reminder of Leviticus 25:9,
"Then you shall sound the horn loud; in the seventh month, on
the tenth day of the month, the Day of Atonement, you shall have
the horn sounded throughout your land." The shofar was sounded
in order to proclaim the beginning of the fiftieth year—the
Jubilee—the time of freedom: "You shall proclaim liberty throughout the land for all its inhabitants" (Lev. 25:10). Thus, it is only
fitting that after the long blast of the shofar we proclaim, "Next
year in Jerusalem!" (In Israel we say, "Next year in rebuilt
Jerusalem.") This declaration signifies the hope for a return to a
city that has symbolized hope and freedom for generations of
Jews; it is an appropriate conclusion for the day of contrition and
an apt beginning of a New Year that is full of hope.[39]

THE EFFECT OF YOM KIPPUR

The tone of Yom Kippur is very different from that of Rosh
Hashanah: the festive atmosphere is missing.[40] Instead, we are

immersed in a world other than our own. We leave ordinary life when we experience the release of our vows and the forgiveness of our past and when we sever our connections with the physical and social dimensions of our daily lives. We plumb the depths of our own lives, contemplating our errors and remaking ourselves. We spend the day in an atmosphere of holiness, separated even from regular time. A poem written by Friedrich Ruckert (1788–1866) and set to one of Gustav Mahler's most haunting melodies expresses this experience of detachment well:

I have become a stranger to the world
Where once I used to waste a lot of time;
It has so long now heard nothing of me,
It may well think that I have died!

Indeed, I am not much concerned
Whether it believes me dead.
I cannot even contradict it,
For really, I am dead to the world.

I have renounced the worldly bustle
And live in peace at a quiet place.
I live alone in this, my heaven,
In my love, in my songs.

For us, however, this "death to the world" is only a temporary event. Having achieved our goal of forgiveness and inner peace through great spiritual effort, we affirm God, heed His summoning trumpet call, and continue with our lives.

10

Biblical Readings for the Yamim Nora'im

Jewish worship has always consisted of a combination of prayer and study; listening to the words of the Torah is no less important than expressing ourselves to God in prayer. In listening to readings from the Torah and the Prophets, we imitate our ancestors who heard the divine word first at Sinai (Exod. 20) and then again in Jerusalem when Ezra proclaimed it (Neh. 8), interestingly enough, on Rosh Hashanah. In both cases, Israel pledged to heed the word of God. The practice of reading sections of the Bible on the Sabbath and Holy Days is an ancient one that dates back to the days of the Second Temple and that formed the basis for the synagogue service.[1]

One of the features of the Torah reading is the act of calling people up to the Torah. The Hebrew word for this act, *aliyah*, means "going up," indicating that the act of saying a blessing over the Torah is one of the greatest honors awarded Jews in the service. The number of people who are called up to the Torah varies according to the sanctity of the day: on weekdays there are three; on Rosh Ḥodesh, the beginning of the month, four; on the festivals, including Rosh Hashanah, there are five; Yom Kippur is a step higher, and so there are six *aliyot* then; and on the Sabbath, the holiest day of all, there are seven *aliyot*.[2]

As early as the time of the Mishnah (200 C.E.), rabbinic authorities suggested what they viewed as appropriate readings for the Days of Awe: "On Rosh Hashanah we read, 'In the seventh month, on the first day of the month' [Lev. 23:23], and on Yom Kippur 'after the death' [Lev. 16:1]" (M. Megillah 3.5). Since Rosh Hashanah was observed for only one day during Mishnaic times in the Land of Israel,[3] the Mishnah does not address a reading for the second day. The recommended reading for Rosh Hashanah describes the way the day is to be observed; the Yom Kippur reading describes the ritual of the High Priest in making atonement for the sanctuary and the ceremony of sending out the scapegoat.

Sometime later, the Jerusalem Talmud (third to fourth century C.E.) describes an alternative reading for Rosh Hashanah: the story of the birth of Isaac, beginning with the verse from Genesis 21:1, "And the Lord took note of Sarah" (J. Megillah 3.7). This talmudic alternative is the Torah reading used today for the first day of Rosh Hashanah.[4]

The Babylonian Talmud (third to fifth century C.E.) suggests that we read "In the seventh month" and recommends a prophetic reading (Haftarah) containing the words, "Truly, Ephraim is a dear son to Me. . . ." The reference is to Jeremiah 31:2–20, which we now read on the second day of Rosh Hashanah. The Talmud then notes that some read the story of the birth of Isaac instead of the passage from Leviticus and that the account of the birth of Samuel (1Sam. 1–2:10) is sometimes substituted as a Haftarah for the reading from Jeremiah. The Talmud continues:

> At this time when we observe two days of the holiday, on the first day we read, "And the Lord took note of Sarah. . ." (Gen. 21:1) and we read the story of Hannah (1Sam. 1–2:10), and on the morrow, "And sometime afterward, God put Abraham to the test" (Gen. 22:1), and "Truly, Ephraim is a dear son to Me" (Jer. 31:20) (B. Megillah 31a).

Indeed, this is our practice today: on the first day of Rosh Hashanah we read of the births of Isaac and Samuel, and on the second day we read of the binding of Isaac along with the text from Jeremiah. The Talmud also mentions that on Yom Kippur afternoon we should read the text concerning taboo sexual relations (Lev. 18) and the Book of Jonah—practices we follow today as well.

TORAH READING FOR THE FIRST DAY OF ROSH HASHANAH

On the first day of Rosh Hashanah, then, we read the story of the birth of Isaac (Gen. 21) and on the second day the continuation of this text, usually referred to as the binding of Isaac (Gen. 22). The connection of these readings to the holiday may not be readily identified at first glance. In view of the fact that Rosh Hashanah is considered the "birthday of the world," it may have been more appropriate to read the account of creation found at the beginning of the Book of Genesis. We must remember, however, that "creation" is actually a minor theme of the High Holy Days, one that was not always universally recognized.[5]

The idea of "remembrance," on the other hand, is one of the primary themes of Rosh Hashanah. It is specifically mentioned in the Torah in connection with the holiday (Lev 23:23) and is one of the three basic themes of the Rosh Hashanah *Musaf Amidah.* The Rabbis designated Rosh Hashanah as *Yom Ha-zikaron* (the Day of Remembrance), a phrase used repeatedly in the prayers. In fact, it was this idea that the Rabbis chose to emphasize in the Torah reading: "remembrance" means God's visitation of His people for their good. He recalls them, remembers His promises, and fulfills His word. In Hebrew, the word for "remembered" is *zakhar.* A widely used synonym is *pakad,* and it is with this word that the Torah reading begins: "The Lord took note of *[pakad]* Sarah."

Yet there is more here than the appearance of the word, since the essence of the story itself illustrates the concept of remembrance. Sarah, who had been childless, is assured by God that she would bear Abraham a son: "I will return to you [Abraham] when life is due, and your wife Sarah shall have a son" (Gen. 8:10). God later "remembers" (*pakad,* or took note of) Sarah, fulfilling His promise. This story serves as a primary example of God's remembrance and as an assurance that God will remember us for our good on Rosh Hashanah, just as He remembered Sarah.

Commentary on the Reading for the First Day

The Name of the Child (Gen. 21:3).   Isaac, in Hebrew *Yitzhak,* is named by Abraham. The word, meaning laughter, appears earlier in Genesis (18:12–15), when Sarah laughs at the thought that a woman her age with a husband so old could have a child:

> And Sarah laughed to herself, saying, "Now that I am withered, am I to have enjoyment—with my husband so old?" Then the Lord said to Abraham, "Why did Sarah laugh?" . . . Sarah dissembled, saying, "I did not laugh," for she was frightened. He replied, "But you did laugh."

The laughter of Sarah, the expression of her doubt, is transformed into the name of the child whose existence demonstrates the miraculous power of God. The meaning of the name is referred to later, when Sarah says: "God has brought me laughter; everyone who heard will laugh with me" (Gen. 21:6). This last phrase has been interpreted in two ways: either Sarah is pleased, saying that every one will rejoice with her, or she is indicating that people will make fun of her.

The Torah continues to echo the word *yitzhak* when it uses it negatively about Ishmael: "Sarah saw the son, whom Hagar the Egyptian had borne to Abraham, playing [*metzahek*] (Gen. 21:9). In biblical Hebrew, the word for "playing," *metzahek,* is the same as the word for "laughing."

The Circumcision of Isaac (Gen. 21:4).   The covenant between God and Abraham represents a promise to make Abraham a great nation, to give his descendants the land of Canaan and to make them a blessing for all humanity (Gen. 17:1–14). Circumcision is the visible symbol of that covenant:

Such shall be the covenant, which you shall keep, between Me and you and your offspring to follow: every male among you shall be circumcised. You shall circumcise the flesh of your foreskin, and that shall be the sign of the covenant between Me and you. At the age of eight days, every male among you throughout the generations shall be circumcised . . . (Gen. 17:10–12).

Abraham himself was ninety when he was circumcised and Ishmael, his son, was thirteen. The circumcision of Isaac, whose future birth was proclaimed when the commandment of circumcision was given, is the first complete fulfillment of the commandment and a further sign that everything promised by God was actually taking place. As such, it was an event of great significance.

The Weaning of Isaac (Gen. 21:8).   The act of weaning has no particular relevance within Judaism today and is not a mitzvah as is circumcision. Nevertheless, it is recorded in the biblical text as an important milestone; it corresponds with the occasion when Sarah observes Ishmael "playing" and determines that he must be sent away. There is dramatic irony here in the fact that a time of joy—celebrating the life of one son—becomes an occasion for a domestic tragedy—losing another son.

Ishmael's "Playing" (Gen. 21:9).   It is clear that something about Ishmael's actions evoked Sarah's sharp reaction. Was he laughing at Isaac and boasting that he was still the elder and therefore the rightful heir? That would explain Sarah's words, "the son of that slave shall not share in the inheritance with my son Isaac" (Gen. 21:10). The Sages offered other explanations of the word "playing":

> Rabbi Akiba explained, "Playing" always means forbidden sexual acts. . . . Sarah saw Ishmael chasing after wives and forcing them. . . . Rabbi Ishmael taught, "Playing" always refers to idolatry. . . . Rabbi Eliezer says, "it means spilling blood" . . . . Rabbi Azariah says, "Ishmael would take a bow and arrow and aim it at Isaac while pretending to be playing". . . .[6]

Whatever the explanation, Sarah's actions here may be seen as those of a mother trying to protect the rights of her son: Sarah wants to eliminate any possibility of Ishmael's usurping Isaac's place. While her actions appear cruel and unfeeling to Abraham, who was "distressed greatly" (Gen. 21:11), God agrees with her, instructing Abraham, "whatever Sarah tells you, do as she says, for it is through Isaac that offspring shall be continued for you" (Gen. 21:12).

Legend has it that the feast celebrating the weaning of Isaac (Gen. 21:8) actually brought about the command to sacrifice Isaac. Satan, the accusing angel, came to the feast disguised as a poor man. Abraham was so busy and so excited that he had no time for the man and forgot his usual charitable behavior. Satan therefore challenged God: "Let's see exactly how pious and obedient this man is. Ask him to sacrifice this beloved child to You and see if he will do it or not."[7] This legend is obviously a recasting of the Book of Job, in which the trial of Job is brought about by *Ha-satan* (the accuser), who challenges Job's piety.

Abraham's Reaction (Gen. 21:11).   Unlike Sarah, who has only one son and can devote all her emotions to him, Abraham is the father of two and cannot be indifferent to the act of exiling a child, much less his firstborn son. He is troubled by this act, as indeed he should be. Yet he carries it out, because God commands him to do so, assuring Abraham that Ishmael will come to no harm and, moreover, that he will yield a nation (Gen. 21:13). Abraham's love and sensitivity are illustrated by the way he personally rises early in the morning—something he does again when leading Isaac to the sacrifice (Gen. 22:3)—and gives Ishmael and Hagar provisions himself before sending them on their way. It undoubtedly would have been easier to leave that difficult act to one of his numerous servants, but that was not Abraham's way.

God's Help to Ishmael (Gen. 21:17).   As God had promised Abraham, God helps Ishmael to survive when he is in danger of perishing in the wilderness. Genesis 21:20 emphasizes God's role in Ishmael's life and in his becoming a great nation: "God was with the boy." The midrash comments on the words, "where he is," at the end of the verse, suggesting that this was a response to the angels, who asked God how He could justify saving Ishmael when his descendants would grow to be the enemies of the Israelites in the future. God responds by asking whether Ishmael is now wicked or innocent. When the angels reply that he is innocent, God says, "I judge people by what they are now [that is, "where he is"] and not by what they may become."[8]

Conclusion.   The Torah reading for the first day of Rosh Hashanah concludes with a section that shows Abraham taking a further step toward the fulfillment of God's promise: he establishes himself in the land by making a pact with the leader of its inhabitants and by planting a tree in Beersheba—clear signs of his intentions to dwell in the area permanently.

Maftir.   The reading from the second scroll, the *maftir* (Num. 29:1–6), describes the observance of the day and its sacrifices. The one mitzvah of the day, sounding the shofar, is recorded here: "You shall observe it as the day when the horn is sounded" (Num. 29:1).

HAFTARAH FOR THE FIRST DAY OF ROSH HASHANAH

The reading from the Torah scrolls is followed by a reading from the Prophets, the Haftarah. On the first day of Rosh Hashanah the reading is 1 Samuel 1–2:10, which parallels the Torah reading in that it tells of the circumstances surrounding the birth of Samuel. Here, too, there is a woman who could not conceive until "the Lord remembered her" (1Sam. 1:19). The woman, Hannah, goes to the sanctuary of Eli the Priest to pray and to beseech God for a child. She pledges that her child would be a nazarite, dedicated to the service of God (1:11). Eli, who sees her lips moving as she prays, mistakenly thinks that she is drunk (1:13). Interestingly enough, the Sages said that many of the laws of prayer were derived from Hannah's actions, including the idea that when we pray we do not merely think the words, but actually mouth them.

The second chapter of the book, with which the reading concludes, is a magnificent psalm of thanksgiving uttered by Hannah when she brings the child to the sanctuary where he is to live and serve God. While the psalm may not have been written especially for this occasion, it is a song of praise for one who has triumphed. The psalm offers examples of those raised from misery to happiness, including the barren woman who bears seven children (2:5),[9] while the wicked are now cast down—and all these circumstances are seen as God's doing.

TORAH READING FOR THE SECOND DAY OF ROSH HASHANAH

On the second day of Rosh Hashanah the story known as *Akeidat Yitzhak* (the binding of Isaac) is read. As we have seen, the *Akeidah* is referred to many times in the liturgy and has come to play a central role in Rosh Hashanah. It is one of the most difficult portions of the Torah to understand, and biblical commentators, rabbinic Sages, and modern biblical scholars and philosophers have continued to puzzle over it.

The outline of the story as presented in the Torah is simple and clear: Abraham is being tested by God. He is told to offer his beloved son Isaac (through whom Abraham has been promised progeny) as an offering upon one of the mountains of Moriah. Silently, without a word of either protest or assent, and in complete contrast to his lengthy discussion with God over the fate of Sodom and Gomorrah, Abraham takes his son, two servants, and an ass and sets out on the journey. Three days later, he sees the place from afar, leaves the lads and the animal behind, and assuring them that he and Isaac will go and worship "and return," continues on with his son. Isaac inquires about the lack of an animal to sacrifice and is assured that "God will provide a lamb." When they arrive at the designated spot, Abraham binds his son, places him upon the altar, and prepares "to slaughter" him. He is stopped by an angel who commands him to do nothing to harm Isaac. Abraham sees a ram caught in a thicket and offers it as a sacrifice. God assures him that because he fulfilled God's request and was willing to offer his son he will now be the recipient of God's threefold promise: to be the father of a great nation, to inherit the land, and to be a blessing to all humanity.

The story is told with great restraint. The relationship and the closeness between Isaac and Abraham are emphasized by the repetition of the words "my father," "my son," and the repeated phrase "And the two of them walked on together."

The story is also filled with paradoxes: the God of justice and mercy gives the most cruel commandment; the God who promised that Isaac would become the ancestor of the nation demands Isaac's death; and Abraham, the passionate advocate of righteousness, consents to the most immoral of deeds. Many questions are raised by this story: Why is it necessary for God to put Abraham to such a trial? Does God not already know the character of the man? Why does Abraham consent to perform such an immoral deed? How could he believe that God, whom he has called "the judge of all the earth," would command the murder of Isaac? Why does Abraham not argue with God about it? Why is Isaac so passive; why does he not resist? Some have seen in this story a rejection of human sacrifice, or a way for the Torah to assert to those pagans who offered their children to their own gods that the God of Israel abhors such acts. Others argue that the story illustrates Abraham's willingness to do whatever God required of him. Whatever the answers to these questions, one thing is clear: the biblical story is intended to show that Abraham was deserving of God's tripartite blessing.[10]

Rabbinic Interpretations

If the Torah told the story of the trial of Abraham, the Sages retold it as the binding of Isaac. According to various midrashic interpretations, Isaac was thirty-seven years old when Abraham told him that he was to be sacrificed, and he tearfully and sadly assented. He went knowingly to his death, since that was the will of God. The following is the text of one such midrash:

"And saw the place from afar" (Gen. 22:4). Abraham said to Isaac, "Do you see what I see?" He said to him, "I see a mountain lovely and beautiful and a cloud resting upon it." He said to the servants, "Do you see anything?" They responded, "We don't see anything." He said to them, *"You stay here with the ass* (Gen. 22:5), since the ass sees nothing and you see nothing. You are no better than it. . . . *The boy and I will go up there".* . . . What is the meaning of "there"? We shall see what is the outcome of the "there" that God said to me: *"There shall your offspring be"* (Gen. 15:5).

"We will worship and we will return to you" (Gen. 22:5). His mouth predicted that the two of them would return in peace. *"He immediately took the firestone and the knife" (Gen. 22:6). "Immediately, Isaac said to Abraham his father, 'Father', and he answered, 'Yes my son'. And he said, 'Here is the firestone and the wood; but where is the sheep for the burnt offering?'"* (Gen. 22:7). At that moment Isaac was greatly afraid for he saw nothing that could be offered up and he sensed what was about to happen. He said, *"Where is the sheep for the burnt offering?"* Abraham said, "Since you have asked, the Holy One has chosen you." Isaac said, "If He has chosen me, my life is offered to Him, but I am greatly sorrowed to have my blood shed." Nevertheless, *"And the two of them walked on together"* (Gen. 22:8), this one to slaughter and this one to be slaughtered.

Isaac was thirty-seven years old at the time of "the binding." *"They arrived at the place of which God had told him. Abraham built an altar there; he laid out the wood; he bound his son Isaac"* (Gen. 22:9). When he was about to slaughter him, Isaac said to him, "Aba [father], tie my hands and feet tightly because the soul is very assertive. When I see the knife I may struggle and then the sacrifice will be rendered unfit. Please do not make any wound [that would render it unfit]." Immediately, *"And Abraham picked up the knife to slay his son"* (Gen. 22:10). Isaac said to him, "Aba, I beg you, do not tell my mother when she is standing on the edge of a pit or on the roof lest she throw herself down and die."

The two of them built the altar and he bound him on the altar and took the knife to slay him and a quarter of a log of his blood poured out of him. . . . When he was doing this, *"an angel of the Lord called to him from heaven, 'Abraham! Abraham!'"* (Gen. 22:11). Why did he call his name twice? Because Abraham was hurrying to complete the slaughter. *"And he said, 'Do not raise your hand against the boy'"* (Gen. 22:12). He said to him, "Who are you?" He replied, "An angel." He said to him, "When I was told: Take your son . . . it was the Holy One Himself who told me. If He wants to stop me, let Him tell me Himself!" Immediately, "*The angel of the Lord called to Abraham a second time*" (Gen. 22:15), because he did not want to listen the first time.

Then Abraham said to the Holy One, "Master of the universe, a man tests another when he does not know his true character, but You know everyone's nature. Why do You have to do this?" He said to him, "*Now I know that you fear God*". . . . (Gen. 15:5). Immediately, the Holy One opened the heavens and said, "*By Myself I swear*". . . . (Gen. 22:16). Abraham said, "You have sworn, now I shall swear that I shall not leave this altar until I tell You all that I wish to say." He said to him, "Speak." "Did You not say to me '*Look toward heaven and count the stars, if you are able to count them*. . . . *So shall your offspring be*'". . . . (Gen. 15:5). He said to him, "Yes." He said, "From whom?" He said to him, "From Isaac." He said to Him, "I could have said to You, yesterday You told me, '*For it is through Isaac that offspring shall be continued for you*' (Gen. 21:12), and now You tell me '*offer him there as a burnt offering*' (Gen. 22:2). But I suppressed my inclination and did not say that. Now when Isaac's descendants sin and are in trouble, remember unto them the binding of Isaac. Consider it as if his ashes were strewn before You on the altar and forgive them and redeem them from their troubles."

Said the Holy One, "You have had your say. Now it is my turn. In the future Isaac's descendants will certainly sin before Me and on Rosh Hashanah I shall judge them. If they want Me to find some merit for them and remember the binding of Isaac, let them sound this shofar before Me." Abraham said to Him, "What is a shofar?' " He said to him, "Look around you." Immediately, "*his eyes fell upon a ram caught in the thicket by its horns*" (Gen. 22:13). The Holy One said to him, "Let them sound the horn of the ram before me and I will save them and redeem them from their transgressions."[11]

Some midrashim go even further and imply that Isaac's blood was actually shed and that he was burned as a sacrifice and only later came back to life.[12] The similarities to the Christian story of the crucifixion are apparent. Was this a Jewish reaction to Christianity's assertions or did it exist earlier?[13] Whatever the answer, the purpose served by the story as reconstituted by the Sages is quite different from that of the original biblical story. It now portrays this act as one of willing martyrdom and as such functions as the prototype for later tales of Jewish martyrdom (which developed for the first time in the days of the Maccabees and became prevalent in the rabbinic period), for which Israel is rewarded by God who forgives them and their sins.

The midrashic interpretations of the *Akeidah* story also add an important strand to Rosh Hashanah: when Abraham demands (in repayment for his show of absolute faith) that God show mercy on the children of Isaac, God agrees and gives Abraham the ram's horn as a symbol of His forgiveness. When Rosh Hashanah comes, it is upon the children of Isaac to sound that horn and thus "remind" God of their merit. The rabbinic reading of the *Akeidah* therefore enhances the idea of "remembrance" and gives new meaning to the sounding of the shofar: "Said Rabbi Abbahu: 'Why do we use a ram's horn? So that I will recall the binding of Isaac for your sake and credit you as if you bound yourselves on the altar before Me.' "[14]

The concluding segment of the Torah reading for the second day, the *maftir,* is the same as that for the first day: Numbers 29:1–6.

HAFTARAH FOR THE SECOND DAY OF ROSH HASHANAH

The reading from Jeremiah 31:2–20 echoes the Torah reading in its description of a parent who is being deprived of a child. In this text, Jeremiah describes the matriarch Rachel, who was not buried in Hebron with the other patriarchs and matriarachs but along the wayside, as watching over the people of Israel when they are exiled by the Babylonians and taken into captivity: "She refuses to be comforted for her children who are gone" (Jer. 31:15).

Just as Abraham was given back his child, so God promises Rachel that her children shall return:

Restrain your voice from weeping,
Your eyes from shedding tears;

For there is a reward for your labor,
declares the Lord:
Your children shall return to their country.

TORAH READING FOR YOM KIPPUR MORNING

On Yom Kippur the Torah reading is Leviticus 16, the description of the ritual cleansing of the shrine, which was performed by Aaron. This ritual was to be performed every year "in the seventh month, on the tenth day of the month . . ." (Lev. 16:29).[15] It is a ceremony of expiation, cleansing the sanctuary of accumulated ritual impurities; this cleansing is achieved by sprinkling the blood of the sin offerings for the priests and for the people within the inner shrine (Lev. 16:14–15) and upon the altar (Lev. 16:18–19). The iniquities of the Israelites are then atoned for by confession (Lev. 16:21) and having them carried away symbolically by the scapegoat (Lev. 16:22).

Clearly, there are two major parts of the ceremony, one concerned with cleansing the sanctuary and its components, the other intended to cleanse the people of sin: "For on this day atonement shall be made for you to cleanse you of all your sins; you shall be clean before the Lord" (Lev. 16:30). For this latter element to be accomplished, the people must also practice self-denial and refrain from work on the tenth day of the month (Lev. 16:29).

Commentary on the Reading for Yom Kippur Morning

The Garments of the Priest (Lev. 16:4). For the ceremony of expiation, the Priest wears simple, white linen garments, as opposed to his usual rich gold, bejeweled garments (Lev. 8:7). The garments themselves represent the purity that the day is intended to produce. The wearing of a simple white garment (a *kittel*) to services is a long-standing practice for the Days of Awe, as is the use of white coverings for the Torah scrolls and the ark.

Expiation for the Priestly Family (Lev. 16:6).   Since the Priest is in charge of the sanctuary, he bears the greatest responsibility for its sanctity and purity.

The Goat for Azazel (Lev. 16:8).   Two goats are chosen, one to be sacrificed to God, and the other to be sent into the wilderness. *Azazel* has been explained variously as the name of a place or the name of a goat-demon.

Entering the Inner Sanctuary (Lev. 16:12).   After sacrificing the sin offerings, the blood is taken behind a curtain, into the innermost reaches of the sanctuary: the Holy of Holies, where the Ark of the Covenant was kept. The presence of God was said to reside there. The incense was intended to protect the Priest who was to be in the presence of God.[16] That is the import of the words "lest he die" (Lev. 16:15). Sprinkling the blood on the various objects is a means of cleansing them from impurity.

The Confession (Lev. 16:20). The confession of sins begins the ceremony of expiating the sins of the people. This confession is made over the goat, which is then sent away so that "the goat shall carry on him all their iniquities to an inaccessible region . . ." (Lev. 16:22).

Self-denial (Lev. 16:29).   The people are commanded to practice self-denial or self-affliction. The verse does not explain what is meant by this term, but tradition has interpreted it to mean fasting. Rabbinic tradition also determined that, by extension, self-denial meant abstinence from bathing, anointing with oil, wearing shoes, and having sexual intercourse.

Maftir.   The reading from the second scroll, the *maftir,* is Numbers 29:7–11, which describes the observance of the day and enumerates its sacrifices.

HAFTARAH FOR YOM KIPPUR MORNING

The magnificent prophetic reading for Yom Kippur is taken from Isaiah 57:14–58:14 and describes the appropriate fast that will earn forgiveness. This reading serves to supplement and correct the impression the Torah portion may have given with regard to the role of ritual in atonement. Isaiah states categorically that starving one's body is useless if it is not accompanied by righteous action:

On your fast day
You see to your business
And oppress all your laborers.
Because you fast in strife and contention
And you strike with a wicked fist (Isa. 58:3–4).

A true fast will include caring for the poor and hungry and showing compassion (Isa 58:7). Only in that way will God's forgiveness be earned.

TORAH READING FOR YOM KIPPUR AFTERNOON

As on the Sabbath, the Torah is read at the afternoon service of Yom Kippur. The reading is Leviticus 18, which delineates a list of forbidden sexual relationships.[17] This list was generated to establish a different standard of conduct for the Israelites from that of the Egyptians or the Canaanites (Lev. 18:1). Forbidden, according to the biblical text, were sexual relations between close relatives, between men and married women, between men, and relations with beasts. Such relationships were considered defiling and were given as the reason that the Canaanites were not permitted to live in the land with the Israelites (Lev. 18:24–28).

This section may have been chosen because of its connection with sanctity, which we attempt to achieve on Yom Kippur; sanctity was connected in the minds of the Sages with the idea of purity of sexual relations.[18] It has also been suggested that because Yom Kippur was one of two days in the year (the other was the fifteenth of Av) when young women would go into the vineyards dressed alike in white—so that the young men could view them and choose a bride (M. Ta'anit 4.8)—the text from Leviticus was read to warn them against selecting women prohibited to them.[19] The simplest possibility is that the *Minḥah* reading (Lev. 18) is a continuation of the morning reading (Lev. 17), which describes the Yom Kippur purification ritual.

HAFTARAH FOR YOM KIPPUR AFTERNOON

The highlight of the *Minḥah* service for Yom Kippur is un-doubtedly the Haftarah, the reading of the book of Jonah.[20] The central concept of this book is repentance—the notion that a hu-man being can change his or her way of life, regret former ac-tions, and be forgiven by God—a concept treated more fully and in a more thought-provoking manner in Jonah than any other book in the Bible. The story of the flood, for example, could have been a perfect opportunity for Noah to have called for repentance; the story of Sodom might have afforded such an opportunity for either Abraham or Lot. Although the rabbinic midrash adds such stories, they are glaringly absent in the biblical text. This absence has led scholars to believe that the concept of repentance devel-oped after the narratives of the Bible were put in writing.[21] It is certainly present in the writings of the prophets, who continually call for repentance:

If you return, O Israel, declares the Lord,
If you return to Me,
If you remove your abominations from My presence (Jer. 4:1).
Return, O Israel, to the Lord your God,
For you have fallen because of your sin.
Take words with you
And return to the Lord.
Say to Him:
Forgive all guilt
And accept what is good. . . .

I will heal their affliction,
Generously will I take them back in love (Hos. 14:2–5).

The background to the Jonah story, interestingly enough, is not the sins of Israel but the sins of a pagan nation. The story therefore functions almost as an alternative version of the story of Sodom and Gomorrah. Whereas the earlier text is concerned with God's justice—that is, God will punish those who are guilty but, as Abraham discerns, He will not sweep away the righteous with the wicked—the Jonah text goes much further: God is concerned here with finding a way to redeem the sinners from their wickedness and to exercise mercy.

The Book of Jonah is a morality tale, a kind of historical novel or allegory based on the prophet Jonah but designed to convey a relatively simple message: God wants sinners to leave their evil ways and to return to Him. God is depicted in the Book of Jonah as a God of mercy, who prefers repentance and forgiveness to inflicting punishment in the form of death and destruction. God loves His creatures and pities them. Yet Jonah seems unable to accept or come to terms with this idea.[22] Does he fear for his own honor? Is he more concerned with his authority than with human beings? Does he believe in justice as opposed to mercy? Jonah is forced to undertake the task of bringing the people the message of repentance, but rebels at it and attempts to flee. When he finally carries out this mission against his will, it is successful, and this is exactly what he seems to have feared.

Although the book of Jonah does not say so specifically, Jonah was a prophet. (He is mentioned in 2 Kings 14:25 as having lived in the time of Jeroboam II, 784–744 B.C.E.) Moreover, Jonah is a reluctant prophet, following in the tradition of other prophets who unhappily undertook a mission of prophecy: Moses initially refused his mission (Exod. 3:11–4:17) but eventually capitulated, and Jeremiah did not want to deliver God's message (Jer. 1:6–8) but was forced to do so. Jonah, however, goes even further than his predecessors and attempts to flee the directive of God. He takes a boat to Tarshish (Jon. 1:3)—thought to refer to a location somewhere in Spain—but God pursues him, creating a terrible storm. Rather than returning to shore, Jonah asks to be cast overboard (1:12), in effect continuing his flight, and perhaps even indicating a desire to die.[23] God will not let that happen and sends a giant fish to rescue Jonah (2:1). When Jonah shows appreciation for God's act and indicates that he will go to the Temple to show his thanks (2:10), God has the fish cast Jonah on dry land, but again tells Jonah that he must go on with his mission (3:1–2) rather than going to the Temple.

Although Jonah is a Hebrew prophet, the story is clearly intended to be universal. The non-Hebrew sailors, who ironically seem more attuned to God than Jonah, are God-fearing, that is, concerned with morality. They respect the Hebrews and their God. The Ninevite recipients of the message, like the inhabitants of Sodom, are not Hebrews. Nevertheless, they respond with alacrity to God's message: the people instinctively undertake a fast (3:5), their king calls on them to forsake evil, and they do so (3:8).

Jonah hopes that the city of Nineveh will be destroyed and waits to see what will happen (4:5). Through a series of events, God attempts to teach Jonah the lesson of compassion and concern for others: God gives him a miraculous plant to increase his comfort and then suddenly takes it away from him, exposing him to a violent wind and to the heat of the sun. Does Jonah learn the lesson that God intended for him? The book leaves that question open. But even if Jonah does not change, the reader certainly can.

The story of Jonah may be read as a parable of human life. It offers us an opportunity to reflect on how we deal with the tasks that we are given in life. How do we respond to the demands God makes of us? Do we flee from them? Are we better at the end of our journeys than at their beginnings? The Book of Jonah is not only an entertaining tale, but also a profound and complex one that is brilliantly suited to Yom Kippur. It is customary to add Micah 7:18–20 to the reading, since this passage reiterates the concept of God as merciful, preferring forgiveness to anger.

Epilogue:
Getting Started

The High Holy Days, the Days of Awe, and the *Mahzor*, the liturgy for those days, are two great creations of the Jewish people and the Jewish tradition. They are spiritual masterpieces that deserve the same attention and scrutiny as any other artistic masterpiece of world civilization, be it in literature, painting, or music. Such masterworks can be appreciated on many levels. Some people come to a museum and gaze for a moment at a great painting and then move on. Others study it for hours. Some analyze it and read about it in order to better plumb its depths. So too with these days and these prayers. We can come into the synagogue and taste them for a brief time, sitting passively and enjoying the atmosphere, or we can make the effort to understand them better and learn to relate them to our own lives, plunging into them deeply and vigorously. As the Sages remarked, "According to the effort, so is the reward." The more we put in, the more we take out.

In a sense, reading this book can be the beginning of a profound experience of the Days of Awe, but it is only a beginning. What makes the difference is active participation. We have perused the growth of these days and seen the way in which they were reinterpreted and magnified by sages and poets. We have discussed the basic themes they embody, themes that plumb the depths of human life and ask ultimate questions, challenging us to scrutinize ourselves and to change. What are our lives, what our worth? What is the nature of sin, and how do we deal with guilt? Is return, repentance, and change possible, and if so, how do we go about it? What are the wrongs human beings do to one another? How can we sensitize ourselves to others and what we do to them? How can we reconcile old differences and make peace where there has been friction and strife? What is the good society, and how can we help to achieve it? All of these and more are the questions and challenges that the High Holy Days, their liturgy, and biblical readings put before us.

For this one period each year we are given the opportunity to back away from the business and busy-ness of life in order to consider what it is all about. Beginning with the first day of Elul we undergo a process of withdrawal from the world that eventuates in the total estrangement of Yom Kippur. The result is a rebirth and a re-emergence into the world with renewed understanding and vigor, having atoned and therefore being at one with God and our innermost beings, knowing that we relate best to God when we relate properly to other people.

Rosh Hashanah and Yom Kippur are times of affirmation: affirmation of our membership in the Jewish people and the Jewish tradition, affirmation of our belief in God, affirmation of the worth of human beings, and affirmation of life itself. We put ourselves through a kind of trial, a period of questioning and self-judgment, so that at the end we can emerge saying "yes" to life. In the words of Isaiah:

Be your sins like crimson,
They can turn snow-white;
Be they red as dyed wool,
They can become like fleece (Isa. 1:18).

The experience of these days must be undertaken together with others. Part of it is done at home and with family and friends, another part within the synagogue. Finding the proper environment is half the secret of success. One who enters the synagogue only at this time can hardly expect to feel at home in it. The experience of the Days of Awe will also differ from synagogue to synagogue. It is best to think, investigate, and choose one's synagogue wisely. What kind of a service suits you best? Is it one in which you can be an active participant and not merely a passive spectator? Does it challenge you and make you think or lull you into forgetfulness? Does it have the ability to move you emotionally?

Of course, when all is said and done, these High Holy Days cannot be isolated from the rest of the year. We can understand and appreciate them best when they are a part of the natural flow of a year in which we participate in the Jewish tradition and live according to its rhythm. Jewish tradition has connected the High Holy Days to the rest of the year in two interesting ways: by leading directly from Yom Kippur into the next holiday, Sukkot, and by extending the period of final judgment to Hoshana Rabba, the seventh day of Sukkot.

The connection of Hoshana Rabba to the constellation of the Days of Awe is an ancient one. We find reference to it in Midrash Tehillim, the rabbinic commentary to the Book of Psalms, which stems from the talmudic period and contains material from the early centuries of the common era.[1] Commenting on Psalm 16:11, "Delights are ever *[netzah]* in Your right hand," the Sages interpret *netzah* not as "forever," the common translation, but as "victory," from the related word, *nitzahon*. They also refer to the ancient custom of placing a wreath of victory in the hands of a winning charioteer. This custom, say the Sages, refers to Israel: on Rosh Hashanah all the nations pass before God as contestants, and their guardian angels declare that they were victorious. However, no one really knows if the victor was Israel or the nations. When Sukkot comes, however, it becomes clear that the people of Israel are indeed victorious, because they "take their festive wreaths in their right hands." This "festive wreath," the lulav (the palms together with the myrtle and willow), is read as the wreath of victory. On the seventh day, when the altar is being circled with this "festive wreath," the angels proclaim, "I bring you good news: at the judgment you are proclaimed victors over the nations" (Midrash Tehillim 17.5).

The custom during the days of the Second Temple was to adorn the altar with specially cut willows and to circle the altar daily carrying willows and chanting the verse, "O Lord, deliver us" (Ps. 118:25). On the seventh day, they circled it seven times and beat the willows against the altar at the conclusion.[2] The Hebrew for "deliver us" is *hoshi'a na,* which has been contracted into the word *hoshanah.* Eventually, the day became known as Hoshana Rabba, the great *hoshanah,* since, as an accompaniment to the seven processions, special prayers of deliverance, *hoshanot,* were chanted.

Since Sukkot is the holiday when, according to the tradition, God determines the amount of water (rain) that will descend that year,[3] there is little doubt that this ceremony, together with others held on Sukkot, such as the "waterdrawing festival," were rites connected with the idea of a fruitful year. How did this ritual become connected with the judgment of human beings? It may be that the phrase "deliver us" was the impetus for reinterpreting this holiday as the day of judgment. What are we asking deliverance from, if not punishment? In the Middle Ages the connection between Hoshana Rabba and deliverance from punishment for sin became common and was canonized in the mystical work, the Zohar.[4] Customs grew up of having the leader of the service dress in white, the color of the Days of Awe, and for people to stay awake all night studying and praying in anticipation of the final rendering of the verdict. Thus, the Days of Awe were moved not only backward to the beginning of Elul, but forward to the end of Sukkot as well.

The other connection is perhaps even more important. It is that we are bidden to begin building our sukkah—at least to drive in the first nail—upon returning home from the *Ne'ilah* service. There is no greater contrast in religious feeling than that between Yom Kippur and Sukkot. Yom Kippur is all deprivation, asceticism, and spirituality; Sukkot is all joy, festivity, dancing, singing, and feasting. On Yom Kippur we are in heaven; on Sukkot we are very much on earth—to our great pleasure. We cannot and should not stay very long in the rarified atmosphere of Yom Kippur. We have to return to earth, to begin to build and make life happy and fruitful, not only for ourselves but for others. If that is the outcome of the Days of Awe, they have been worthwhile.

The call to connect Sukkot with Yom Kippur in this way is symbolic of what Judaism wants us to take away from the Days of Awe. They are not to be isolated, but are to be integrated into a total Jewish life, one that includes celebration and a full relationship with God and with other human beings. In this way, we actualize the Torah's command, "choose life."

NOTES

Chapter 1. The Days of Awe: Origins and Development

1. Rabbinic tradition has assigned certain historical events to these dates. For example, the Midrash states that the first of Elul is the time when Moses went up Mount Sinai (Exod. 24:12) to receive the second tablets. The people then sounded the shofar to remind themselves to avoid idolatry (*Pirke derebbi eli'ezer,* 46). Rosh Hashanah is the day upon which Sarah, Rachel, and Hannah conceived; Joseph left prison; and the bondage of the Israelites in Egypt ceased (B. Rosh Hashanah 10b–11a). Yom Kippur is the day upon which Moses descended with the second set of tablets, indicating that the people had been forgiven (*Seder Olam Rabba* 6). While these midrashic interpretations play only a minor role in the theology and liturgy of the *Yamim Nora'im,* they do inform our understanding of the historical significance of the dates on which the holidays are observed.

2. "Remember that you were a slave in the land of Egypt and the Lord your God freed you from there with a mighty hand and an outstretched arm; therefore the Lord your God has commanded you to observe the Sabbath day" (Deut. 5:15).

3. For a scholarly reconstruction of the ancient Israelite calendar and a comparison of the various calendars, see H. L. Ginsberg, *The Israelian Heritage of Judaism* (New York, 1982), Chapters 5 and 7. See also Yehezkel Kaufman, *The Religion of Israel* (Chicago, 1960), 154.

4. In Deuteronomy 16 the list of the holy days is confined to the three festivals alone. Since Deuteronomy is the code that outlawed other sanctuaries and required attendance at the Temple in Jerusalem, it may have been concerned only with those times when people were to come to the central sanctuary (see Deut. 16:16–17).

5. Kaufman, *Religion of Israel* (Chicago, 1960), 306–309. He states that "the new year festival was conceived in early times as the day when the destiny of the world was fixed." This is one of three motives in the parallel Babylonian festival. The others had to do with the lives of the gods and naturally "could not be adopted into the religion of Israel" (308). See also Sigmund Mowinckel, *The Psalms In Israel's Worship,* vol. 1 (Oxford, 1962), 120ff.

6. See Kaufman, *Religion of Israel,* 306, n. 7.

7. Moshe Segal, "The Religion of Israel Before Sinai," *Jewish Quarterly Review* 52 (1963): 242. Leon F. Liebreich is quite right, however, in criticizing Segal's conclusion that these themes in later Judaism are identical with the contents of these psalms and that "the New Year liturgy of the Synagogue is the direct descendant of the older liturgy of the Temple . . ." ("Aspects of the New Year Liturgy," *Hebrew Union College Annual* 34 [1963]: 175–176.) The most we can infer is that the psalms celebrate God's coronation. The rabbinic interpretations are quite different.

8. See Jacob Milgrom, *The JPS Torah Commentary: Numbers* (Philadelphia, 1990), 246.

9. Segal, "Religion of Israel," 244–245. See also Kaufman, *Religion of Israel,* 119.

10. Baruch Levine, *The JPS Torah Commentary: Leviticus* (Philadelphia, 1989), 160. Levine suggests that this is the intention of Psalm 81:4, "Blow the horn on the New Moon/on the full moon for the day of our pilgrimage festival."

11. The Hebrew term *Rosh Hashanah* is found only once in the Bible, in Ezekiel 40:1, and the reference is not to the first day of the seventh month but to the tenth day—Yom Kippur.

12. Kaufman, *Religion of Israel,* 308.

13. Segal, "Religion of Israel," 245–255. See also Kaufman, *Religion of Israel,* 117–120.

14. See Isaiah 58:3, 5, and 10. As Milgrom points out, other acts of self-denial may also have been understood, something that the Rabbis made explicit (*JPS: Numbers,* 246). See B. Yoma 74b.

15. Milgrom, *JPS: Numbers,* 246.

16. Levine, *JPS: Leviticus,* 99. See also Everett Fox, *The Five Books of Moses* (New York, 1995), 584.

17. See James Frazier, *The Golden Bough, Abridged Edition* (London, 1922). Frazier describes other scapegoat rites in Rome and Greece (756–768) and among Indians, Chinese, and Asiatics (736–756).

18. Theodor H. Gaster, *Festivals of the Jewish Year* (New York, 1952), 138ff. For an excellent discussion of this entire issue see Milgrom, *JPS: Numbers,* 444–447. Milgrom points out that the two goats serve two different purposes: the sacrificed goat purges the sanctuary of "Israel's impurities," while the scapegoat carries off "all of Israel's transgressions." Since Israel is holy, it requires purification no less than the sanctuary (Milgrom, 446).

19. Gaster, *Festivals,* 144.

20. Gaster, 138, n. 1.

21. *Pirke derebbi eli'ezer,* 46.

22. Levine, *JPS: Leviticus,* 102.

23. Kaufman, *Religion of Israel,* 105.

24. See Segal, "Religion of Israel," 250. The name *Aza'el* is found in the Ethiopic Book of Enoch as the tenth in the list of fallen angels.

25. Segal, 250ff.

26. Some commentators consider that this is a vestige of pre-monotheistic belief, others that it is only symbolic. Levine also points out the element of sympathetic magic, that is, a goat being sent to counteract the goat-demons. See Levine, *JPS: Leviticus,* 252. See also Milgrom, *JPS: Numbers,* 446.

27. Gaster, *Festivals,* 141ff.

28. Naftali Herz Tur Sinai, *Biblical Encyclopedia* (in Hebrew) (Jerusalem, 1976), 3:598. He attempts to discern various stages within the development of Yom Kippur during biblical times. Some believe that fasting was associated with the day only at a later time or that Yom Kippur was an invention of the post-exilic era. Others think that at first the observance was only for Temple purification, while human atonement was done separately (see Lev. 4:13–21). Only later was this idea added to Yom Kippur. It is virtually impossible, however, to prove such reconstructions, and they must be left to the realm of interesting speculation.

29. See Tur Sinai, *Biblical Encyclopedia* 3:595, and Levine, *JPS: Leviticus,* 162.

30. *Biblical Encyclopedia,* ibid.

31. Philo, *Special Laws* (Cambridge, 1962), 2:188–192.

32. Ibid.

33. This idea raises a question about the possible celebration of the New Year during the First Temple period. Had it been forgotten? It also seems strange that the New Year was so firmly established in the rabbinic tradition only a few hundred years later.

34. Philo, *Special Laws* 2:196.

35. In T. Kippurim 2.1 this is cited as the opinion of Rabbi Meir, while the Sages change the order placing "sin" first, arguing that the list should progress from the lesser to the more severe sin.

36. Saul Lieberman, *Tosefta Kifshutah: A Comprehensive Commentary on the Tosefta* (New York, 1962), 4:792ff.

37. Azazel is understood as coming from the Hebrew words *azaz*, meaning rugged and *el*, meaning strong. See B. Yoma 67b and Segal, *Religion of Israel*, 249.

38. Segal, *Religion of Israel*, 249.

39. Eliezer Halavi Greenhut, ed., *Midrash shir ha-shirim* (Jerusalem, 1981), 3:6. See also J. Yoma 6:3.

40. See T. Rosh Hashanah 2.17.

41. See also T. Rosh Hashanah 2.

42. *Avot derabbi natan-a,* 4.

43. See also B. Yoma 85b and following.

44. B. Betzah 4b.

45. Tradition has it that the two days were ordained by the early prophets. See Y. Eruvin, end of chapter 3. Some scholars believe that the celebration of two days in the Land of Israel was very ancient, both days being equal and using the same Torah readings. See E. Fleisher, "The Calendar of the Festivals in the *Piyyut* of R. Eleazar beRebi Kalir" (in Hebrew), *Tarbiz* 52.2: 223–273. There is evidence, however, that it began only in the eleventh century when Jews from Provence settled in the Land of Israel and insisted on it because of the sacredness of the holiday. Because of the fact that this holiday fell on the first of the month (unlike others which come on the tenth or on the fifteenth) there could have been circumstances in which it was celebrated for two days in the Land of Israel. The New Month was proclaimed only when witnesses came. Since one could not wait for witnesses to proclaim Rosh Hashanah, the holiday was always celebrated on the 30th of Elul and sometimes on the next day as well, if that was the real day of the New Year. There is a great deal of evidence, however, to indicate that the current practice of two days of Rosh Hashanah in Israel came about only in the eleventh century when Jews from Provence settled there and insisted upon it because of the sacredness of the holiday. See Max Arzt, *Justice and Mercy: Commentary on the Liturgy of the New Year and the Day of Atonement* (New York, 1963), 26, and Mordecai Margolioth, Hilukhim She-ben Anshei Mizrah U-vene Eretz Yisra'el (in Hebrew) (Jerusalem, 1938), 162.

46. See *Abudarham Hashalem*, 1, p. 334 where he described Hoshana Rabba as the day of "completing the sealing." See also J. Rosh Hashanah 4.8 and Midrash Tefillin 17:5. It is therefore possible that the origins of this concept are from an earlier period in the second half of the first millenium. See Hayyim Schauss, *Guide to Jewish Holy Days* (New York, 1938), 306, n. 229.

47. *Hag Hasukkot,* 6.

48. S. Y. Agnon, *Days of Awe* (New York, 1948), 30.

Chapter 2. The Meaning of the Yamin Nora'im

1. See discussion of these themes in Chapter 5.
2. Sifre Numbers 77.
3. Viktor E. Frankl, *The Will To Meaning* (New York, 1969), 16.
4. The reading in the Mishnah of *benei marom* (those on high) has long been recognized as a corruption of the Latin word *nomiron* (troop).
5. See discussion of this *piyyut* in Chapter 5.
6. See discussion of this *piyyut* in Chapter 4.
7. Franz Kafka, *The Trial* (New York, 1937), 286.
8. See Reuven Hammer, *Entering Jewish Prayer* (New York, 1994), Chapter 8.
9. See discussion of these themes in Chapter 5.
10. T. Rosh Hashanah 2.12.
11. See Chapter 3. See also Milgrom, *JPS: Numbers*, 392ff.
12. Moses Hayyim Luzzatto, *Mesillat Yesharim* (The Path of the Upright), ed. Mordecai M. Kaplan (Philadelphia, 1966), 76.
13. See the full discussion of this book in Chapter 10.
14. Sefer *Ha-ḥinukh* (Jerusalem, 1960), 403, n. 321.
15. Luzzatto, *Mesillat Yesharim*, 76ff.
16. Saadia Gaon, *The Book of Beliefs and Opinions*, ed. Samuel Rosenblatt (New Haven, 1948), 220.
17. Saadia Gaon, 222.
18. *Hilkhot Teshuvah* 2.1.
19. *Hilkhot Teshuvah* 2.2.
20. *Hilkhot Teshuvah* 2.4.
21. Y. Makkot 31:d; Pesikta de Rav Kahana 158b. For a full discussion of forgiveness and repentance see Solomon Schechter, *Some Aspects of Rabbinic Theology* (New York,1936), 293–345.
22. Frankl, *Will to Meaning*, 73.
23. See discussion of *Tashlikh* in Chapter 5.

Chapter 3. Beginning the Journey: Preparing for the High Holy Days

1. One custom is to visit the graves of relatives and of the righteous prior to Rosh Hashanah.
2. Agnon, *Days of Awe*, 25.
3. *Pirke derebbi eli'ezer*, 46.
4. *Mahzor Vitry*, ed. Simha ben Samuel (Nuremberg, 1923), 345.
5. M. Ta'anit, 2.1–4.
6. Ibid.
7. *Tanna deve eliyahu zuta*, 23. The conclusion concerning the Thirteen Attributes is derived from B. Rosh Hashanah 17b.
8. B. Rosh Hashanah 17b.
9. For an extensive article on the development and various rites of *Selihot* see the *Jewish Encyclopedia* (New York, 1905) 11:170–177. See also Daniel Goldschmidt, *Seder Selihot* (in Hebrew) (Jerusalem, 1965).

10. Commentary "Mordecai" of the B. Yoma, beginning. This code was written by Mordecai ben Hillel Ha-kohen of Nuremberg in the thirteenth century. See Ismar Elbogen, *Jewish Liturgy: A Comprehensive History* (Philadelphia, 1993), 181. Elbogen suggests a connection to fasts during the ten days of penitence.

11. Agnon, *Days of Awe*, 32.

12. Ibid.

13. B. Horayot 12a.

Chapter 4. The Rosh Hashanah Liturgy I: Arvit and Shaḥarit

1. See Va-yikra Rabba 29.1 and parallels. See also Louis Ginzberg, *Legends of the Jews* (Philadelphia, 1954) 1:82 and notes. While it is usual to interpret the story of Adam and Eve as one in which God punishes them severely, the rabbis saw it as containing an element of pardon and forgiveness. The biblical text therefore provides a doctrine not of original sin, but of original forgiveness.

2. See Chapter 2.

3. See Lawrence A. Hoffman, *The Canonization of the Synagogue Service* (Notre Dame, 1979), 90–114 for a detailed discussion.

4. Daniel Goldsmidt, *The High Holy Day Maḥzor* 1, 6.

5. See Daniel Goldsmidt, *Studies in Prayer and Piyyutim* (in Hebrew) (Jerusalem, 1979), 376–380 for other examples of *piyyutim* for the evening service.

6. See Hammer, *Entering Jewish Prayer* (New York, 1994), 156ff for a full explanation.

7. Originally written for Rosh Hashanah, *U-vekhen* is recited at every service of Rosh Hashanah and Yom Kippur. See Louis Ginzberg, *A Commentary on the Palestinian Talmud* (New York, 1961) 4:234.

8. The entire prayer is devoted to the theme of kingship. Its presence in the *Kedushah*, the sanctity blessing, may be understood in light of the dispute in the Mishnah where Rabbi Yohanan ben Nuri says that the section of kingship should be placed in the third blessing (M. Rosh Hashanah 4.5). In Babylonia the idea of including kingship in the blessing was accomplished by changing the conclusion of the blessing from the usual "the holy God" to "the holy King." It has been suggested that the *U-vekhen* prayer was composed and inserted into the *Amidah* in order to introduce this new formula properly.

9. Louis Ginzberg, *A Commentary on the Palestinian Talmud* (New York, 1961) 4:173.

10. Yosef Heineman believes that the original place for this prayer was in the special addition to the Grace After Meals for Rosh Hashanah. See Shraga Abramson and Aaron Mirsky, ed., *The Book of Haim Sherman* (in Hebrew) (Jerusalem, 1970), 101.

11. This section, which originated in Babylonia, is recited only on Rosh Hashanah. It replaces the usual holiday prayer *Ve-hasi'enu* (lift us up), recited at one time in the Land of Israel on Rosh Hashanah.

12. It is interesting to note a more ancient version of this signature, no longer in use: . . . "King of the entire world who sanctifies Israel, the beginnings of the year *[roshei shanim]*, renews years, remembrance of shofar blasts, times of rejoicing, the seasons and the holy convocations." See Ezra Fleisher, *Prayer and Prayer Rituals in the Land of Israel* (in Hebrew) (Jerusalem, 1988), 124. This ancient formula places Rosh Hashanah within the cycle of regular festivals, but in so doing diminishes its unique importance and obscures the central theme of sovereignty.

13. See Hammer, *Jewish Prayer,* 100–197 for an explanation of these sections.

14. Ismar Elbogen, *Jewish Liturgy* (Philadelphia, 1993), 219–37.

15. See Goldschmidt, *Mahzor,* 39–42 on the *piyyut.*

16. The ancient tradition calls for the ark to be opened for practical purposes—in order to remove or replace a scroll. In the course of time, the open ark was seen as indicating a greater degree of sanctity or of closeness to God. Indeed, in the *Ne'ilah* service (the closing service of Yom Kippur), the open ark becomes a symbol of the gates of heaven, which remain open to receive our prayers.

17. He includes his son's name as well: "Elhanan my son, may he be granted life eternal." This unusual mention gave rise to the legend that Elhanan was abducted as a child, baptized, raised as a Christian, and eventually became pope. When the Vatican promulgated an anti-Jewish edict, Simeon was sent to Rome. His son recognized him and came back with him, returning to Judaism. Other legends have it that the son killed himself, in which case, "may he be granted life eternal" would be understood as a plea for one already dead. There is no solid evidence upon which to base any of these legends, but in any case Simeon's poems allude to great persecutions and sufferings of the Jews at that time.

18. The *Amidah* itself for *Shaharit* is identical to that of *Arvit.* There are two versions of the middle blessing of the *Amidah* for Rosh Hashanah—the one recited in the evening *(Arvit),* in the morning *(Shaharit),* and in the afternoon *(Minhah);* and the one recited during the additional service *(Musaf).* The detailed description of the *Amidah* found in the Mishnah (M. Rosh Hashanah 4.5) is of the version we recite during *Musaf.* It contains nine blessings (paragraphs) and includes the framework for the sounding of the shofar, the central mitzvah of Rosh Hashanah. This *Amidah* was originally recited at *Shaharit* but later was moved to *Musaf.*

19. M. Tamid 4.1.

20. M. Berahot 4.3–4.

21. See Hammer, *Jewish Prayer,* 169–173 on the *Kedushah.*

22. If the first day of Rosh Hashanah falls on the Sabbath, the poem is then recited on the second day. *Ta'ir ve-tari'a* is not said on the Sabbath because it is based on shofar blowing, which is not performed on the Sabbath.

23. M. Rosh Hashanah 1.1–2.

24. The specific Torah readings for Rosh Hashanah are discussed in Chapter 10.

25. Hammer, *Jewish Prayer,* 61.

26. Theodor H. Gaster, *Festivals of the Jewish Year* (New York, 1953), 113.

27. B. Rosh Hashanah 16b.

28. This connection will be discussed in detail in Chapter 10, on the Torah readings for the High Holy Days.

29. Although a horn from any kosher animal may be used to make a sho-far, it is customary to use a ram's horn because of its association with the story of the binding of Isaac.

30. Sefer Avudarham (Amsterdam, 1726), 100.

31. M. Hilkhot Teshuvah 3.4.

32. See Herman Kieval, *The High Holy Days* (New York, 1959), 115–132 for an extensive list of old and new interpretations.

33. According to M. Megillah 2.4 the shofar may be sounded any time during the day. Nevertheless, it is not usual to postpone the performance of a mitzvah so long. See B. Megillah 20b and Rashi's comments.

34. J. Rosh Hashanah 4.8, 59c.

35. See Tractate Sofrim 18.11.

36. Another Lurianic practice introduced the recitation of selected verses from the psalms that have the acrostic *kera satan* (destroy Satan), such as *Min ha-meitzar*. According to talmudic tradition, Satan performs his task as the ac-cuser on 364 days a year, but on one day, Yom Kippur, this power is taken from him. This idea served as a basis for the kabbalists' attempt to deprive Sa-tan of power on Rosh Hashanah as well. The blowing of the shofar has there-fore been used as a means of exorcising demonic power, such as a dybbuk.

37. T. Rosh Hashanah 33b.

Chapter 5. The Rosh Hashanah Liturgy II: From Musaf to Tashlikh

1. See Herman Kieval, *The High Holy Days: Book One* (New York, 1959), 135 on Yossi of Slonim.

2. It is worth mentioning that this issue is still a matter of scholarly de-bate. Gedalia Alon contends that the shofar was originally blown in *Musaf* and that the various arguments that it was moved are not historical. Alon reasons that the shofar was blown in the Temple over the sacrifice specific to the day, that is, the additional—Musaf—sacrifice and that the custom was taken over from there to the synagogue service (quoted in J. Heinemann, *Studies In Jewish Liturgy* [Jerusalem, 1983], 57). Saul Lieberman, on the other hand, argues that in the days of Hillel and Shammai, when the Temple existed, the shofar blow-ing was part of the morning service. See *Tosefta Kifshuta* 1.41, n 58.

3. See Leon J. Liebleich, "Aspects of the New Year Liturgy," *Hebrew Union College Annual* 34 (1963): 125ff, and Joseph Heinemann "The Ancient Order of Blessings for Rosh Hashanah" (in Hebrew), *Tarbiz* 45 (1970): 258ff.

4. Sifre Numbers 77.

5. Baruch Levine, *The JPS Torah Commentary: Leviticus,* 160.

6. Quoted in Levine, 135.

7. M. M. Kalisch, *A Historical and Critical Commentary on the Old Testa-ment: Leviticus* (London, 1872), Part 2:506.

8. Jacob Milgrom, *The JPS Torah Commentary: Numbers* (Philadelphia, 1990), 75.

9. Sifre Numbers 77.

10. Hammer, *Entering Jewish Prayer,* 206–209.

11. This line was omitted because of Christian censorship based on the mistaken notion that *Aleinu* was written as an anti-Christian prayer.

12. See Bernard Mandelbaum, ed. Pesikta derav kahana, 333; Leon Liebleich, "New Year Liturgy," 159; and Leviticus Rabba 29.1.

13. Leibleich, 160.

14. Genesis Rabba 82.2.

15. Eric Werner, *The Sacred Bridge* (London, 1959), 253. See also Gabriel A. Sivan, "Hymns of the Isles," *Judaism* 39, no. 3 (Summer, 1990): 327ff on the attribution of this hymn to Amnon of Mainz and Kalonymus ben Meshullam Kalonymus, "which heightened this *piyyut's* martyrological associations and its appeal to Ashkenazi Jews who had experienced all the horrors of the most recent Crusades."

16. See Kieval, "The Paradox of Kol Nidre," 141ff.

17. B. Rosh Hashanah 27a.

18. Gaster, *Festivals of the Jewish Year* (New York, 1952), 122. See also Hayyim Schauss, *Guide to Jewish Holy Days* (New York, 1938), 160–164.

19. For kabbalists, the shaking of the garments was symbolic of shaking away the *kelipot,* the husks of evil spoken of in the Lurianic Kabbalah.

Chapter 6. Opportunities for Change: The Ten Days of Penitence

1. J. Rosh Hashanah 1.3, 57a. See also Joseph Tabory, *Jewish Festivals in the Time of the Mishnah and Talmud* (in Hebrew) (Jerusalem, 1955), 221ff.

2. In the Pesikta derav kahana, which was edited in the fifth century B.C.E., the expression "ten days of repentance" is used: "Therefore it says, 'Seek the Lord while He can be found' (Isa. 55:6), during the ten days of repentance when He is in your midst . . ." (*Pesikta,* Discourse on "Seek the Lord," edition B. Mandelbaum 2, 472).

3. See Leviticus Rabba 10.5. Vol. 1, 204, ed. M. Margulies.

4. Ibid, 206.

5. This remark was made in a class taught by Professor Lieberman at the Jewish Theological Seminary of America, 1958.

6. B. Berahot 12b.

7. Ibid.

8. See Tractate Sofrim 19.8.

9. B. Rosh Hashanah 18a.

10. Joseph Tabory, *Jewish Festivals,* 222–223.

11. The verses from Hosea served as the basis for many rabbinic homilies concerning the importance of repentance, such as this one, quoted in the Midrash:

> Return, O Israel, to the Lord your God (Hos. 14:2). This teaches that the Holy One informed Israel that when suffering would come upon them, they would repent at the conclusion of their exile. For the moment they repent, they will be redeemed. . . . Rabbi Levi said, "Great is repentance. It reaches to the very throne of God!" For you have stumbled because of your sin (Hos. 14:2). Rabbi Isaac said, "This may be compared to a huge

boulder placed at the crossroads. All who passed by stumbled because of it. The king said, 'Move it a little until I remove it completely.' Thus the Holy One said, 'My children, the evil inclination is a great stumbling block in this world. Just move it a little bit until the hour comes when I will remove it completely. . . .'" Resh Lakish said, "Great is repentance for it transforms deliberate transgressions into positive virtues, as it is said, 'And if a wicked man turns back from the wickedness that he practiced . . . he becomes righteous . . . he shall live'" (Ezek. 18:27–28). Rabbi Meir said, "Great is repentance for if one repents, both he and the entire world are forgiven" (Midrash Ha-gadol Deuteronomy, Nitzavim 30).

12. Joseph Tabory, *Jewish Festivals,* 223, n. 34.

13. This is one of two special Shabbatot when sermons were always given. The other is the Shabbat before Passover—Shabbat Ha-gadol, or the Great Sabbath—when it was customary to speak at length about the laws of Passover.

14. For more information on *Tashlikh,* see Chapter 5.

15. Theodor H. Gaster, *Festivals of the Jewish Year* (New York, 1952), 133–144.

16. S. Y. Agnon, *The Days of Awe* (New York, 1948), 150.

17. See Jacob Z. Lauterbach, "The Ritual for the Kapparot Ceremony," in *Studies In Jewish Law, Custom and Folklore* (New York, 1970), 133–142.

18. Orhot Haim, Hilkhot Yom HaKippurim, 605. See Agnon, *Days of Awe,* 146–50. In his glosses to the work, however, Moses Isserles stated the opposite: This practice is in all our lands (of Ashkenaz) and must not be changed.

19. This biblical verse was also used as the basis for the idea that the fast itself must begin before dark, that is, on the 9th of the month. See Tabory, *Jewish Festivals,* 282.

20. Agnon, *Days of Awe,* 169.

Chapter 7. The Yom Kippur Liturgy I: Kol Nidre

1. Nahum N. Glatzer, *Franz Rosenzweig: His Life and Thought* (New York, 1953), xvii–xviii.

2. Theodore Reik, *Ritual: Psychoanalytic Studies* (London, 1931), 167ff.

3. In the Ashkenazic tradition this gesture is performed through a prayer called *Tefillat zaka.* The Sephardic tradition has a different prayer, "My desire is unto You," which expresses similar thoughts. See Shlomo Deshen, *The Kol Nidre Puzzle: An Anthropological and Historical Study* (Sefer Katz, 1981), 189. This expression of contrition can, however, be made simply in one's own words.

4. B. Nedarim 77a. See also Israel Davidson, "Kol Nidre," in *American Jewish Yearbook* 25 (Philadelphia, 1923), 189.

5. See Daniel Goldschmidt, *The High Holy Day Mahzor* (in Hebrew) (Jerusalem, 1970), 28.

6. See also S. Y. Agnon, *Days of Awe* (New York, 1948), 210. In many congregations, however, all the scrolls are removed and held.

7. Deshen, *The Kol Nidre Puzzle,* 140ff.

8. B. Keritot 6b.

9. Ismar Elbogen, *Jewish Liturgy* (Philadelphia, 1993), 128.

10. This practice, too, was introduced by Rabbi Meir of Rothenburg.

11. Herman Kieval, "The Paradox of Kol Nidre," 91.

12. Reik, *Ritual,* 173.

13. Kieval, "The Paradox of Kol Nidre," 91. See also Reik, *Ritual,* 173–177. And see especially the addition to the *Mahzor,* printed in Vilna by Romm in 1866, in which *Kol Nidre* is is prefaced by a declaration that the vows referred to are not those taken "before authority or at law courts, or vows and oaths which concern the interest and well-being of others, irrespective of creed or race."

14. The threefold recitation has been explained variously as the normal way of reciting a legal formula and as a way of permitting latecomers to arrive and still hear it. See M. Menahot 10.3 and *Encyclopedia Judaica* 11:1166.

15. The context here is the prohibition upon a woman of making certain vows without the permission of her husband and has nothing to do with the subject of *Kol Nidre.* However, many of the legal terms cited in *Kol Nidre* are used here as well.

16. Incentive vows are those made in business dealings when all assumed that positions were taken only for bargaining purposes; exaggeration vows refer to ways of speaking that are not meant to be taken seriously, such as "I saw as many people as crossed the Reed Sea"; erroneous vows are those where one had incorrect information; and vows under pressure refer to vows that were made but could not be kept because of unforeseen circumstances, such as a flood that prevented one from reaching one's destination.

17. Kieval, "The Paradox of Kol Nidre," 84.

18. Joseph Block, quoted in Davidson, "Kol Nidre," 186.

19. Baruch Levine, "The Language of the Magical Bowls" in *A History of the Jews of Babylonia,* ed. J. Neusner (Leidon, 1970) 5:343–375. See especially p. 359.

20. Deshen, *The Kol Nidre Puzzle,* 145ff.

21. Goldschmidt, *Mahzor,* 26. It should be noted that the word "prayer" does not really apply to *Kol Nidre,* since it is not something addressed to God. It is more of a statement or a proclamation.

22. Moshe David Herr, "Matters of Halakhah in the Land of Israel in the Sixth and Seventh Centuries" (in Hebrew), *Tarbiz* 59 (1990): 74ff.

23. See Kieval, "Paradox of Kol Nidre" and Goldschmidt, *Mahzor.*

24. Reik, *Ritual,* 170–171.

25. A. Z. Idelsohn, "The Kol Nidre Tune," *Hebrew Union College Annual* 8–9 (1931–1932): 498.

26. Kieval, "Paradox of Kol Nidre," 94.

27. *Mahzor Vitry,* 351.

28. Idelsohn, "Kol Nidre Tune," 495.

29. *Jewish Encyclopedia* 7:543.

30. Idelsohn, "Kol Nidre Tune," 499.

31. Kieval, "Paradox of Kol Nidre," 95.

32. Idelsohn, "Kol Nidre Tune," 501.

33. This attempt at substitution was made either through original prayers composed on the subject of sin or through the substitution of Psalm 130. See Kieval, "Paradox of Kol Nidre," 92.

34. *Jewish Encyclopedia* 7:539.

35. Reik, *Ritual,* 186.

36. Reik, 210.

37. Reik, 194.

38. Deshen, *Kol Nidre Puzzle,* 139–143.

39. The *Mahzor Vitry* also refers to Yom Kippur as the day of the year when Satan has no power over us.

40. Elbogen, *Jewish Liturgy*, 128.

Chapter 8. The Yom Kippur Liturgy II: Arvit

1. Mekhilta derabbi yishma'el, Beshallah, Chapter 4.

2. See Hammer, *Entering Jewish Prayer*, 121–197.

3. Hammer, *Prayer*, 128ff.

4. Deuteronomy Rabba, ed. S. Lieberman (Jerusalem, 1964), 68–69.

5. Joseph Tabory, *Jewish Festivals in the Time of the Mishnah and Talmud* (Jerusalem, 1995), 283, n. 97.

6. See Chapter 4.

7. For variations of this blessing that were found in the Cairo Geniza—some of which include even more verses and more of the regular sections of the Festival *Amidah,* and which reflect the prayers used in the Land of Israel—see Ezra Fleischer, *Prayer and Prayer Rituals in the Land of Israel* (in Hebrew) (Jerusalem, 1988), 142ff.

8. The Mishnah (M. Yoma 7.1) indicates that the High Priest recited seven blessings on Yom Kippur: Torah, Temple Service, Thanksgiving, the forgiveness of sin, the Temple, Israel, and the Priests and Prayer. See also T. Kippurim 3.18. According to Tzvi Groner, the blessing "King who forgives and pardons" was part of the blessing for the confession, which was added to the blessing "King who forgives," rather than having a special *hatimah* for the confession. See "The History of the Blessing for the Confession" (in Hebrew), *Bar Ilan Yearbook* 13 (1976): 164.

9. The text in *Mahzor Vitry* is virtually identical but does not include the section, "for You are a forgiving and pardoning [God]" prior to the *hatimah.* Instead, it reads, "For you are a God of truth and your words, O our King, are truth and endure forever." These same words appear in the blessing for Rosh Hashanah.

10. Tractate Sofrim 19.4.

11. See the list of variations found in the Geniza quoted in Fleischer's discussion in *Prayer and Prayer Rituals*, 137ff.

12. See Max Kadushin, *The Rabbinic Mind* (New York, 1952), 215–221.

13. On this subject see Jacob Milgrom's illuminating discussion, "Judgment and Mercy: Vertical Retribution and 'Salah,'" in *JPS Torah Commentary: Numbers* (Philadelphia, 1990), 392–396.

14. Daniel Goldschmidt, *The High Holy Day Mahzor* (New York, 1970), 12, n. 3.

15. Goldschmidt, *Mahzor,* 6.

16. Ismar Elbogen, *Jewish Liturgy: A Comprehensive History,* 178.

17. The same format is used in a series of verses that appears in the daily preliminary service. This was an ancient method of creating liturgical units.

18. The verse actually reads, "'shall come to worship before Me,' said the Lord." It has been altered slightly to make it suitable for liturgical purposes.

19. This verse, too, has been altered slightly: instead of "my iniquity" the plural "our iniquity" is used. The previous lines are not biblical quotations.

20. In some *Mahzorim,* "The Thirteen Attributes" are recited only once, even though each of the four *piyyutim* is recited.

21. See Mekhilta derabbi yishma'el to the verse in the Ten Commandments and B. Eruvin 22a.

22. All that remains of this *piyyut* in most *Mahzorim* is the refrain. The full text of this and of many other *piyyutim* that are no longer in common use may be found in the Daniel Goldschmidt *Mahzor*.

23. Gabriel Sivan, "Hymns of The Isles," *Judaism* 39.3 (Summer 1990): 330–331.

24. In the original, all of these are in the singular. They have been placed in the plural in order to make them appropriate for community prayer.

25. See Gershon D. Cohen, "The Song of Songs and the Jewish Religious Mentality" in *Studies in the Variety of Rabbinic Cultures* (Philadelphia, 1991), 3–18.

26. See also M. Yoma 3.8 and 4.2.

27. For biblical examples see Gen. 4:13 and 38:26, Exod. 32:31, and Ezra 9:6.

28. *Mishneh Torah, Hilkhot Teshuvah* 1.1.

29. T. Kippurim 4:14.

30. T. Kippurim 4:15.

31. M. Yoma 3.8. This formula was not incorporated into the synagogue liturgy. See also the discussion in the Talmud to this passage on the exact order of the terms.

32. B. Yoma 77b.

33. Leviticus Rabba 3.3. See also J. Yoma 8:7.

34. See Lawrence A. Hoffman, *The Canonization of the Synagogue Service* (Notre Dame, 1979), 104.

35. Goldschmidt, *Mahzor,* 10.

36. Elbogen, *Jewish Liturgy,* 125.

37. Hoffman, *Canonization,* 105.

38. *Abudarham Hashalem* (in Hebrew) (Jerusalem, 1995), 1, 317.

39. *Mahzor Vitry,* 391. See also Elbogen, *Jewish Liturgy,* 126.

40. See Tzvi Groner, "Blessing for the Confession," 159–160.

41. *Mahzor Vitry,* 394.

42. See Groner, "Blessing for the Confession," 164.

43. Hoffman, *Canonization,* 105.

44. B. Yoma 77b.

45. Midrash Rabba to the verse and *Abudarham Hashalem,* 1, 315.

46. Also attributed to Rabba, B. Berahot 17a.

47. B. Yoma 9a.

48. Ecclesiastes Rabba to Eccles. 7:2.

Chapter 9. The Yom Kippur Liturgy III: Services of Yom Kippur Day

1. Ismar Elbogen, *Jewish Liturgy: A Comprehensive History,* 125.

2. B. Megillah 23a. See also Joseph Tabory, *Jewish Festivals in the Time of the Mishnah and Talmud,* 283.

3. In Hebrew, sections such as these are referred to as *seder* (order), as opposed to *tefilah* (service). This distinction is more difficult to maintain in English.

4. For a discussion of these sections see Reuven Hammer, *Entering Jewish Prayer,* 100–120.

5. Rav Amram Gaon includes Psalms 17, 25, 51, 65, 67, 103, and 104 as well. See Elbogen, *Jewish Liturgy,* 127.

6. See *Seder Olam Rabba* 6.

7. J. Makkot 2.6, 31d.

8. Rosh Hashanah is the exception, having nine blessings.

9. See Chapter 4.

10. These sections were not recited at all on Rosh Hashanah or on Yom Kippur in the ancient liturgy of the Land of Israel. See Ezra Fleisher, *Prayer and Prayer Rituals in the Land of Israel,* 125.

11. Elbogen, *Jewish Liturgy,* 127.

12. Fleisher, *Prayer,* 142.

13. Ibid.

14. While Judaism frequently paints optimistic pictures of human life and worth (for example, "You have made him little less than divine and adorned him with glory and majesty" [Ps. 8:6]), the mood of Yom Kippur encourages a more somber view of life. Why were human beings created last of all, asked the rabbis? So that if a person is not worthy or becomes overly proud he could be told: even a fly, a gnat, a worm was created before you (Genesis Rabba 8.1).

15. The urgency that the Hebrew conveys by its staccato rhythm and repetition of the word *na* (please) is not transmitted all that well by the English translation.

16. Sifre Deuteronomy, Piska 31. The midrash continues: He is Lord over Israel and over all the creatures of the world.

17. See Gershom Scholem, *Major Trends In Jewish Mysticism* (New York, 1941), 58.

18. On the origins of *Yizkor* see Hammer, *Jewish Prayer,* 285–6.

19. This was the explanation given by the Geonim. See Tabory, *Jewish Fesitvals,* 291.

20. *Avot derabbi natan* a4, b8. Another version says, "We have an atonement in place of it."

21. The reference here is to Abraham.

22. This reference is to Jacob. See Gen. 25:27.

23. For one of many discussions of Milton's epic poem, see Roger Sattuck, *Forbidden Knowledge* (New York, 1996), Chapter 11.

24. Goldschmidt, Mahzor, 538.

25. The official who gave the command to slaughter the Jews.

26. Adolf Jellinek, *Beit ha-midrash* II (Jerusalem, 1938), 64; vi

27. See Louis Finkelstein's "The Ten Martyrs," in *Essays and Studies in Memory of Linda R. Miller,* ed. Israel Davidson (New York, 1938), 29–55.

28. B. Berahot 61b.

29. See Chapter 10 for a discussion of the reading.

30. Elbogen, *Jewish Liturgy,* 127.

31. B. Yoma 87b.

32. See J. Ta'anit 67c.

33. Ibid.

34. Those who are physically unable to stand that long are, of course, permitted to sit.

35. See Chapter 2.

36. See pages 162–165.

37. *Mahzor Vitry,* 395.

38. B. Berakhot 33b.

39. These customs developed in France but were later adopted in most European communities, sometimes in different configurations. See Daniel Goldschmidt, *The High Holy Day Mahzor,* 32.

40. There is a certain aspect of joy, during the day, but it is the joy of knowing relief from sin and acceptance of repentance, and not the celebration of festivity connected with other holidays. See, for example, *Seder Eliyahu Zuta* 4.181, where Yom Kippur is identified as the day when Moses returned from Mount Sinai having obtained forgiveness for the sin of the Golden Calf. See also Tabory, *Jewish Festivals,* 294ff. The release from sin is, further, given as the explanation of the custom described in M. Ta'anit 4.8 of maidens dancing on Yom Kippur dressed in white. See also B. Ta'anit 30b.

Chapter 10. Biblical Readings for the Yamin Nora'im

1. See Hammer, *Jewish Prayer,* 61.

2. This system is according to the ruling of Rabbi Ishmael. Rabbi Akiba thought that there should be six *aliyot* on the Sabbath and seven on Yom Kippur (M. Megillah 4.2 and T. Megillah 3.11). The Talmud explains that Rabbi Akiba thought there was more time for reading on Yom Kippur, while Rabbi Ishmael felt that since the prayers on Yom Kippur were so long the reading should be shorter (J. Megillah 4.3). Still, we cannot be certain that this was their real feeling or whether it had to do with the sanctity of the various days.

3. Ezra Fleisher, however, thinks that from early times two days were observed and the same Torah reading was repeated on both of them. See "The Calendar of the Festivals in the *Piyyut* of R. Elazar beRebi Kalir" (in Hebrew), *Tarbiz* 52, 250.

4. See also T. Megillah 3.6.

5. As late as the second century, there was a dispute among rabbinic authorities concerning the time of creation: "Rabbi Eliezer says, 'The world was created in Tishre . . . on Rosh Hashanah Sarah, Rachel, and Hannah were remembered'. . . . Rabbi Joshua says, 'The world was created in Nissan [the spring] . . . on Rosh Hashanah Sarah, Rachel, and Hannah were remembered'". . . (B. Rosh Hashanah 10b–11a). Even those who thought that creation took place in the fall rather than in the spring were not certain of the date. Some of the midrashim place creation a week earlier, suggesting that it was not the world, but human beings who were created on Rosh Hashanah (see Leviticus Rabba 29.1). See also the Pesikta derav kahana (Mandelbaum edition, 2, 334), where the argument is made that Adam was created on Rosh Hashanah—which would mean that the creation of the world took place six days earlier, in the month of Elul.

6. Genesis Rabba 53.11.

7. Louis Ginzberg, *The Legends of the Jews* (Philadelphia, 1954) 1: 271–273 and notes. In the older versions it is the angels who accuse Abraham.

8. Genesis Rabba 53.17–18.

9. This may be the origin of the legend of another Hannah and her seven sons, all of whom were martyred in the Maccabean period.

10. The story of the *Akeidah* is also one of those biblical narratives that explains the meaning of a place-name. Just as the end of Genesis 21 offers an explanation of the name Beersheba (the well of seven—*be'er sheva,* or the well

of the oath—*be'er shevu'ah*), this story explains the name Moriah as "the mount of the Lord upon which there is vision" (Gen. 22:14), or provision (since God provided the ram). The Septuagint understands Moriah as "the mount on which the Lord appears." The letters in the word *Moriah* are used in various combinations throughout the story, in the meaning of "to see," "to provide," or "to revere." In later tradition Moriah came to be identified with Mount Zion in Jerusalem upon which the Temple was built (2Chron. 3:1).

11. Midrash Tanḥuma Vayera.

12. The origins and development of this tradition have been detailed brilliantly by Shalom Speigel. See *The Last Trial* (New York, 1967).

13. See Spiegel, *Trial,* 86–89.

14. See B. Rosh Hashanah 16a.

15. See Baruch Levine's excellent commentary in *The JPS Commentary: Leviticus* for a complete and detailed explanation of the reading.

16. Levine, *JPS Commentary: Leviticus,* 104.

17. B. Megillah 31a.

18. See for example Solomon Schechter, *Some Aspects of Rabbinic Theology* (New York, 1936), 206ff. See also Tabory, *Jewish Festivals in the Time of the Mishnah and Talmud,* 292.

19. See Max Arzt, *Justice and Mercy: Commentary on the Liturgy of the New Year and the Day of Atonement* (New York, 1963), 260.

20. B. Megillah 31a.

21. See Yehezkiel Kaufmann, *The Religion of Israel* (Chicago, 1960), 282–286. H. L. Ginsberg, in *The Five Megilloth and Jonah* (Philadelphia, 1969), 114–116, disagrees with Kaufmann's early dating of Jonah but not with his analysis of the message.

22. See the fine study of Jonah by Jonathan Magonet, *Form and Meaning: Studies in Literary Techniques in The Book of Jonah* (Sheffield, 1983). See especially Chapter 5, 83–112, and the Postscript, 173–84.

23. See Magonet, *Form and Meaning,* 86.

Epilogue: Getting Started

1. William G. Braude, *The Midrash on Psalms* (New Haven, 1959) 1:xxvii.

2. M. Sukkah 4.5–6.

3. See M. Rosh Hashanah 1.2.

4. Zohar vayehi 12a. See also Yaacov Vainstein, *The Cycle of the Jewish Year* (Jerusalem, 1953), 98–99.

GLOSSARY

This glossary provides definitions for the most important of the Hebrew terms contained in *Entering the High Holy Days*. More detailed descriptions may be found within the text itself.

Akeidah—the binding of Isaac. The story from Genesis 22 that is read on the second day of Rosh Hashanah and is an important motif in the High Holy Day prayers. The merit of this near-sacrifice is invoked before God so that He will forgive Isaac's descendants when they sin.

Aleinu—a prayer expressing God's sovereignty and a hope for the future recognition of His kingship by all mankind. It is the prologue to the *Malkhuyot* (Sovereignty) verses on Rosh Hashanah and has become an independent prayer recited at the end of all services.

Al ḥet—"for the sin." The long confession listing sins in a double acrostic. It is recited at the services of Yom Kippur.

Amidah—"the standing prayer." The central prayer of each service, which consists of three parts: praise of God, petition or discussion of the specific day, and thanksgiving. On Rosh Hashanah and Yom Kippur it consists of seven blessings, except in the *Musaf* on Rosh Hashanah, when it has nine.

Aseret yemei teshuvah—the ten days of repentance. A reference to the ten-day period from Rosh Hashanah through Yom Kippur. During this time period, one is to repent through recognizing and making up for wrongdoing, offering special prayers and performing acts of charity.

Ashamnu—"we have sinned." A brief, alphabetical listing of sins; the "short confession."

Avinu Malkeinu—"our Father, our King." A prayer recited on both Rosh Hashanah and Yom Kippur. It is based on a formula developed by Rabbi Akiba and pleads for God's mercy.

Avodah—a special service introduced into the Yom Kippur *Musaf*; a *piyyut* based on the description in the Mishnah of the way in which the service of Yom Kippur was conducted by the High Priest in the days of the Second Temple.

Azazel—possibly the name of a demon or of a place to which a goat was sent on Yom Kippur, symbolically carrying away the sins of the people. The goat is sometimes called the "scapegoat" in the sense of "escape."

Cohen (plural: *cohanim*)—the priests descended from Aaron who officiated at the Temple.

Eileh ezkerah—"these I will remember." A *piyyut* concerning ten martyrs of the second century C.E., recited as part of the Yom Kippur *Musaf*.

Elul—the sixth month of the Jewish year. It precedes Rosh Hashanah and is used as a time of preparation for the Days of Awe. The shofar is blown each day, and a special psalm is recited. Tradition considers the name to be a Hebrew acronym for the phrase, *ani le-dodi ve-dodi li*—"I am my beloved's and my beloved is mine" (Song of Songs 6:3).

Hineni—"Here I am." A *piyyut* recited by the *hazzan* prior to *Musaf* on Rosh Hashanah and Yom Kippur. It expresses the *hazzan's* humility and anxiety concerning the important task of representing the people before God.

Kaparah—atonement, the rituals of purification both of the sanctuary and of the individual from sin.

Kaparot—the folk-ritual performed on the morning before Yom Kippur, in which either a fowl or money is substituted for the individual and his/her sins.

Ki anu amekhah—"for we are Your people." A brief *piyyut* that precedes the confessions in the Yom Kippur services. It stresses the close relationship between God and Israel.

Kiddush—the blessing inaugurating a festival or the Sabbath. It is recited over a cup of wine.

Ki hinei ka-homer—"behold like clay." A famous *piyyut* inserted into the *Selihot* prayers of Yom Kippur, emphasizing God's ability to mold us according to His will and calling upon God to remember His covenant of mercy.

Kol Nidre—"all vows." The service and declaration with which Yom Kippur begins. A quasi-legal formula releasing us from unfilled vows. The melody is one of the most well-known of all liturgical compositions. It is recited three times.

Le-el orekh din—"God who arranges judgment." A famous Rosh Hashanah *piyyut* on the theme of the Day of Judgment.

Le-shanah tovah tikateivu—"may you be inscribed for a good year." The traditional greeting for Rosh Hashanah.

Mahzor—the High Holy Day prayer book. The word means "cycle" and is also used to refer to any festival prayer book.

Malkhuyot—"kingship." One of three special sections recited in the *Musaf* service of Rosh Hashanah. It proclaims God as *melekh*—King—of the universe; like *Shofrot* and *Zikhronot*, it consists of ten biblical verses, preceded by a prologue and followed by a concluding prayer and the sounding of the shofar.

Minhah—the afternoon service consisting of an *Amidah*, a psalm, and the *Aleinu*. On the Sabbath and on Yom Kippur the service includes a brief Torah reading as well.

Musaf—The additional service recited on the Sabbath and on all holidays.

Ne'ilah—"the closing." The fifth and last service of Yom Kippur, referring either to the closing of the gates of the Temple or the closing of the heavenly gates.

Payytanim—liturgical poets throughout the ages who embellished the services with special poems known as *piyyutim.*

Piyyut (plural: *piyyutim*)—liturgical poems inserted into the basic liturgy to enhance and beautify it.

Rosh Hashanah—"the head of the year." The first and second days of the seventh month, Tishre, which are observed as the days of judgment of all humankind. This is the time when God is acknowledged as sovereign of the universe and is called upon to remember us by fulfilling His promises to us.

Selihot—prayers asking for forgiveness, which are included in the Yom Kippur liturgy. *Selihot* is also the name of special services held before Rosh Hashanah, especially the service recited on the Saturday night before the New Year.

Shabbat Shuvah—the Sabbath of returning. The Sabbath between Rosh Hashanah and Yom Kippur, so named because of the prophetic reading that begins with the call, "Return O Israel."

Shaharit—the morning service. It consists of the *Shema*, the *Amidah*, and a Torah service. On Rosh Hashanah there is also a shofar service. *Shaharit* is introduced by special morning blessings and verses from Psalms.

She-heheyanu—"who has kept us in life." A blessing recited when reaching a new season or an important event in life or when eating something or donning a new garment for the first time during a given year. It expresses thanksgiving for having lived to participate in that event.

Shema—three sections from the Torah recited as part of the morning and evening services. Sometimes this term refers to the line, *Shema Yisra'el*, "Hear O Israel," recited as a confession of faith.

Shevarim—one of the sounds of the shofar, consisting of three short blasts.

Shofar—the horn, usually from a ram, blown on Rosh Hashanah following the Torah service, during the *Musaf* service and at the end of Yom Kippur. It has been associated with the story of the binding of Isaac, in which a ram was sacrificed in place of Isaac.

Shofrot—"horns." One of three special sections recited in the *Musaf* service of Rosh Hashanah. Like *Malkhuyot* and *Zikhronot*, it consists of ten biblical verses referring to the shofar, preceded by a prologue and followed by a concluding prayer and the sounding of the shofar.

Tallit (plural: *tallitot*)—prayer shawl adorned with fringes at the corners and worn at daytime services and on the eve of Yom Kippur.

Tashlikh—"casting." A ceremony conducted on the afternoon of Rosh Hashanah near a body of water, symbolically casting our sins into the water to be carried away.

Tefillin—prayer phylacteries. Small boxes containing sections from the Torah, attached to the arm and head by straps and worn during morning services on weekdays.

Teki'ah—one of the sounds of the shofar, consisting of one long blast.

Teru'ah—one of the sounds of the shofar, consisting of nine short, staccato blasts.

Teshuvah—repentance (from the Hebrew word *la-shuv*, "to return"). The act of *teshuvah* includes acknowledgment of wrongdoing, regret, and change of conduct.

U-netanah tokef—one of the most important of the *piyyutim*. It is recited during *Musaf* both on Rosh Hashanah and on Yom Kippur and vividly depicts the Day of Judgment.

U-vekhen—"therefore." Three paragraphs on the subject of kingship introduced into the *Musaf Amidah* of Rosh Hashanah and Yom Kippur.

Vidui—"confession." A central part of the prayers of Yom Kippur in which we confess our sins. There are two such prayers, the short *Ashamnu* and the long *Al het*.

Ya'aleh—"may (our prayer) arise." A famous *piyyut* recited on Yom Kippur evening, emphasizing the fact that Yom Kippur is a day entirely devoted to prayer.

Ya'aleh Ve-yavo—the special prayer recited on all holidays asking God to remember us with favor and to restore the city of Jerusalem and the Temple.

Yamim Nora'im—the Days of Awe. The common term for Rosh Hashanah (the New Year), Yom Kippur (the Day of Atonement), and the entire period surrounding them. "Awe" is a term referring to something of utmost holiness that evokes a feeling of extreme reverence within us. When Jacob awoke from his dream of the ladder in which he beheld God, he exclaimed, "How awesome—*nora*—is this place (Gen. 28:17).

Yizkor—the service of remembering the dead, recited on Yom Kippur. *Yizkor* is also said on the last day of each festival throughout the year.

Yom Ha-din—"the Day of Judgment." Another name for Rosh Hashanah, the day when God judges all humankind.

Yom Ha-zikaron—"the Day of Remembrance." Another name for Rosh Hashanah, based on the concept that on that day God remembers us and fulfills His promises to us.

Yom Kippur—the Day of Atonement, which falls on the tenth day of Tishre, the seventh month of the Jewish year. It is observed through day-long prayer, fasting, and refraining from other pleasures.

Zikhronot—"remembrances." One of three special sections recited during the *Musaf* service of Rosh Hashanah. Like *Malkhuyot* and *Shofrot*, it consists of ten biblical verses, preceded by a prologue and followed by a concluding prayer and the sounding of the shofar.

Bibliography

For Further Reading

Agnon, S. Y. *Days of Awe*. New York, 1948.

Arzt, Max. *Justice and Mercy: Commentary on the Liturgy of the New Year and the Day of Atonement*. New York, 1963.

Elbogen, Ismar. *Jewish Liturgy: A Comprehensive History*. Philadelphia, 1993.

Finesinger, Sol B. "The Shofar." *Hebrew Union College Annual* 8 (1931): 193–228.

Fox, Karen L., and Phyllis Zimbler Miller. *Seasons for Celebration*. New York, 1992.

Gaster, Theodor H. *Festivals of the Jewish Year*. New York, 1952.

Goodman, Philip, ed. *The Rosh Hashanah Anthology*. Philadelphia, 1970.

———. *The Yom Kippur Anthology*. Philadelphia, 1971.

Greenberg, Irving. *The Jewish Way: Living the Holidays*. New York, 1988.

Hammer, Reuven. *Entering Jewish Prayer*. New York, 1994.

Jacobs, Louis. *A Guide to Rosh Hashanah*. London, 1959.

———. *A Guide to Yom Kippur*. London, 1957.

Kieval, Herman. *The High Holy Days*. New York, 1959.

Millgram, Abraham. *Jewish Worship*. Philadelphia, 1971.

Munk, Elie. *The World of Prayer*. New York, 1961.

Schauss, Hayyim. *Guide to Jewish Holy Days*. New York, 1962.

Seidman, Hillel. *The Glory of the Jewish Holidays*. New York, 1968.

Siegel, Richard, Michael Strassfeld, and Sharon Strassfeld, eds. *The Jewish Catalogue*. Philadelphia, 1973.

Vainstein, Yaacov. *The Cycle of the Jewish Year*. Jerusalem, 1953.

Other Works Consulted in Preparing This Volume

Agnon, S. Y. *Days of Awe*. Jerusalem, 1937.

Braude, William G. *The Midrash on Psalms*. New Haven, 1959.

Cohen, Gershon D. "The Song of Songs and the Jewish Religious Mentality." In *Studies in the Variety of Rabbinic Cultures*. Philadelphia, 1991.

Davidson, Israel. "Kol Nidre." In *American Jewish Yearbook* 25, 180–194. Philadelphia, 1923.

———. "Poetic Fragments from the Genizah." In *Jewish Quarterly Review* N.S. 8 (1918): 425–453.

Deshen, Shlomo. *The Kol Nidre Puzzle: An Anthropological and Historical Study* (in Hebrew), 136–153. Sefer Katz, 1981.

Encyclopedia Judaica. Jerusalem, 1972.

Finkelstein, Louis. "The Ten Martyrs." In *Essays and Studies in Memory of Linda R. Miller,* ed. Israel Davidson, 29–55. New York, 1938.

Fleisher, Ezra. "An Addition to R. Se'adya Gaon's Second *Seder Avoda*" (in Hebrew). *Tarbiz* 58 (1989): 191–205.

———. "The Calendar of the Festivals in the *Piyyut* of R. Elazar beRebi Kalir" (in Hebrew). *Tarbiz* 52 (1983): 223–272.

———. *Prayer and Prayer Rituals in the Land of Israel* (in Hebrew). Jerusalem, 1988.

Frankl, Viktor E. *The Will to Meaning.* New York, 1969.

Ginsberg, H. L. *The Five Megilloth and Jonah.* Philadelphia, 1969.

———. *The Israelian Heritage of Judaism.* New York, 1982.

Ginzberg, Louis. *A Commentary on the Palestinian Talmud.* New York, 1961.

———. *Legends of the Jews.* Philadelphia, 1954.

Glatzer, Nahum N. *Franz Rosenzweig: His Life and Thought.* New York, 1953.

Goldschmidt, Daniel. *The High Holy Day Maḥzor* (in Hebrew). Jerusalem, 1970.

———. *Studies in Prayer and Piyyutim* (in Hebrew). Jerusalem, 1979.

———. *Seder Seliḥot.* Jerusalem, 1965.

Gordis, Robert. *The Book of God and Man.* Chicago, 1965.

Greenhut, Eliezer Halevi, ed. *Midrash Shir Ha-shirim.* Jerusalem, 1981.

Groner, Tzvi. "The History of the Blessing for the Confession" (in Hebrew). In *Bar Ilan Yearbook* 13 (1976): 158–169.

Hammer, Reuven. *Entering Jewish Prayer.* New York, 1994.

———. "The Role of the Two Covenants in Biblical Theology." In *Threescore and Ten,* ed. Abraham Karp, Louis Jacobs, and Zalman Dimitrovsky, 17–32. Hoboken, 1991.

Heinemann, Joseph. *Studies in Jewish Liturgy* (in Hebrew). Jerusalem, 1981.

———. "The Ancient Order of Blessings for Rosh Hashanah" (in Hebrew). *Tarbiz* 45 (1976): 258–267.

———. "The History of the Blessing 'Boneh Yerushalayim.'" In *Sefer haim sherman,* ed. Shraga Abramson and Aaron Mirsky, 93–101. Jerusalem, 1970.

Herr, Moshe David. "Matters of Halakhah in the Land of Israel in the Sixth and Seventh Centuries" (in Hebrew). *Tarbiz* 59 (1990): 62–80.

Hoffman, Lawrence A. *The Canonization of the Synagogue Service.* Notre Dame, 1979.

———. *Jewish Music in its Historical Development.* New York, 1929.

———. "The Kol Nidre Tune." *Hebrew Union College Annual* 8–9 (1931–1932): 493–510.

Jacobs, Louis. *We Have Reason to Believe.* London, 1957.

Jellinek, Adolf. *Beit ha-midrash II.* Jerusalem, 1938.

Jewish Encyclopedia. New York, 1905.

Kadushin, Max. *The Rabbinic Mind.* New York, 1952.

Kafka, Franz. *The Trial.* New York, 1937.

Kaufmann, Yehezkel. *The Religion of Israel.* Chicago, 1960.

Keival, Herman. "The Paradox of Kol Nidre." In *The Yom Kippur Anthology,* ed. Philip Goodman, 84–98. Philadelphia 1971. Also published as "The Curious Case of Kol Nidre." In *Commentary* 46, no. 4 (October, 1968): 53–58.

Lauterbach, Jacob Z. "The Ritual for the Kapparot Ceremony." In *Studies in Jewish Law, Custom and Folklore.* New York, 1970.

———. "Tashlikh." *Hebrew Union College Annual* 11 (1936): 207–340.

Levine, Baruch. *The JPS Torah Commentary: Leviticus.* Philadelphia, 1989.

———. "The Language of the Magical Bowls." In *A History of the Jews of Babylonia.* Vol. 5. Ed. Jacob Neusner. Leiden, 1970.

Lieberman, Saul. "Yannai's Piyyutim" (in Hebrew). *Sinai* (1939): 221–250.

———. *Tosefta kifshutah.* New York, 1955.

Lieberman, Saul, ed. *Deuteronomy Rabba.* Jerusalem, 1964.

Liebleich, Leon J. "Aspects of the New Year Liturgy." *Hebrew Union College Annual* 34 (1963): 125–176.

———. "The Insertions in the Third Benediction of the Holy Day Amidoth." *Hebrew Union College Annual* 35 (1964): 79–101.

Luzzatto, Moses Hayyim. *Mesillat Yesharim* (The Path of the Upright), ed. Mordecai Kaplan. Philadelphia, 1966.

Magonet, Jonathan. *Form and Meaning: Studies in Literary Techniques in the Book of Jonah.* Sheffield, 1983.

Mann, Jacob. "Changes in The Divine Service." *Hebrew Union College Annual* 4 (1927): 241–310.

——. "Genizah Fragments of the Palestinian Order of Service." *Hebrew Union College Annual* 2 (1925): 269–338.

Margolioth, Mordecai. *Disputes between Authorities in Eastern Lands and the Land of Israel* (in Hebrew). Jerusalem, 1938.

Milgrom, Jacob. *The JPS Torah Commentary: Numbers*. Philadelphia, 1990.

Moore, George Foot. *Judaism*. Cambridge, 1946.

Mowinckel, Sigmund. *The Psalms in Israel's Worship*. Oxford, 1962.

Philo. *Special Laws*. Cambridge, 1962.

Reik, Theodor. *Ritual: Psycho-Analytic Studies*. London, 1931.

Saadia Gaon. *The Book of Beliefs and Opinions*, ed. Samuel Rosenblatt. New Haven, 1948.

Samuel, Simha ben, ed. *Maḥzor Vitry* (in Hebrew). Nuremberg, 1923. Reprint. New York, n.d.

Sattuck, Roger. *Forbidden Knowledge*. New York, 1996.

Schechter, Solomon. *Some Aspects of Rabbinic Theology*. New York, 1936.

Schirmann, Jefim. "Hebrew Liturgical Poetry and Christian Hymnology." In *Jewish Quarterly Review* 44 (1953): 123–161.

Scholem, Gershom G. *Major Trends in Jewish Mysticism*. New York, 1941.

Sefer Ha-ḥinukh (The Book of Education). Jerusalem, 1960.

Segal, Moshe. "The Religion of Israel before Sinai." In *Jewish Quarterly Review* 52 (1963): 240–256.

Sivan, Gabriel A. "Hymns of the Isles." In *Judaism* 39, no. 3 (Summer, 1990): 326–337.

Speigel, Shalom. *The Last Trial*. New York, 1967.

Tabory, Joseph. *Jewish Festivals in the Time of the Mishnah and Talmud* (in Hebrew). Jerusalem, 1995.

Werner, Eric. *The Sacred Bridge*. London, 1959.

Weinfeld, Moshe. *Justice and Righteousness in Israel and the Nations* (in Hebrew). Jerusalem, 1985.

Wieder, Naftali. *The Formula of the Blessing of God's Holiness on Rosh Hashanah and Yom Kippur* (in Hebrew). *Tarbiz* 34 (1965): 43–48.

Transliteration Guide to Hebrew Prayers

Av yeda'aka	"The patriarch recognized You"	אב ידעך
Avinu Malkeinu	"Our Father our King"	אבינו מלכנו
Adirei ayumah	"Those mighty and awesome"	אדירי אימה
Ana elohim hayim	"Please, living God"	אנא אלהים חיים
Or olam	"Everlasting light"	אור עולם
Az be-yom kippur	"Then on Yom Kippur"	אז ביום כפור
Ezkerah elohim	"I remember, O God"	אזכרה אלהים
Ein Kamokhah	"There is none like You"	אין כמוך
El dar ba-marom	"God who dwells on high"	אל דר במרום
Eileh ezk'rah	Martyrology	אלה אזכרה

El melekh	"God, King"—Thirteen Attributes	אל מלך
Eimekha nasati	"I am in awe of You"	אימך נשאתי
Amnam ken	"Indeed it is so"	אמנם כן
Amitz koah	"Vast in power"	אמיץ כח
Imru l'elohim	"Speak of God"	אמרו לאלהים
Enkat mesaldekha	"The cry of those who beseech You"	אנקת מסלדיך
Upad me-az	"This day was designated from of old"	אפד מאז
Areshet sefateinu	"May the prayers of our lips"	ארשת שפתינו
Ashamnu	"We have trespassed"	אשמנו
Ashrei	Psalm 145	אשרי

Ata vehartanu — "You have chosen us" — אַתָּה בְחַרְתָּנוּ

Ata hivdaltah enosh me-rosh — "From the very beginning, You set humans apart" — אַתָּה הִבְדַּלְתָּ אֱנוֹשׁ מֵרֹאשׁ

Ata hu eloheinu — "You are our God" — אַתָּה הוּא אֱלֹהֵינוּ

Ata noten yad la-posh'im — "You extend Your hand to transgressors" — אַתָּה נוֹתֵן יָד לַפּוֹשְׁעִים

Atiti le-ḥanenakh — "I have come to implore" — אֲתִיתִי לְחַנְנָךְ

Eten le-fo'ali tzedek — "I will proclaim my Master's justice" — אֶתֵּן לְפָעֳלִי צֶדֶק

B'sefer ḥayim — "In the Book of Life" — בְּסֵפֶר חַיִּים

Barekhu — "Bless" — בָּרְכוּ

Darekha — "It is Your way" — דַּרְכְּךָ

Ha-aderet veha-emunah — "Might and faithfulness" — הָאַדֶּרֶת וְהָאֱמוּנָה

Transliteration	Meaning	Hebrew
Adonai ori	Psalm 27	ה' אורי
Heyeh im pifiyot	"Be on the lips of the messengers of Your people"	היה עם פיפיות
Ha-yom	"Today"	היום
Ha-yom harat olam	"Today the world was born"	היום הרת עולם
Ha-melekh	"The King"	המלך
Hineni	"Here I stand"	הנני
U-vekhen	"Therefore"	ובכן
U-vekhen va-Adonai pakad et Sarah	"And the Lord visited Sarah"	ובכן וה' פקד את שרה
V'ye'etayu	"They shall come"	ויאתיו
Vidui	Confession	וידוי

Transliteration	English	Hebrew
Ve-khol ma'aminim	"All believe"	וכל מאמינים
U-khtov l'ḥayim tovim	"Inscribe for a good life"	וכתוב לחיים טובים
U-mi ya'amod	"Who can withstand"	ומי יעמוד
U-mipnei hata'einu	"Because of our sins"	ומפני חטאינו
U-netaneh tokef	"We shall ascribe holiness to this day"	ונתנה תקף
Zekhor brit Avraham	"Remember the covenant of Abraham"	זכר ברית אברהם
Zikhronot	Remembrance verses	זכרונות
Zokhreinu l'ḥayim	"Remember us for life"	זכרנו לחיים
Yigdal	Closing hymn	יגדל
Yizkor	Memorial prayer	יזכר

Ya'aleh	"Let our supplication arise"	יעלה
Ya'aleh Ve-yavo	"May our remembrance arise and come before You"	יעלה ויבא
Yareiti	"I am in awe"	יראתי
Kevodo iħel ke-hayom	"Or this day He stretched His glory"	כבודו אהל כהיום
Ki anu amekhah	"For we are Your people"	כי אנו עמך
Ki hinei ka-homer	"Behold like clay"	כי הנה כחמר
Kol Nidre	"All vows"	כל נדרי
Kol shinanei shaħak	"All the hosts of heaven"	כל שנאני שחק
Le-el orekh din	"God who sits in judgment"	לאל עורך דין
Moreh hata'im	"You instruct sinners"	מורה חטאים

Mi khamokhah	מִי כָמֹכָה	"Who is like You"
Melekh azur gevurah	מֶלֶךְ אָזוּר בִּגְבוּרָה	"King girt with glory"
Melekh amon	מֶלֶךְ אָמוֹן	"Faithful King"
Melekh elyon	מֶלֶךְ עֶלְיוֹן	"Most high King"
Melokh al kol ha-olam	מְלֹךְ עַל־כָּל־הָעוֹלָם	"Rule over the entire world"
Malkhuyot	מַלְכֻיּוֹת	Kingship verses
Malkhuto bi-kehal adati	מַלְכוּתוֹ בִּקְהַל עֲדָתִי	"His Majesty I acknowledge"
Min ha-meitzar	מִן־הַמֵּצַר	"Out of the depths"
Mi-sod hakhamim	מִסּוֹד חֲכָמִים	"From the teachings of our Sages"
Ma'aseh eloheinu	מַעֲשֵׂה אֱלֹהֵינוּ	"The works of our God"

Merubim tzorkei amkha	"Your people's needs are great"	אֵל מֶלֶךְ
Na'amirakh be-eimah	"We will acknowledge You in fear"	אַנְמִירְךָ בְּאֵימָה
Ne'ilah	Closing service	אַנָּא כֵן
Selah na	"Please forgive"	אָנָּא כִּי
Seliḥot	Forgiveness prayers	אָמְרוּ לֵאלֹהִים
Avodah	Temple Service	אַקְרְבָה מַפִלְךָ
Ad yom moto	"Until the day of his death"	אֱמֶת כְּנָא
Alḥet	"For the sin"	אֱלֹהֵינוּ שֶׁבִּשְׁמֵי
Aleinu	"It is our duty"	אֲמְנַנוּ
Al yisra'el	"Upon Israel"	עַל יִשְׂרָ

Kadosh adir   "The Holy One"   קדוש אדיר

Kedushah   Sanctification   קדושה

Kiddush   Sanctification   קידוש

Romemu el melekh ne'eman "Exalt God the faithful King"   רוממו אל מלך נאמן

She-heḥeyanu   "Who has kept us in life"   שהחיינו

Shofrot   Shofrot verses   שופרות

Shema   "Hear, O Israel"   שמע

Shema koleinu   "Hear our voice"   שמע קולנו

Sha'arei armon   "Gates of the palace"   שערי ארמון

Ta'ir ve-tari'a   "Rouse Yourself and sound the shofar"   תאיר ותריע

Tefen be-makom   "Turn from Your Place"   תפן במקום

Index